THE FORT THAT BECAME A CITY

THE FORT THAT BECAME A CITY

An Illustrated Reconstruction of Fort Worth, Texas, 1849-1853

Drawings by William B. Potter

Text by Richard F. Selcer

Texas Christian University Press

Fort Worth

Drawings copyright © William B. Potter, 1995

Text copyright © Texas Christian University Press, 1995

Library of Congress Cataloging-in-Publication Data

Selcer, Richard F.
    The Fort that became a city : an illustrated reconstruction of
Fort Worth, Texas 1849-1853 / drawings by William B.
Potter : text by Richard F. Selcer.
        p. cm.
    ISBN 0-87565-146-1 (pbk. : alk. paper)
    1. Fort Worth (Tex.)—History. 2. Fort Worth (Tex.) in art
    I. Potter, William B. II. Title.
    976.45315—dc20

                                                95-7572
                                                  CIP

Cover illustration By Dawn's Early Light *by William B.Potter*

*To my loving wife Betty Smith Potter who kept me
supplied with coffee, accompanied me on countless visits
to fort ruins and reconstructions, and acted as a constant
sounding board throughout this project.*

*To our sons, William Bradley (Brad) and Barry
Smith (Buck) Potter for their helpful support, assistance
and encouragement.*

*To my late father and mother, Frank B. and
Birdie Blow Potter, who taught me to love history, my
city, my state and my country.*

—Bill Potter

*To Debbie, Ashley and Brett: This one's for you!
With love always.*

—Rick Selcer

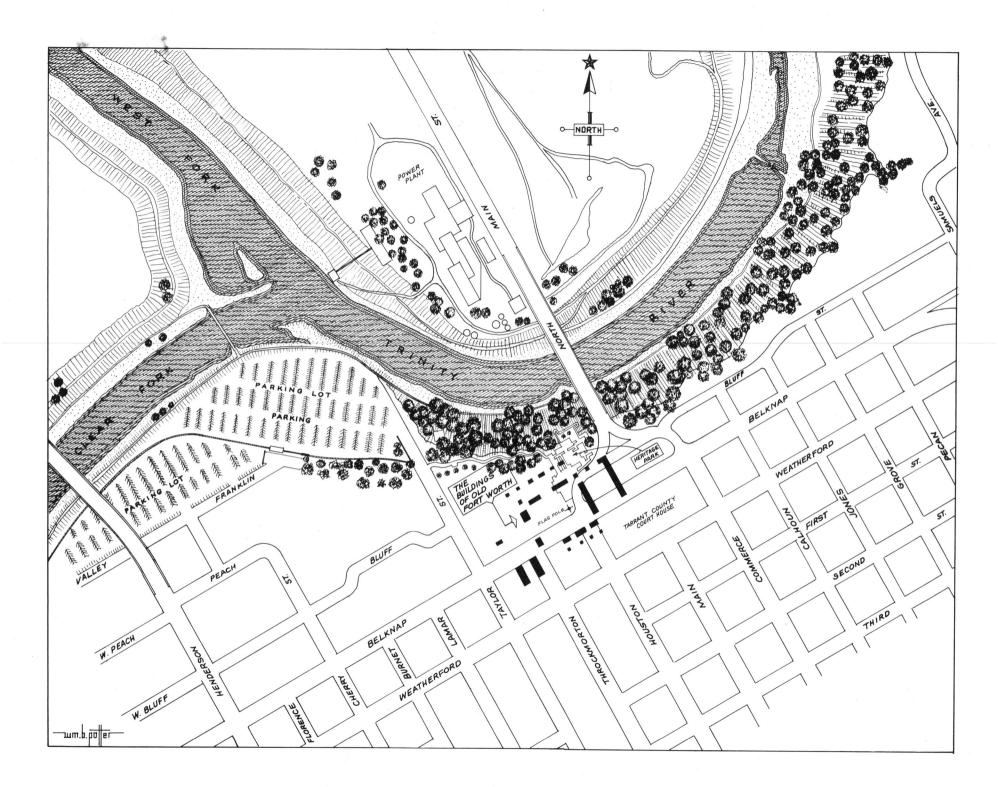

CONTENTS

On the facing page: the original site of Fort Worth is superimposed on the present-day courthouse area.

ACKNOWLEDGEMENTS

Two projects led to the publication of this book, neither of which has become a reality at this date. First: a full scale replica of the original "Fort Worth." Second: a Fort Worth cyclorama and historical museum. Many persons were supportive of these and deserve my sincere appreciation. As for the book, *The Fort That Became a City*, I would like to express my gratitude to the following individuals who offered their support, information, and encouragement during it's creation. Judy Alter and Tracy Row of TCU Press, Ed and Ruby Briscoe, Betty Regester, Frank Perkins, Bill Wardlaw-Brown, Bill Norris, and Rick Selcer, whose comprehensive text and tireless effort combine to give this book the final touch.

—William B. Potter

No historian can hope to write a properly researched book without the contributions of many anonymous helpers. This book represents the combined efforts of lots of people in the last two years, only a few of whom I can mention by name here. Thanks to Bill Potter who first had the idea for a volume on Fort Worth and followed his dream; to Betty Regester, former curator at Log Cabin Village in Fort Worth, for turning over a wealth of research collected over years of diligent work; to Ruby Schmidt for proofing an early draft of the manuscript and for sharing her expertise on many occasions; to Dee Barker for opening up the Tarrant County Historical Commission to me on holidays and off-times and pitching in with the research; to Ken Hopkins for digging out the obscure and the forgotten from the Fort Worth Public Library files; to the underpaid and overworked staff of the Military Reference Branch of the National Archives, Washington, D.C., for helping me make sense of arcane U.S. Army records; to Cornelia Pym at the Fort Worth Public Library for double-checking countless footnote references; to John Shiflet for being my tour guide through Pioneer's Rest Cemetery; to my editor Tracy Row for his unflagging patience during countless rewrites. And a special note of gratitude to Lois Biege for typing footnotes late into the night and for too many little research errands to enumerate. To anyone else I left out, I apologize and I salute your contributions.

—Richard F. Selcer

1
BOOTS AND SADDLES

A small party of mounted dragoons and scouts rode in a rough line of march through thick woods, following a course roughly parallel to the Trinity River, several hundred yards to their right. A faint trail provided a narrow path through the dense undergrowth of trees, bushes and vines all around them. With their view to the river blocked by the tangled thicket, each man studied the back of the man in front of him or cast nervous glances at the undergrowth around them. The creaking of saddle leather and jangle of harness gear barely disturbed the still air as they proceeded in columns of two. A string of pack horses was strategically placed in the middle of the column where the men could guard it against possible attack. Food, supplies, tools, and extra ammunition were on those horses. The men's wariness was born of experience, not the presence of visible Indian signs. As far as they could tell, they were the only people in the world—or at least in this part of Texas.

This late spring day promised to be hot, the morning sun already a bright yellow ball climbing in the sky. Even at this early hour, it was already warm enough to make the troopers' nonregulation blue flannel blouses cling damply to sweaty bodies. In blatant defiance of regulation, most also had their shirt-tails pulled out and their galluses looped down their legs. Nor did uniform regulations mention the large silk handkerchiefs of red or yellow that covered their faces "to keep off the sun and pestiferous gnats." Their carbines were lashed loosely to their saddle pommels, out of the way but within easy reach.[1]

Their arms and uniforms marked them as more than simple hunters or emigrants. They had an air of purposeful confidence about them that ragtag uniforms and unkempt appearance could not disguise—"young men high in health and vigor." These were soldiers—maybe not veterans of the long-running Indian wars, but men not to be trifled with or unnecessarily provoked. Any watching native who observed their passage would have quietly slipped away and gone to warn his tribesmen.

After riding only a mile from the the previous night's campsite, they emerged from the dense groves of oak, sycamore, cottonwood, and hickory trees that grew in profusion along the river and onto a broad, grass-covered plateau formed by a lazy bend in the stream. Now buffalo and mesquite grasses pressed in on both sides of the trail, tickling their horses' stomachs. Farther out, broken by patches of rocky ground, wildflowers and an occasional scrawny mesquite appeared. They continued on, turning to the west and riding across the plateau until they reached a vantage point high above the river where they had an unrestricted view. To a man they sat up straight, their weariness forgotten, and gazed about them. There were audible murmurs of awe at the surrounding country that stretched out as far as the eye could see. The river was a sluggish brown snake coiled between treeless cliffs. It flowed east at the foot of the bluffs in front of them, making a large horseshoe bend to their right before continuing on eastward. Off to the left, it forked just before disappearing out of sight.

The previous twenty-four hours had drained their energies. They had spent a long day in the saddle covering some sixteen miles at a steady pace. Their route that day had taken them through the Trinity River valley, up onto the prairie, across several creeks, and then back to the river valley. About mid-afternoon, the commanding officer decided they would make an early camp and arrive at their destination, rested, the following morning. Their campsite had been on a point of land among live oaks overlooking the river. Thankfully, the site had plenty of firewood and fresh water, the latter due to a cold, natural spring.[2] A small, shabby rough-hewn cabin—which had been unoccupied for some time—stood nearby, abandoned like so many other of the white man's efforts to establish himself in the area.

One of the men shot a deer, so they ate fresh venison for supper. One deer was more than enough for the handful of men around the campfire that night. It was also a welcome relief from their normal diet of salt pork or jerked beef which they always carried with them. They supplemented the tasty venison steaks with standard army rations of hardtack biscuits and red beans, washed down with strong black coffee. There was no need to save any of the meat because it was apparent that game was abundant in this area. In fact, they had seen all sorts of wild game on their journey northward, beginning with bob whites, prairie chickens, jack rabbits, deer, and the swift pronghorn antelope that bounded over the plains in panicked flight. When they got closer to the Cross Timbers, they had caught glimpses of wild turkeys, squirrels, raccoons, and opossums.

The land near the creeks and the Trinity River looked fertile, too. It was blackland prairie, the sort of country where a man could settle down and raise a family. Most of the men were single, and few, if any, planned to make a career out of the army. In fact, many had signed up hoping to get a start in the West, among them a fair number of European immigrants who had never seen so much unoccupied land in their lives. It was the principal motivation for enlisting in the peacetime army of the mid-19th century.[3]

All in all, their luck had been uncommonly good, and the men had a good feeling about this expedition, certainly better than they had felt when they left Fort Graham on the Brazos two days earlier. At that point, all they knew was they were heading into Indian country to locate a site for a new military post that was intended to make North Texas safe for civilization. There had not been an attempt to create a permanent settlement in the area since the short-lived Bird's Fort experiment ended in 1842.[4]

From Fort Graham they had followed a trail north by northeast that brought them to Johnson's Station, formerly a licensed trading post and militia station on the boundary between Indian and white lands. What remained was a dying community—the last settlement on the Trinity before Indian country. If they had headed northwest out of Fort Graham, following the route of the Brazos River, they would have come to the domain of the Delaware and the Shawnee, the Ioni, the Keechi, and the Caddo, and beyond them, the lands of the Waco and the Tawakoni. The nearest of those tribes were only thirty-two miles upriver from Fort Graham, but that did not concern these men; they were headed in the opposite direction. There was some comfort in that fact.

There were no more than a dozen in the party including five civilians. They joked and cut up as if they were on a lark instead of a military expedition. That sort of mood was good for morale, but dangerous for the safety of their scalps in hostile country. The commanding officer let them have their fun because he knew what hard work lay ahead. But he worried about the recent reports of marauding Indians in this vicinity.

The night before, having almost reached the end of their journey, they finally began to realize they were genuine trailblazers in the tradition of Daniel Boone, John C. Frémont, Lewis and Clark. This fair land appeared to even the most calloused man among them as virgin wilderness "fresh from the hands of the Maker."[5] For a few moments that morning they had almost forgotten why they were there. The major's quiet orders brought them back to reality. They gathered their horses from the picket line, stowed their gear on the pack animals and stood "to horse" waiting for the major's signal to mount. Now, a short ride later they found themselves on a bluff high above the surrounding country.

One of the civilians in the lead held up his hand to halt. He turned in his saddle dramatically sweeping his arm in a great arc that invited them to look around. They slowly turned their heads in every direction, "reviewing the scenery from all points." Most of the flora they could see was bright yellow, turned prematurely dry by the same hot sun that made them sweat profusely despite the early hour. There was, everyone agreed, a remarkable clearness and purity to the hot, dry air, giving them visibility up to two miles. No one needed to say a word, but they knew this was the place they were looking for.[6]

The officer conferred briefly with a large, florid-faced man riding beside him, dressed in nondescript frontier garb that gave little sign that he was a former member of the state legislature and held a lieutenant colonel's commission in the state militia known as the "rangers." That man was Middleton Tate Johnson, called "Tate" by all who knew him. The two men held each other in high regard, not only as fellow soldiers, but as brother Masons pledged by sacred oath to assist each other in every way possible. On this expedition, however, Johnson was not a ranger or a Freemason. He was a civilian guide, and beyond that his interest was personal.[7]

Johnson had come up to the West Fork of the Trinity River about three years earlier at the head of a company of mounted rangers to make an effort at establishing a military presence in the region under the direction of the state of Texas. Authorities in Austin were determined to secure their Indian borderlands by building a chain of militia stations along the frontier. Johnson's Station was one of those posts. But the rangers were no more sucessful in 1846 than their predecessors had been in 1841 and Johnson's Station suffered the same fate as most of the others—it was deserted after the Mexican War started and its garrison was mustered into federal service. And like Bird's Fort before it, Johnson's Station was ultimately abandoned as a military post, but it remained a well-known landmark and rendezvous point on the upper Trinity.[8]

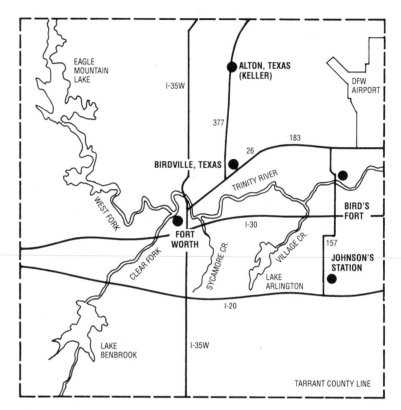

Above, the earliest place-names in today's Tarrant County are keyed to current landmarks.

Tate Johnson was "a man of energy and more than the ordinary man in point of intellect," according to Simon Farrar who had served under him in the Mexican War.[9] He was also a fearless pioneer and a shrewd land speculator who was equally adept at leading a mounted charge or making a buck. After the war, he was one of the first settlers to make his home on the north Texas frontier. When he was mustered out of state service on February 3, 1849, he received a generous land grant on the upper Trinity for services rendered to his state and country. Since February, however, he had been living in Shelby County, 200 miles to the east, itching to develop his holdings on the Trinity.[10] Now he was acting as scout and guide for the soldiers, leading them west from Johnson's Station, some sixteen miles behind them in the direction of Dallas.

Johnson had brought along four friends from Shelby County—Charles Turner, Dr. William B. Echols, Simon B. Farrar and his brother-in-law Joe Parker. None of the men were rangers at this time, as those part-time soldiers usually only served for six-month stretches during emergencies. Only Farrar had any significant military experience. Echols was a physician and one-time state legislator; Turner was a trader by profession. They were just along for the ride. It was Johnson who would have to keep the "bluejackets" out of trouble while looking out after his own private interests.[11]

They all stood to profit if the region of the upper Trinity could be opened up to settlement under army protection: land would be available and the first ones on the scene would get the choicest pieces. That is why they did not have to be asked twice to serve as guides. They agreed to meet with Arnold at the station first established by Johnson three years earlier. They arrived at the rendezvous a week ahead of the dragoons, set up camp, and waited.[12]

The soldiers were members of the Second Dragoons under the command of Major Ripley Arnold on an official mission for the United States government. The trip from Fort Graham had been uneventful. They left civilization behind on the Brazos River and did not see signs of it again until they reached Johnson's Station. For most of their trip they had followed a well-marked trail across high rolling prairie, occasionally crossing stretches of hilly and rocky ground cut up by the beds of small streams and dry arroyos. This land had never been broken by the plow, but some of the men who had been farmers in civilian life commented on the deep reddish loam, how it should prove easily tillable and very productive some day when it was cleared of Indians. They saw the first signs of human habitation when they reached the broad band of forest known as the lower Cross Timbers just before arriving at Marrow Le Bone Spring, the site of Johnson's Station.

The road they had followed up from Fort Graham skirted the edge of the lower Cross Timbers, a forbidding, dense thicket where one could hide an army. They kept a wary eye out for ambushes because this was Indian country. The Cross Timbers in particular were favored by several tribes for wintering. And not too far to the west, the ominously named Comanche Peak reminded them who really controlled the country.[13]

The dragoons travelled fast, covering twenty to thirty miles a day in their first two days out. The prairie was covered with almost-waist-high buffalo and mesquite grass interspersed with clumps of wild rye and oats. They had seen nothing but scrawny oaks and mesquite trees dotting the prairie in the beginning, but since meeting up with the Johnson and his partners, they had passed through a section of the lower Cross Timbers, starting about five miles east of the bluffs where they now stood. They had also crossed several creeks along the way and passed what appeared to be marble outcroppings, all of which the commanding officer duly noted in his log. Although they had traversed prairie where one might naturally expect to see the great woolly buffalo, no one had seen any because the creatures had already retreated farther westward to avoid the relentless encroachment of white men.[14] They did see herds of wild horses in the distance, however, and some of the men were eager to give chase, but the commanding officer put a stop to that sort of talk immediately.

It was, everyone agreed, a "wild and beautiful country" which one of the civilians informed them was "inhabited only by Indians, wild horses, [and] innumerable quantities of deer, wolves" and other wild creatures.[15] They had seen and heard enough on the trail to accept his description as gospel. At night, coyotes and wolves had serenaded them with a chorus of "dismal howls and yelps." The keen, quick cries, they knew came from the coyotes; the prolonged howls were from yellow wolves. So far, no Indians.

Arnold inspected the site and pronounced it good. Simon Farrar could not have agreed more, although he was not looking at it with a military eye. He was more interested in staking out a headright. "I thought it was the most beautiful and grand country the sun ever shone on," he recalled many years later. From a more pragmatic view, the major, who was still recovering from a recent bout of illness, was simply glad their journey was at an end.[16] He issued crisp orders: "Company, halt! Dismount!"—then walked over to a nearby copse of gnarled oaks where he tied his horse. The men followed his example, then fanned out to explore the area. Later with no fanfare they named this untrammelled piece of ground for an officer they all knew and respected, whom most had served under in the recent Mexican War—"that grand old hero," General William Jenkins Worth. They called it "Fort Worth."[17]

The usually meticulous commanding officer failed to note the exact date. It was sometime near the end of May 1849. A little later, the troopers remounted and rode back down the trail the way they had come, leaving the little spot atop the bluffs quiet once again. They knew they would be back, and the next time, to stay.

2
TO ARMS

The man at the head of the column was a thirty-two-year-old, no-nonsense officer and veteran campaigner. A graduate of West Point, Ripley Arnold had been a soldier since 1838, the same year, ironically, that Congressman and former President John Quincy Adams introduced a successful resolution in the House of Representatives barring the annexation of Texas by the United States. Now Arnold was deeply involved in extending the United States' claim over Texas with Congressional blessings.

The 1838 class at West Point was one of the more distinguished in academy history, not far behind the legendary class of 1846. Among Arnold's classmates were such future luminaries of the Union and Confederate armies as Pierre Gustav Toutant Beauregard, Irvin McDowell, William J. Hardee, Henry Hopkins Sibley, and Hamilton Wilcox Merrill, all of whom ranked higher upon graduation than Ripley Arnold, who was number thirty-three out of forty-five.[1] That number meant more than just personal pride or accomplishment; it determined which branch of the service a graduating officer might go into. The highest class rankings got to serve with the engineers. The lowest class rankings, which included Ripley Arnold, were limited to the infantry, mounted rifles and dragoons.

Merrill, Hardee, Sibley, and Arnold all wound up on the Texas frontier and distinguished themselves there. Merrill succeeded Arnold in command at Fort Worth and was given the job of shutting down the post that Arnold had first established, while Hardee's more rapid rise in command made him the superior to both men during their service in Texas. Sibley made something of a reputation for himself before the Civil War as a quartermaster extraordinaire, inventing both the Sibley tent and the Sibley stove. Unfortunately, like so many other officers on the frontier for long tours of duty, he developed a great love of liquor, so great in fact that one soldier said "it exceeded his love of home, country, and God."[2] Many other officers had similar drinking problems; Ripley Arnold, however, was not one of them.

By the original terms of his appointment to West Point, Arnold had been obligated to a single year of service after graduation, but he chose to be a career soldier from the beginning. In the peacetime army, that meant low pay, postings far from civilization, and little chance of reaching the top ranks. But he accepted those limitations and made duty, honor, and country his professional creed.

In the years after leaving West Point as a young shave-tail brevet second lieutenant, Arnold had a life for himself in the Second Dragoons, advancing steadily through the ranks to captain and eventually brevet major. Two wars did not hurt. He had been cited for bravery twice, first for "gallant conduct" in the Seminole Indian Wars, and then for "gallant and meritorious conduct" in the Mexican War.[3] In May 1846, with his promotion to captain, he was given a staff assignment as assistant quartermaster, a job that did more to prepare him for his Texas service than all the fighting he had been in up to that time. His first posting in Texas after the Mexican War was at Fort Graham.

Brevet Major Arnold was hard-working, conscientious, and attentive to detail. He kept track of every soldier in his command (even those absent on detached duty for months), forwarded regular reports to his superiors, balanced his books, and in general kept up with the piles of paperwork that the army demanded.[4] His forte, in fact, was not fighting but managing, organizing, and building. All these were characteristics which led the army to pigeonhole him first as a recruiter, then as a quartermaster. The quartermaster corps where he spent most of his career was not the most desirable branch of service for an ambitious and aggressive officer, certainly less desirable than the dragoons. At best, the movement from field command in the dragoons to quartermaster duty could be described as lateral. When it came time to select officers for garrison duty on the frontiers of Texas, Arnold was a natural: his supervising abilities, organizational skills, and Indian fighting experience made him an easy choice.

The red-haired commander was also a proud and profane man, not the least intimidated by being placed in charge of a motley bunch of rambunctious, semi-disciplined, and ill-bred doughboys.[5] He had led worse than this lot through the swamps of Florida and the deserts of Mexico. He was taller than most of his men, and while far from burly, had a certain air about him that demanded respect. As a commander, he was blunt in his criticisms, but not averse to singling out good soldiers for praise. He noted approvingly in one report that Private Francis Knaar, the post "saddler," was "always at work on old equipment." In the same report, however, he castigated Private Matthew Patterson as "perfectly worthless, can't trust him with horse or equipment."[6] Such harsh language was not confined to reports. Later in his career, Arnold once publicly accused his post surgeon of "drunkenness and falsifying" and in a loud voice ordered him to his quarters, leading to a duel.[7] With little provocation, it seemed, the major could be as vulgar and brutal as any of his men.

Despite some rough edges, Ripley Arnold was the kind of man the U.S. Army wanted holding the line on the frontier because, far removed from higher authority and the reassuring chain of command, he still insisted on doing things by the book. He represented the best of the United States antebellum army, often called the "Old Army."

Arnold's initial visit to the Twin Forks in May 1849 is not the date celebrated in local history and lore. That came two weeks later. While June 6, 1849, marks the accepted founding date of Fort Worth, it was actually Ripley Arnold's second official visit to the site. His first trip at the end of May had been what is known in military parlance as a "locating expedition." And Arnold so advised his superiors in Washington, D.C., upon his return. Writing to Major General Roger Jones, Assistant Adjutant General of the Army, on June 2, he said, "I have located a new Post on West Fork Trinity River. My address will be 'Dallas, Dallas County, Texas,' a town about thirty-five miles east of me."[8] Arnold wrote that letter from Fort Graham, his headquarters at the time, but by designating his future mailing address as Dallas, it is clear he intended to be at Fort Worth for some time.

By June 4 he was back in the saddle, this time at the lead of his company, retracing his steps back up to the Trinity. The route he took was not exactly the same because this time they did not detour by way of Johnson's Station. They came directly to the site on the bluffs, arriving on June 6.[9]

The decision to establish Fort Worth was made in Texas, not Washington, but beyond that simple fact, the origins of that decision are shrouded in uncertainty. Two men are usually given complete credit—General William Jenkins Worth and Major Ripley Arnold.[10] The specific orders, however, came from General William S. Harney, commanding the Second Dragoons. To be sure, Worth and Arnold deserve most of the credit.

The story starts with Worth, the untrained military officer who first recognized the strategic necesssity for a military post on the north Texas plains. Then Arnold, with help from Middleton Tate Johnson, chose the site, constructed the post, and served as its first commander. Worth's name was given to the fort and later the city that grew at that location. Arnold's name was not similarly honored until a century later when it was attached to a public housing project near the original site of the fort. Other officers, commanding the Eighth Infantry Regiment, Second Dragoons, or Eighth Military Department (which became the Department of Texas in 1853) played more or less significant roles.

The genesis of the idea for establishing Fort Worth came much earlier than the events of 1849. The military importance of the upper Trinity had long been recognized. During the years of the Republic of Texas (1836-1845) officials planned to establish a fort at the head of the Clear Fork of the Trinity, one of a series of frontier strong points, the others being at Comanche Peak on the Brazos and on the San Saba. Though these plans were never realized because of the impending war with Mexico, the U.S. government would later establish Forts Worth, Graham, and Martin Scott at the same respective locations.

After annexation in 1845, the state government also faced the problem of frontier security, deciding to station companies of rangers or mounted militia at five locations, one of which was the West Fork of the Trinity River in present-day Tarrant County. That site became Johnson's Station. (The other locations were Castroville, San Antonio, the Little River in Bosque County, and Torrey's trading post in Johnson County.)

Neither the Republic nor the state was capable of mounting an effective defense of the frontier with their limited financial resources and military establishment. The federal government, on the other hand, suddenly had plenty of troops available with the end of the Mexican War. In February 1848, the Texas legislature asked Congress for protection from hostile Indians threatening its western frontier. The U.S. government was entirely agreeable to strengthening its authority over the vast, lightly held domain of Texas, then the newest state in the Union. For years, Texas borderlands had been under constant threat from both Mexicans and Indians and statehood had not changed that. Expansion-minded Texans, in turn, posed a threat to long-term peace with Mexico by trying to use Texas as a base for filibusters south of the border.

They had to be watched, and if necessary stopped from provoking an international incident.

Furthermore, Washington bureaucrats were interested in knowing just what the government owned in the southwestern borderlands. While the general outlines and geography of the state were known, the country west of the 100th meridian was largely an enigma. And with the discovery of gold in California at the beginning of 1848, thousands of gold seekers were beating a path across the state, eager to reach El Dorado. For good military reasons, as well as interests of general knowledge, the area needed to be explored and secured. That was Worth's assignment as commander of the Eighth Military Department. He inherited this assignment and a general blueprint for operations from his predecessor, Brigadier General (Brevet Major General) David E. Twiggs, the first commander of the Eighth Military Department.

The Eighth Military Department had been created by the War Department on August 31, 1848, and encompassed all of Texas. Among the troops assigned to the department were the Eighth Infantry Regiment and the Second Dragoons, both of whom were to play prominent roles in the establishment of Fort Worth.[11]

Twiggs arrived in Texas on November 1, 1848, nine months after the formal end of the Mexican War. He came to his new assignment as something of a tarnished hero, having risen to the rank of Brevet Major General during the war for "highly distinguished services," but acquiring numerous enemies along the way, including William Jenkins Worth. Amongs Twigg' war trophies was a "U.S. Congressional Sword," the equivalent of today's Congressional Medal of Honor (presented by President James Polk on March 2, 1847 "in testimony to the high sense entertained by Congress of his gallantry and good conduct in storming Monterey [sic]") and another honorary sword from the state of Georgia.[12] The Mexican War also gave Twiggs a chance to hone his administrative skills as military governor first at Matamoros, then at Monterrey, and finally at Vera Cruz. In March of 1848, he left Vera Cruz and took an extended leave of absence before reporting to his new assignment in Texas. By dint of Orders No. 7, dated September 24, 1848, Twiggs was directed to take the Second Dragoons with him and "assume command of the Eighth Military Department."[13]

David Twiggs was nearly six feet tall, with a robust physique, bull neck, and cherry-red face. He started out as a captain with the Eighth U.S. Infantry in 1812 and won his spurs fighting British, Indians, and Mexicans over the next thirty-six years. In 1836 he was promoted to colonel and placed in command of the newly created Second Dragoons. Utterly lacking in charisma, Twiggs was "not a man well beloved by officers or soldiers," according to Samuel French, who served under him as a lieutenant in the Mexican War. French added that the dragoon commander was "not genial in temperment or disposition."[14] He issued orders without proper authority and quarrelled incessantly, but held the grudging respect of his superiors because he got things done. Still, he had too many rough edges and unconventional ways for West Point trained officers.[15]

Now, promoted to a high administrative post, David Twiggs had to tone down some. He immediately set about trying to organize his new department. Initially, he was not encouraged by what he saw. He characterized Texas as a "troubled state" and bemoaned his lack of troops, the poor communications with his far-flung command, and the unsettled state of the frontier. "There will be some difficulty in locating posts on the northwestern frontier of Texas," he warned, because so much of the land was already in private hands and the owners would expect generous compensation. He was determined not to let greedy settlers extort rent from the army either. "If the land is owned and rent demanded, I will move the troops and continue to do so until I find some position not claimed by the citizens of Texas." He also stated he was in desperate need of qualified engineering officers.[16]

In subsequent orders, he outlined his Indian policies. Every effort, he stressed, must be made "to cultivate a friendly understanding with the different tribes." Both the white population of Texas and the Indians must be kept from warring on one another. The key, as he saw it, was keeping the two sides as far apart as possible. "The Indians will be required to remain north and west of a line connecting the different posts established . . . except on friendly visits to the posts for purposes of trade."[17]

This is the first mention of a cordon of posts in the official records of the Eighth Military Department. On November 7 he ordered companies of dragoons to take up positions on the Brazos, the Bosque, the Colorado, and the Medina rivers; he ordered additional detachments to Fredericksburg and Austin.[18] An imaginary line drawn between these positions represented the intended Indian frontier. But the line was intrinsically weak. There was no long-term plan to turn the dragoon encampments into permanent forts, and the northern end of the line left a distance of over 120 miles of unguarded frontier stretching from the Brazos to the Red River. Whether Twiggs had a more substantial defense in mind will never be known.

Less than a week after his arrival, the zealously self-serving Twiggs was already writing to Washington asking that his brevet rank of major general be confirmed in light of the enormous responsibilities that went with commanding the Eighth Department. He reviewed the extent of his domain and the number of problems he faced in support of his case for immediate confirmation. Apparently the army was not impressed with either his arguments or his problems because not only was he not promoted, his command was taken away. On December 10, 1848, Secretary of War William L. Marcy relieved him from his position at the head of the department and ordered Brigadier General William Jenkins Worth to Texas to take over. Twiggs' brief command ended when Worth landed in Texas with the Eighth Infantry as his escort. Twiggs stayed on in the Lone Star State until July 5, 1849, when

Orders No. 8 placed him in charge of the army's Western Division with headquarters at Pascagoula, Mississippi. With mail service characteristically slow, the troopers in North Texas did not learn of his transfer until the middle of August.[19]

Though vain and thin-skinned, William Worth was a considerable improvement over David Twiggs. Like Twiggs, Worth had achieved his high rank via politics, long service, and fortuitous circumstances. Also like Twiggs, he was a product of the militia, not West Point, though he had served honorably as the first commandant of cadets at the United States Military Academy in the 1820s.

Worth had come up from the ranks, starting out as a private three decades earlier and fighting in three major wars: against the British in 1812, the Seminole Indians from 1840 to 1842, and most recently against the Mexicans. Along the way he had introduced precision drill into the curriculum at West Point and had taught the science of tactics to three men who went on to become legends in American military history—Jefferson Davis, Albert Sidney Johnston and Robert E. Lee. Joining Winfield Scott's invasion of Mexico in 1847, he commanded the amphibious landing at Vera Cruz and the heroic assault on Chapultepec Palace. He led the last troops out of Mexico City on June 12, 1848, after the peace settlement was implemented.[20] For his outstanding service he was promoted to major general and awarded a U.S. Congressional Sword of Honor. Like Twiggs he also had a disputatious temperment and an overabundance of pride.

General William Jenkins Worth. Because he died of cholera at a lonely frontier posting in peacetime, William Jenkins Worth is the antebellum army's forgotten general. Meanwhile, his contemporaries, Winfield Scott, Zachary Taylor, Franklin Pierce, Gideon Pillow, and David Twiggs all went on to greater accomplishments. (Courtesy of the Fort Worth Museum of Science and History.)

Unlike Twiggs, however, he had a bright mind and a genuine fighting spirit.

It has been suggested that Worth was posted to Texas after the Mexican War because he had provoked a "rancorous quarrel" with Winfield Scott, the army's senior commander and a popular national hero, and Texas was the most dead-end assignment that could be found for him.[21] This scenario is unlikely, however, considering the great importance that Washington placed on the Southwest and the commitment the government was making at this time in terms of troops and money to keep the region. Texas, with its huge land area and huge problems, needed a commanding officer the caliber of William Worth.

On January 2, 1849, less than a month after being ordered to Texas, Worth and the Eighth U.S. Infantry landed at Galveston Island, moving inland soon thereafter to set up regimental headquarters at San Antonio, where departmental headquarters were already located.

The men arrived on January 17 and went into camp five miles from the center of the historic town at a site they named Camp Worth in honor of their popular commanding officer. Eschewing the comforts of San Antonio, the commanding general set up housekeeping with his men. This choice, while admirable from a soldier's standpoint, would produce fatal consequences because the men of the Eighth were doing battle with a more dangerous enemy than Comanches—cholera. The sickness had struck while they were bivouacked on the coast and they carried it north to Camp Worth with them. The entire regiment was suffering from the devastating effects of a raging epidemic, which left them with no more than 200 men, one-fifth of their authorized strength, capable of taking the field. During its first weeks in Texas, the Eighth was barely able to function as an active regiment, with scarcely a single company reporting more than fifteen men present for duty on a daily basis. Their first orders from Worth, modified as a result of their weakened condition, were to relieve troops of the First and Third Regiments in establishing positions on the Indian border. But those orders were withheld until the regiment was "renovated in health and recruited in men."[22]

While suffering from cholera the same as his men, Worth nonetheless threw himself into the work of his new command. At the time, the Lone Star State was still administered as a single command, designated by the Military Department of Texas and New Mexico. Worth came to Texas with specific instructions from the war department to station troops on the course of the Rio Grande below San Antonio and along the frontier settlements.[23] This meant establishing a number of new posts, but the details were left up to the commanding general. These orders would have far-reaching consequences. Eventually, Texas would become home to more military posts than any other section of the Southwest (nineteen in 1851) and tie up more than one-fifth of the U.S. Army regular forces in the antebellum period.[24]

As the new commander of the Eighth Military Department, Worth encountered a situation that was both good and bad. On one hand, he inherited all the Texas-sized problems that Twiggs had cited in his demand for promotion. On the other hand, he also inherited the rudiments of a frontier policy initiated by Twiggs.

Worth found that the first post on the frontier line had already been established by Captain Seth Eastman and the First Infantry Regiment. It was just outside the small German town of Fredericksburg in the central Hill Country near the Pedernales River. A year later the post received an official name: Fort Martin Scott. The garrison's job was to protect traffic on the military road between San Antonio and Fredericksburg from hostile Comanches, who, at the time, raided at will across the area. David Twiggs was the moving force behind the establishment of Fort Martin Scott, and its importance is indicated by the fact that for a brief time, from May 1851 through November 1852, it served as the headquarters of the Eighth Military Department and was still an active post when the Civil War broke out.

Worth's first concern—after seeing to the health of his men—was the volatile Rio Grande border, where Texans, Mexicans, and Indians all warred on each other periodically. Worth's initial move was to send Lieutenants William F. Smith of the Topograhical Engineers and William H. C. Whiting of the Engineers west toward El Paso with instructions to "select eligible sites" along the way for military posts. They set out from San Antonio on February 12, 1849, and did not return for more than two months.[25]

Whiting was soon off again to the central portion of the state on a similar mission. His preliminary orders sent him to New Orleans in July to purchase the survey instruments needed to locate "a line of posts from the Red River to the Rio Grande."[26] This second expedition kept him in the field most of the rest of the year, taking him from Eagle Pass on the Rio Grande to Coffee's Bend on the northern boundary, and securing vital information that the army needed to set up a chain of forts across the middle of the state.[27]

While the Eighth Infantry settled into its new encampment, General Worth issued his first official dispatch from "Camp Worth" on February 25, 1849. Subsequent correspondence between departmental headquarters and the fort on the upper Trinity River led to considerable confusion in names.[28] The history of Fort Worth and Camp Worth are connected, but only extraneously.

Of more immediate concern to any inquiry into the origins of Fort Worth were the Second Dragoons, the troops who built and first garrisoned the site. The regiment was organized by an Act of Congress on May 23, 1836, not, as some sources claim, to do service in Texas, but to fight Seminole Indians in Florida.[29] Their first colonel was the insufferable David E. Twiggs, who went on to eternal infamy as the officer who surrendered the entire U.S. military establishment in Texas without a fight at the beginning of the Civil War.

Troops of the U.S. dragoons often received the unwelcome assignment of locating and building new posts because cavalry was the most effective frontier force the U.S. Army had. Not only could they cover the vast distances involved in patrolling the frontier, but they were the best answer to the well mounted and highly mobile Plains Indians who were the principal enemy in the western territories.

In its relatively brief history, the American army had not prominently featured cavalry. The mounted arm was completely disbanded for nearly twenty years after the War of 1812. Even with the creation of the First Dragoon Regiment by act of Congress in 1833, the troops were still expected to ride to the battlefield on horseback but then fight dismounted.[30] When necessary, they could also fight mounted. The United States Army in the antebellum period had just two regiments of dragoons, designated the First and Second Dragoons. Each regiment consisted of ten companies, usually posted so far apart they rarely saw each other, much less gathered together as a regiment. In 1842, belt-tightening and changing tactical doctrines led to the Second Dragoons being dismounted for the next four years, but when the Mexican War started they got their horses back. They were assembled at something close to regimental strength for the first time ever, and authorized strength was set by Congress in May 1846 at 100 men per company. Both dragoon regiments were sent off to fight in Mexico. After the war, however, their companies were scattered again across the western frontier—most, but not all, of

General William Selby Harney as he appeared late in life after a checkered career in the U. S. Army. As a colonel of the Second Dragoons in Texas in 1849, he issued the orders that established Fort Worth. This is the only known picture of Harney. (Reproduced from L.U. Reavis' The Life and Military Services of General William Selby Harney [St. Louis: 1878].)

the Second Dragoons winding up in Texas. Company strength was reduced to fifty enlisted men and twelve officers.[31] Even at this strength, authorized numbers were seldom achieved in the field.

During the Mexican War a strange shift in attitude toward the dragoons occurred in the U.S. Army. Their consistently high *esprit de corps* and sparkling combat record made them elite. Adding to their new aura was the fact that the officers were all graduates of West Point and "gentlemen of intelligence." Private Samuel Chamberlain of the First Dragoons observed with a measure of pride and more than a hint of chauvinism, "The Dragoons were far superior in materials to any other arm of the service. No man of any spirit and ambition would join the 'Doughboys' [infantrymen] and go afoot, when he could ride a fine horse and wear spurs like a gentleman." He also noted a bit defensively that dragoon officers were "often harsh and tyrannical, yet they took pride in having their men well clothed and fed, in making them contented and reconciled to their lot."[32]

Despite their hard-riding, hard-fighting ways, the dragoons were not universally admired. They did not care much for drill or normal camp routines and they did not take well to orders from non-dragoon officers. Early in the Mexican War, when Worth's Eighth Infantry was bivouacked with the Second Dragoons, he labelled the horse soldiers, "a notoriously disorderly regiment in the encampment."[33] That reputation stuck with them for the remainder of the war.

Yet these were the same men who were given the monumental task after the Mexican War of patrolling and, when necessary, subduing the great Texas frontier. As the army's principal mounted troops (not to be confused with a regiment of "mounted infantry" created in 1846), the dragoons proved particularly adept at frontier warfare, a fact recognized by both the high command and members of Congress. In 1850 the Committee on Indian Affairs for the House of Representatives reported on the difference between infantry and mounted troops for Indian warfare:

> Beyond the mere guarding of posts, infantry are entirely useless for such service. If out of musket shot, the infantry might as well be a hundred miles from the scene of depredations. . . . Well mounted cavalry, armed with six-shooters and rifles, are the only force of any practical utility in overawing the western prairie Indians.[34]

Colonel George McCall, after an inspection of New Mexico Territory following the Mexican War, agreed. "I am persuaded that the nature of service to be required of the Army for the next ten years will be such as to require that the cavalry arm shall greatly predominate in its organization."[35] The vigorous service of the Second Dragoons in Texas confirmed that estimation time and again.

Their appearance alone should have scared away all but the most belligerent Indians. The troopers of the Second Dragoons were a raffish bunch, swaggering and heavily mustachioed. Many wore their hair unfashionably long, and more

David Emanuel Twiggs, about 1848, displaying his brevet major general's insignia and wearing one of the three ceremonial swords he received for his Mexican War service. He is sometimes confused in photographs with fellow Mexican War hero William Jenkins Worth. Twiggs' career spanned more than half a century and his popularity in the Army at this time was second only to Zachary Taylor's. (Courtesy of the National Archives.)

than a few even adorned themselves with gold earrings in defiance of long-standing army regulations.[36] Their closest military cousins were the legendary Texas Rangers of law enforcement fame, who shared a similar contempt for rules, regulations, and military protocol.

Dragoons always travelled heavily armed, every man carrying a saber, a carbine, and a brace of pistols, with a knife probably tucked away somewhere. To the uninitiated, they might resemble a band of common outlaws more than some of Uncle Sam's finest. Appearances aside, all this firepower made them a formidable fighting force, and explains why the Indians tended to leave them alone when they traveled en masse.

Conventional wisdom, derived partly from Sam Chamberlain, Ulysses Grant, and other soldiers of the day, states that the dragoons had a higher percentage of native-born Americans than the other arms of the regular army.[37] This may have been true elsewhere, but at Fort Worth, Company F of the Second Dragoons was nearly fifty percent foreign-born. This percentage was similar to that in the rest of the army at the time. Large numbers of Irish and Germans in particular filled the ranks of the infantry, many of them veterans of service in European armies. Fort Worth's founders included eleven Germans, six Irish, and an assortment of Swiss, Scots, and Poles. And these numbers do not include those whose country of origin is unknown but whose names suggest some heritage other than Anglo-Saxon.

The dragoons shared responsibility for securing the frontier with the infantry. Soldier for soldier, the infantry were cheaper and easier to train. So in the making of strategy and in post assignments, the two arms often served side by side.

While this arrangement suited the government, the citizens of Texas had their own opinions. One Texas newspaper complained a few years later, "The people of [this] country think themselves much exposed, as all they have to depend upon for protection are the soldiers at the posts, *but these being all Infantry* [emphasis added] the people, very naturally, place little reliance on their ability to aid them."[38]

In Texas, the Eighth was the principal infantry regiment. It was the newest in the army in 1849, having been created by Act of Congress in July 1838. As a colonel, William Worth commanded in the beginning and kept a close association with the regiment throughout the rest of his foreshortened military career. During the next seven years the regiment saw service on the Canadian border and in Florida against the Indians. The regiment was first posted to Texas in 1845 as part of General Zachary Taylor's "Army of Occupation" to keep an eye on Mexico. Their first introduction to Texas-brand hospitality occurred at Corpus Christi, which the regimental historian described as "the most murderous, thieving, gambling, cut-throat, God-forsaken hole in the Lone Star State or out of it."[39]

When hostilities commenced with Mexico in 1846 they marched into northern Mexico with Taylor, 394 men and twenty officers strong. They subsequently were transferred to General Winfield Scott's army at Veracruz to participate in his bravura advance on Mexico City, and ended the war in occupation of that place. Seventy-one members of the regiment were decorated during the conflict. On the numerous battlefields where it was fought, they were "second to none in the performance of distinguished services."[40]

They finally headed home from Mexico in July 1848 and settled in at Jefferson Barracks, Missouri, to await their next assignment. It was not long in coming. Four months after leaving the land of Cortez they were ordered to Texas via New Orleans, arriving at Port Lavaca on December 18 "in apparent good health, cheerful, comfortably clothed . . . and in first rate condition for the field." Three days later the "right wing" (five companies) was ordered to Victoria on the Guadalupe River to take up their new duties guarding the Mexican border. That same day Asiatic cholera broke out among the five companies of the "left wing" remaining at Port Lavaca, which included Company F. The right wing was also victimized, but missed the worst part of the epidemic. All together, one-third of the troops were infected, and one-half of those died in the first few hours. The epidemic did not break until December 27, but by then it had "nearly destroyed" the regiment. As the Eighth slowly recovered during early 1849, its companies were scattered among the forts and camps of Texas, where they remained for the next twelve years.[41]

When the Eighth Infantry was stricken by a second cholera outbreak in the spring of 1849, all of Worth's military plans were in jeopardy. Frontier settlements wanted protection and the war department wanted action. Work had to go ahead on the defensive line with whatever manpower was available. By some strange benevolence, the epidemic did not devastate the dragoons. While the infantry rested and recuperated in their camps, the Second Dragoons were busy establishing Fort Croghan (March 18), Fort Graham (March 27), and Fort Worth (June 2). In the latter half of 1849, the Eighth was able to return to the field, establishing Fort Lincoln (July 7) and Fort Gates (October 26).[42] Thereafter, the infantry and dragoons shared responsibility for manning this chain of forts, often combining elements from both at the same location, while at other places they rotated in and out during the life of the post. While elements of both the dragoons and infantry would have shared the task of garrisoning Fort Worth sooner or later, fate played the biggest part in putting the dragoons there first.

When General Worth died on May 7, 1849, command of the Eighth Department devolved immediately upon Colonel (and Brevet Brigadier) William Selby Harney who was at Second Dragoon headquarters in Austin when word of Worth's death came. Harney was described by a contemporary as "one of the most extraordinary men in the army," having entered the service as a second lieutenant of infantry in 1818. In 1836 he was appointed lieutenant colonel, Second Dragoons, under David Twiggs. During the Mexican War he fought with Winfield Scott in the campaign to capture Mexico City, rising to the rank of full colonel. He was warmly commended by the commanding general on more than one occasion and came out of the war a brevet brigadier general. He was, however, widely acknowledged as a "very eccentric" character.[43]

As the second ranking officer in the Department of Texas in May 1849, Harney was next in line to take over as acting commander. He retained his position at the head of the Second Dragoons and simply added the duties of department commander. For the time being, he had to answer to no one any closer than Washington, a fact he found particularly appealing. At a barrel-chested six feet two inches, he was one of the most athletic men in the army. But his judgement was another matter. He was hot-headed and impetuous, which helped make him a hero on several battlefields, but equally made him a problem for his superiors. He had an absolute genius for stirring up controversy. Once, he got into a public brawl with a teamster and whipped the man soundly. On another occasion, he outfitted his dragoons in Mexican sombreros, to the considerable dismay of his superiors and the complete delight of his men. In later years General of the Army Winfield Scott felt nothing but contempt for his "ignorance [of military decorum], passion, and caprice."[44]

Flaws and all, General Harney was nonetheless the nominal head of the department when Arnold rode north to the Trinity at the end of May 1849. By the time the new commander, Major General George Mercer Brooke, took over on June 4, Arnold had located a site and taken the first steps to found a new post near the Twin Forks. It can be said, therefore, that Fort Worth was established on William S. Harney's watch.

After Brooke took over and reviewed the actions taken by Harney, he disagreed with the latter's disposition of "forces on the frontier of Texas" but refrained from ordering any hasty changes before communicating with the War Department.[45] In the end, no changes were made, and Fort Worth remained on line guarding the Twin Forks.

There is some debate about whose orders established Fort Worth. Arnold's own orders cannot be found in the records of the National Archives or the state of Texas, though many have claimed to quote them. All the evidence points toward Harney as the hand that signed the orders, and his authority came not from his elevation to acting departmental commander, but from Worth himself. On February 13, Worth had issued Orders No. 13, dealing with the organization of his department. He showed he could delegate authority by dividing his vast command into two districts, the Rio Grande and the Frontier. Over the Frontier District he placed Harney, "the senior officer on the southwestern frontier." Harney's authority covered the area from San Juan Bautista in south Texas to the Washita River on the Texas-Oklahoma border, "including the posts on the Leona, Fredericksurg, San Antonio, and the Towash Village [near Waco]."

Worth further instructed Harney "as soon as practicable [to] make a personal inspection of, and give the necessary orders for the construction of such practical defensive arrangements as may be sufficient to guard against hostilities, and for the security of the families, stores, animals, farms." One of these "practical defensive arrangements" would become Fort Worth.[46]

Harney was acting under the orders he had received three months earlier. On May 10, three days after Worth's death, Orders No. 16 from Harney's headquarters in Austin directed "Bvt. Major Arnold with his Company to the West Fork of the Trinity." These orders were received by Arnold at Fort Graham on May 15.[47] Unfortunately, they only exist today in transcribed form as part of Fort Graham's Post Returns for May 1849. Arnold's adjutant simply noted the arrival of Orders No. 16 under "Orders Received."

For the rest of his military service, Arnold was never out from under Harney's authority. Harney remained in place as commander of the Second Dragoons in Texas even after being replaced as interim departmental commander. In December 1852, he returned for another tour of duty as head of the Eighth Military Department, replacing Persifor Smith in that position. His second tour lasted until May 1853 when he again stepped down, but he remained at the head of the Second Dragoons until July 20, 1854.

As a department commander, Harney had very little influence on events in Texas, but as the senior officer of the Second Dragoons he had a major impact on the twin problems of Indian relations and frontier defense. Harney did not believe in keeping his dragoons sitting in forts while the Indians bypassed them and raided settlements at will. The raiders must be pursued, brought to bay, and punished severely. His hard-nosed attitude toward all Indians was summed up when he was sent to the North Platte River in 1855 to pacify the Brule Sioux. Soon after arriving, he informed both the Indian Bureau and any subordinates who happened to ask, "By God, I'm for battle—no peace!"[48]

The other senior officers who came and went in the Eighth Military Department after June 1849 had little direct effect on affairs at Fort Worth or on Arnold's activities in particular. The major carried on his necessary correspondence with headquarters but had no personal dealings with his immediate superiors—George M. Brooke and Persifor Smith—in the chain of command.

Brooke was a native Virginian and career army officer who had first entered the service in 1808. He soldiered through two major conflicts, the War of 1812 and the Mexican War, before attaining major general's rank in 1848 as a reward for "meritorious conduct particularly in the performance of his duties in prosecuting the war with Mexico."[49] By the time he took over departmental command he was nearing sixty years old, an advanced age for any military officer of that day except the ageless Winfield Scott. Brooke died on the job on March 9, 1851.

Major General Persifor Smith, who followed Brooke as commander of the Eighth Department, was another old-line officer, born in Pennsylvania while John Adams was President.

He made his first career in law and politics before joining the militia and then the regular army. He distinguished himself on the field in both the Seminole and Mexican wars. In May 1848 as military governor of Veracruz, he oversaw the embarkation of U.S. troops headed back to the states. He met with many of those same troops again in Texas three years later when he took over command of the Eighth Department. By that time he had been promoted to brevet major general. Less than two years later, he was transferred to the Western Department at St. Louis, leaving a faint but significant imprint on military affairs in Texas: He was the "architect" of the second line of frontier forts in Texas, constructed between 1851 and 1859.[50] During Smith's brief tenure, his decisions from San Antonio had no noticeable impact on Arnold's command. When he had problems, Arnold preferred to write directly to the Adjutant General's Office in Washington, D.C., bypassing the chain of command.[51]

General Worth's plan from the beginning was to establish "six points on a general line from the Rio Grande in the direction of the Washita" in present-day Oklahoma. His defensive arrangements would incorporate the points first selected by the government of the Republic of Texas six years earlier. To illustrate his plan he sent a sketch of the Texas frontier along with his written report to the War Department in Washington, D.C. The map was quite accurate, being drawn up by Lieutenants Francis T. Bryan and Nathaniel Michler of the Topographical Engineers.[52] Qualified engineers were a rarity on the frontier and their services were always at a premium whether mapmaking, laying out forts, or surveying roads. As of February 18, 1849, Worth's plans were not developed to the point of marking any sites on the map. Nonetheless, the army supported his plans completely.

In spite of Worth's battle with cholera, he was able to travel, make inspections, and carry on correspondence with his superiors and subordinates. More importantly, he saw to the establishment of Fort Inge (March 13), Fort Croghan (March 18), and Fort Graham (March 27) on his proposed defensive line. He now had two-thirds of the frontier covered.[53] There were still gaps to the west of San Antonio, south of Fort Graham between the Brazos and the Colorado, on the Nueces River between San Antonio and Corpus Christi, and on the upper Trinity. Fort Worth, initiated by his successor, would fill the gap on the upper Trinity. Fort Lincoln, established by elements of the Eighth Infantry fifty miles west of San Antonio on July 7, 1849, filled that gap. Fort Gates, founded on the Leon River on October 26, 1849, and Fort Merrill, established on the Nueces River fifty miles from Corpus Christi in March of 1850, filled the last two gaps.

Completed in less than a year, the chain roughly followed the Balcones Escarpment, crossing six rivers and nearly 300 miles from north to south. General Worth, however, never lived to see his defensive system in place. At 1:00 P.M. on May 7, 1849, he succumbed to the same disease that had taken so many of his men, dying at his headquarters in San Antonio.

A hundred years later, William Jenkins Worth would be remembered as a hero in only two places in this country: New York City where his neglected and often overlooked monument stands, and the city posthumously named for him.

It is clear from examining army records that Fort Worth was not part of a master plan from the War Department in Washington. It was one link in a chain, with the number and location of the posts that formed the chain left up to the judgement of commanders on the scene. The initiative taken by Arnold and other local commanders like William Jenkins Worth and William S. Harney was neither presumptuous nor surprising in light of the fact that the U.S. Army had no comprehensive plan in the antebellum period for mounting a frontier defense and no budget for establishing new posts as they were needed. Before 1855 the government did not even consider creating a line in the budget to cover "selecting sites for [new] posts."[54]

Fort Worth's humble origins are typical. It started, literally, as an "outpost" for Fort Graham. The garrison was always understrength and often poorly equipped, its mission vaguely defined. The place could only be located on a map by tracing the route of the Trinity River to the junction of the twin forks and proceeding another mile upriver. There, at latitude 32 degrees 47 minutes and longitude 97 degrees 25 minutes stood Fort Worth.

Fort Graham had been founded three months earlier also by Company F, Second Dragoons, under the personal com-

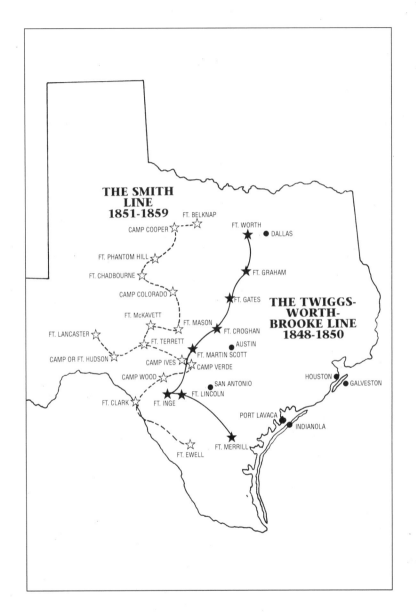

mand of Colonel Harney. Major Arnold took over the post in the middle of April and completed the work begun by his predecessor. Using Graham as a base, he could extend the defense line another fifty-six miles north to the Trinity. Fort Graham was the main post, Fort Worth, the outpost.[55] Neither place fit the popular conception of an armed fort. As one unimpressed visitor to Fort Graham commented, "This is not strictly speaking, a fort, but merely a Military Depot with a small detachment of troops, a few traders and the hangers on, of such places."[56] The Fort Worth-Fort Graham relationship was not unusual. The U.S. Army favored a system of primary and secondary posts to defend the frontier. Companies of soldiers from the main post could then be rotated in and out of the outpost, or "picket post" as it was called, on a regular basis. This approach to frontier defense had the twin benefits of economizing on both construction and garrison costs. It was especially useful in Texas where there was so much frontier to be defended. Thus, Fort Martin Scott was founded as an outpost for San Antonio, and Fort Chadbourne for picket details sent out of Fort Concho. Fort Stockton, on the road between San Antonio and El Paso, had outposts at Escondidos, Rainbow Cliffs, and Frazier's Ranch. After the Civil War, Fort Phantom Hill served as the outpost for Fort Griffin.[57]

There was an urgency in the summer of 1849 to get this line laid out and its component posts constructed and manned. Without them the frontier was wide open to Indian raids, particularly roving bands of Comanches who had been relatively quiet since signing a peace treaty in 1846. Now they were on the warpath again as they found themselves being inexorably squeezed out of their traditional hunting grounds in central Texas. After returning from his reconnaissance expedition to El Paso in the spring of 1849, Lieutenant Whiting reported in September that the southwestern frontier was "exceedingly unsettled [and] the Comanches are preparing for war." This underscored a dire prediction he had written two months previously that, "A genuine Indian war [in Texas] will shortly obtain."[58]

Whiting's alarming reports merely confirmed what the army knew: the western frontier needed a stronger defense than the state of Texas was able to provide. The solution to the problem was clear. In the next decade, fully one-fourth of the army's total manpower would be committed to Texas.

3
REVEILLE AND FATIGUE

Major Arnold's second trek to the Twin Forks region went as smoothly as the first. Once again they stopped at the cold spring. The dragoons were more heavily loaded down this time because they brought with them all the tools and equipment it would take to carve their new home out of the wilderness. Everything they would need was stowed in several four-wheeled baggage wagons, each pulled by six sturdy mules. It was a form of army conveyance that would not change for another quarter century—and the Quartermaster Department seemed determined to keep some of the wagons in service that long.[1] He issued brief orders to his men as soon as they reached their destination—some to unload the wagons, others to set up camp among the trees or to fan out and search for game; and, of course, he was careful to post several men as pickets. The campsite was not a natural defensive position; it would be easy for a hostile force to sneak up close and surprise them without proper safeguards.

Arnold was also concerned that his men had not had a real rest in seven months. Since leaving Pascagoula, Mississippi, on November 1, 1848, they had travelled by ship and horseback to Austin, Texas, and from there to Camp Inge on the Rio Bosque, arriving on December 8. They left Camp Inge on February 26, 1849, and marched to Camp Thornton, then to Fort Graham, arriving on April 4. During those six months of service in the field, six men had died of natural causes, leaving Company F with only thirty-two men present for duty at Fort Graham at the end of April. Eight men were on sick call. A month later, Arnold himself reported sick, but there was no time to take leave. He would have to recuperate while establishing the new post on the Trinity.[2]

Since the dragoons were on a construction assignment, they anticipated no serious trouble, and so they came better equipped for carpentry than for fighting. They had brought no artillery with them for the simple reason that they did not have any. None of the dragoons in Texas did, and this was a major concern second only to the manpower shortage. The only available guns were at the Eighth Infantry depot in San Antonio, but they were not assigned to the dragoons. Soon after taking over the department in June, Major General G. M. Brooke wrote the War Department "suggesting" that each company of dragoons in the state "be furnished with a mountain howitzer."[3] In the meantime, Company F began its service on the upper Trinity without the comforting back-up of a big gun. Major Arnold was acutely aware of what a disadvantage that was for his command: in the event of an Indian attack, they would have to repel the raiders with only their sidearms. Before the end of June, Arnold wrote to San Antonio requesting artillery. "All is well," he reported, "but we would be better equipped to deal with our problems if a howitzer could be sent to us."[4] A twelve-pound mountain howitzer (series 1840-41), so named because it was lightweight and easily transportable, was eventually sent up from San Antonio but not for several more months. The Indians feared the weapon because it could toss an explosive shell as far as a mile at an elevation of five degrees. There is only the most dubious historical evidence that it was ever fired in anger.[5]

Ever since their first bivouac, the mood had been light, though the troopers had no idea whether they were being watched by hostile eyes. There was even a touch of bravado as they professed themselves to be "perfectly indifferent to Indians, wolves and all the wild enemies of the white man."[6]

Still, they were trespassing on Indian lands, not as innocent wayfarers but as intruders bent on pushing the white man's claims into new territory.

Arnold's initial encampment with his full company was not on the site of the future fort, nor even in the immediate vicinity, but at the "elegant cold spring" where he had spent the night with his locating party a week earlier. There in the familiar grove of live oaks, about one mile from the bluff, he ordered his men to put up their tents and lay out their camp. In those days the location was commonly known as Live Oak Point, and in the years to come old-timers were able to point it out without hesitation. Today, the site cannot be located. The best that can be said is that it was on the upper end of Samuels Avenue, just north of Pavilion Street and near the Treaty Oak—"in the bend of the Trinity," according to the old-timers. The troops stayed for two months while constructing the fort, but this encampment was never intended to be a permanent home.[7]

Among the folklore about Fort Worth is a story that the dragoons initially camped in the river bottom, but there is no evidence to support this notion. In fact, even the humblest private would have known better. No West Point-trained officer would have set up camp in a noxious river bottom where his men were vulnerable to sudden attack from hostile Indians and infestations of mosquitoes—not when the nearby bluff offered a better strategic position. Arnold was quiet on the subject, but his first quartermaster, Lieutenant Samuel Starr, hinted at the obvious problems in one of his early reports: it was too close to the river on relatively soft, low-lying land covered by dense undergrowth. The fresh-water spring, which was the only real attraction of the site, was no trade-off for the negatives. Plus the heavy tree growth would have multiplied the work to be done clearing the ground for a fort.

Whether the dragoons ever intended to stay longer at Live Oak Point than was absolutely necessary is open to debate. The earliest city history describes their encampment as "temporary quarters," and army reports explain the reason for moving as soon as possible. As Starr recorded some months later, "The first location was thought to be unhealthy," so it was "removed to its present site." His evaluation was confirmed by Lieutenant W.H.C. Whiting who came through in 1849 and found the whole Trinity locale to be very unhealthy.[8] Starr, of course, was not at Fort Worth in the summer of 1849, but his report is probably the origin of the lore.[9]

Further clouding the issue are the claims of settler Press Farmer, who reminisced that he first visited the dragoon camp in the summer of 1849, looking for the surgeon to treat his friend Edmund S. Terrell. He found sickness "prevailing among the soldiers" and recommended the high bluffs as a better spot for the post. Whether Arnold had already decided to move is moot, but in later years, Farmer received credit: "The advisability of the change commended itself, and as soon as the proper arrangements could be made a removal was effected."[10]

Standing on the bluff, Arnold surveyed his new domain with the practiced eye of a trained officer. There was a relatively level area of several well-drained acres for a parade ground, and plenty of wood and water nearby. The boundaries of the "reservation" would be determined by how much land he wanted to clear and how many men he had to accommodate—at this early date a single company. There was no master plan for building frontier posts. Each one was built to fit its surroundings and available building materials.

The fact that most frontier posts had an unremarkable sameness about them was more by circumstance than design. The officers who built them came from a common background. Every graduate of West Point after 1830 had studied civil and military engineering under the brilliant Dennis Hart Mahan, and his teachings were drilled into their heads. But on the frontier every officer in Arnold's position was also his own architect, contractor, and builder.

Arnold set about building a fort to fit the needs of his command and to meet the requirements of his mission. While contemplating this challenge, he was reminded of the words of Tate Johnson when the dragoons first arrived at Johnson's Station: "Major, we've been in need of you. Our homes have been burned; our women and children kidnapped and held for ransom; and our livestock stolen by the Indians from reservations north of Red River. We have sent protest upon protest to Governor George T. Wood but to no avail. Thank heaven the President has heard and answered our plea."[11] The major did not bother to tell him that

President Zachary Taylor had no knowledge of their plight and was unaware of their plea.

Arnold's mission, as outlined in Orders No. 13, was simple and straightforward: establish the first outpost of United States troops in this desolate region as a necessary step to protect the several small and struggling frontier settlements nearby. The largest of those villages was Dallas, thirty-five miles to the east and therefore under no imminent threat from raiding Indians. Of more immediate concern were the nearby settlements of Birdville and Alton (present-day Keller), each with fewer than fifty residents and no military protection closer than Fort Graham. Johnson's Station also had great potential for growth. If these places were to prosper and other settlements were to be planted in the area a regular garrison would have to be established.

The prime directive contained in Worth's orders recognized this fact: "The first and highest duties of the troops throughout the line of forts . . . is to afford security in persons and property to the citizens residing within, or near, such lines."

There was a second part of his mission, which would not please land-hungry settlers, and that was, "By kindness and all proper forebearance, to conciliate the Indian tribes—protect them from violence and injustice, and make them understand this true interest and their obligations."[12] The idea of protecting the Indians from the whites was not a popular one with men like Tate Johnson and Simon Farrar, but it was part of Arnold's orders nevertheless.

Ownership of the land on the Trinity was not an issue in the beginning. The only residents in the immediate area in the summer of 1849 were two squatters, Press Farmer and Edmund S. Terrell, who were "camped" southwest of the bluff and hardly likely to dispute land claims.[13] For all practical purposes, the land where Arnold settled down with his company was unoccupied and unclaimed. If anything, the Army was a welcome neighbor to every other property owner within a day's ride. In the bigger picture, Texas was the landlord of record since the state had retained the right to all its public lands when it entered the Union in 1845. Unlike every other state, Texas' public lands did not automatically become part of the federal domain. In the years after 1845 the U.S. Army was forced to negotiate with the state for sites upon which to build its forts and depots. The laws of Texas permitted the U.S. Government to "purchase sites in organized counties," but in the summer of 1849 Tarrant County was still unorganized, so the Fort Worth site could not be properly deeded to the Army even if Washington and Austin had agreed to do so.[14]

The government seldom held title to the land on which its Western forts were located so troops constructed temporary, inexpensive quarters whenever possible and added to them or upgraded them as necessity required. On the frontier, the garrisons constituted little more than squatters. None of the frontier posts erected in Texas between the Mexican War and the Civil War were on land owned free and clear by the U.S. government. Sometimes, as in the case of Fort Chadbourne, land was secured through long-term lease for nominal annual payments.[15] More often, the army simply preempted unsurveyed country and maintained possession as long as necessary. The state and its citizens were forced to accept this extralegal arrangement if they wanted U.S. Army troops to guard the frontier.

Initially, the land was gladly ceded in strategic parcels known as "reservations" to the government by a state legislature anxious about frontier security. This produced some curious arrangements. When the Eighth Infantry first set up headquarters in San Antonio, they moved into the Alamo, put a new roof on the old mission, and proceeded to use it for many years as a Quartermaster Depot—all without title to the property. The regiment's operating budget was so poor, the commanding general of the Eighth was forced to rent his personal quarters in a modest building elsewhere in the city (the corner of Houston and St. Mary's streets).[16]

In the years that followed, with more than three dozen posts and camps scattered across Texas, the army was forced to deal with the thorny problem of land claims. Neither of the traditional alternatives, preemption or renting, was ideal. In 1867 the secretary of war noted the "difficulty as well as expense [that] attends the renting of land for military sites in Texas," and the legal complications resulting from preemption had been demonstrated time and again. He recommended purchasing sites wherever possible or, when the land was left in private hands, building temporary structures.[17] Finally, in 1867, Congress took the matter out of the army's hands by set-ting up a board for the purchase of military sites in Texas. The board was to set the value of military reservations, determine the legal owners of the land, and, where long-term occupation was desirable, make an offer to the owners to purchase.[18] None of this concerned Ripley Arnold. Any corrective to fix the problem, or even recognition that a problem existed, remained far in the future at the time Fort Worth was formally established, so Major Arnold's little outpost was located under the older policy of preemption.

When Arnold first surveyed his new realm, he must have felt like Robinson Crusoe: practically everything he could need was right in his back yard. All the basic materials necessary to build a post—what the official documents described as "an abundance of stone and timber"—were to be found nearby.[19] And once the place was built, no other post on the frontier would be so well fixed in terms of forage and subsistence. The "little villages" of Dallas and Alton plus "numerous hamlets" dotting the Cross Timbers could supply "nearly everything that [was] required for consumption by the troops."[20]

The challenge was to turn raw materials into stables, storehouses and living quarters. On the level tableland atop the limestone bluffs the troopers went to work under Arnold's watchful eye. In the next few weeks they began carving a post out of the wilderness by sheer sweat and back-breaking toil. The first order of business was to lay out a parade ground, the traditional center of any military post. Here they first raised Old Glory over the unfinished works, lashing a pair of thin tree trunks together to make a rough-hewn flagstaff. The first flag-raising ceremony was a moment of great pride. The flag they saluted bore one star for each of the thirty states in the Union in 1849.

Next they had to lay in a supply of timber so that work could proceed steadily. Fort Worth troopers were lucky—men at some other Texas posts, where wood was scarce, literally had to break up "old bacon boxes" and gun chests just to make coffins.[21] The broad river bottom and the nearby creek environs were full of trees. Farther away but still easily accessible was the dense expanse of the Cross Timbers. Tall, straight cottonwoods were cut down first for use in the barracks. But there were not enough cottonwoods nearby, so the work details were not picky. Pecan, elm, and post oak grew profusely in the rich bottom land, interspersed with hackberry and cedar. Turning this resource into usable lumber was a problem that demanded the right kind of wood—mesquite and post oak, for instance, were useless—plus skilled labor and a fully functioning sawmill.

They had brought along a "horse-powered saw mill," and soon put it to work. But their portable technology proved inadequate to the demands placed on it; the saw was slow and inefficient. Making the job worse, none of the trees the men hauled up to the bluff were really suitable for making boards, and the planks that could be fashioned had to be worked at least partly by hand. Squared timber for framing and flat pieces for shingles and scantling had to be hauled in from Johnson's Station, site of the nearest heavy-duty sawmill. In a few months Tate Johnson had an operation going that was capable of turning out 300,000 board feet of post-oak planking and 3,000 of oak and cedar scantling per year. Better yet, he was willing to supply all of the army's lumber needs at a good price. Thanks to the abundance of trees, and to Johnson, the men at Fort Worth were better off than those at other posts. At Fort Belknap, for instance, building materials had to be hauled in at exorbitant prices from as far away as forty-five miles.[22]

The main problem at Fort Worth was that the timber harvested had to be used before it had time to season. It dried, warped and split under the blistering Texas sun, leaving cracks in the buildings big enough for a man to peer through. When fall showers came, followed by winter winds, the men suffered greatly, cursing the day they had been assigned to the tiny post on the Trinity.

Slowly, what had been unbroken prairie was transformed into something resembling a true military post of sturdy log structures. Other than signs of military occupation, however, the future fort looked like any construction site, with tools and materials scattered about among half-finished structures and temporary quarters. Waist-high grass still grew in the vicinity of what is now Commerce Street, and present-day Main Street was nothing but a wagon trail. Just outside the front gate two roads converged—one from Dallas and the other from Fort Graham via "Little's Ford." If not watched carefully, post horses sometimes wandered off on one of the roads and had to be chased down.[23]

Arnold's "construction foremen" were the four non-commissioned officers—sergeants and corporals—attached to Company F. The major himself was the only commissioned officer on the site; not a single captain or lieutenant was present during those early weeks to share the burdens of command and shoulder some of the work. Indeed, there had been no junior officers with Company F since the previous January though two were assigned. Without the usual chain of command, Arnold relied a great deal on Sergeant Jacob Dearing and Corporal Daniel McCauly to see that his orders were carried out.[24]

The troopers went about their work without benefit of trained engineers or civilian contractors. To the best of their ability, they performed the jobs of bricklayer, carpenter, stonemason, millwright, and draftsman. This put the buildings of Fort Worth in marked contrast to the way those in Fort Graham had been built. There, members of the Second Dragoons had been assisted by skilled laborers.[25]

Through June, July and into August, Arnold drove his men. The work was hard, the days were long, and there is every reason to suspect that the men relieved the loneliness and eased their aches and pains with something stronger than army-issue coffee. There is no direct testimony to this effect, but it is hard to believe somebody did not sneak a bottle or more along when they rode out of Fort Graham. Liquor was often considered the soldier's best friend: cheap, easy to procure, readily stored, and not prone to spoil. It could slake a man's thirst in the summer, warm his bones in the winter, and

ease the pain of his labors. It also made bad food tolerable and could serve as a handy, self-prescribed medication.

Day after day the men had to do double duty as both soldiers and laborers, and after just three weeks Arnold's men were worn out. Out of the forty-one men who had accompanied him north, ten privates were on sick report and only one of his two regular sergeants, Jacob Dearing, was with him. William Slade, his other sergeant, had been left ill at Fort Graham, as had Privates Frederick Kleinsmith and William Whitburn, both of whom died before rejoining the company. Even the bugler was sick. In their weakened state, Company F could not have withstood a determined Indian attack during those weeks. Their senses dulled with fatigue, they showed scant resemblance to the crack fighting unit the dragoons were supposed to be.[26]

About the first of August, Company F moved its camp from Live Oak Point up to the bluff "immediately opposite the junction of the West and Clear Forks of the Trinity."[27] Construction continued unabated. While they sawed and hauled and cleared, the men lived in field tents made of light-weight tarpaulin material. Arnold established his first official headquarters at Fort Worth in such a tent, "on the block just west of the [later] courthouse square," while his command camped around him "according to army regulations." Those flimsy canvas walls formed their first home. Even months later, after winter had descended, some new additions to the garrison were forced to sleep in tents out of necessity. In

January 1850, three weeks after he reported to Fort Worth, for example, Lieutenant Samuel Starr wrote his wife that he had "lived in a tent till two or three days ago."[28]

If the pattern followed in the early days of other Texas posts is any indication, the men may have used those same tarpaulins as the first roofs on their quarters until shingles and clapboards could be obtained.[29] Some probably even slept on the open ground under the stars, though they had to be careful of snakes and spiders. Since the weather was characteristically hot and dry that summer, those arrangements were adequate. Slithering and crawling creatures were not as much of a problem at night to men tucked away in a bedroll as during the day while laboring in the river bottom. There, the danger of poisonous bites and stings was ever present from centipedes, scorpions, and tarantulas, not to mention copperheads, moccasins, and rattlesnakes. Because of primitive medical care, a bite from any of these could easily prove fatal. One later visitor to Texas warned, "Snakes of every variety, hue and description abound." He reserved his greatest fear to the undeserving centipede, however, as "the most fatal of all the wild or creeping things. . . . He does not bite; but each of his thousand legs contains the venomous sting which is so fatal to life. There is no cure—no hope. . . ." But the least fear-invoking creature was also the most dangerous. The mosquito was not just a maddening pest, but the greatest danger to health because it carried malaria.[30]

From their elevated vantage point, approximately 100 feet above the Trinity, the soldiers enjoyed an unobstructed view of the countryside in all directions, bracing breezes, and some relief from the biting, stinging creatures that infested the bottoms.[31] On the other hand they were also now at the mercy of summer's scorching sun and, even worse, winter's icy blasts that came whistling down from the north. In the years that followed, the dreaded "northers," or "blue whistlers" as Texans often called them, would be cursed more vehemently and remembered longer by the soldiers and settlers who experienced them than the sweltering summers. The trade-off between malaria in one location versus pneumonia or sunstroke in another was hardly cheering.

Indians, dangerous varmints and inadequate shelter from the weather were not the only problems Arnold had. His biggest concern after securing the area against attack was to locate an adequate supply of drinking water, not just for his work parties, but for the garrison that would take up residency on the post. Despite the fort's perch over a river, the problem was not as simple as it might seem. Trinity River water was brackish at best and its seasonal flow was highly unpredictable, dwindling to a muddy trickle and "pool beds of stagnant water" in the hottest months of the year. When it was in full flow, the river could serve many essential purposes, but human consumption was only a last resort; for all practical purposes it was not potable.

There was the clear, cold spring at Live Oak Point, but that water had to be hauled nearly a mile which would never do as a long-term solution. The first fresh water enjoyed by the troops was hauled by bucket "from a pool on the Clear Fork near the junction with the West Fork," only half the distance from the fort to the cold spring.[32] But as nice as that was, it was still too far away for the regular needs of the post. They needed a well within the perimeter for reasons of convenience and security. That meant digging.

One of Arnold's first assignments, therefore, was to put his men to work digging for water. Since the real work of building a fort could not proceed until a close-by water supply was found, it is likely that Arnold put a good number of the company on that task. Digging for water was very much a hit or miss thing; there was no science to it, just intuition, trial and error. The experience gained by these same men building Fort Graham was put to good use at Fort Worth. Digging a hole and finding water at the bottom of it did not guarantee a long-term reserve. There was always the fear that the water might prove salty, not a rare occurrence even far inland. Standard operating procedure called for digging down to a depth of sixty feet, and if nothing was found by that level, giving up and trying another location. As he watched his men dig down through the layers of soil and limestone that formed the top of the bluff, Arnold was aware of reports that it seldom rained in this region. What he did not know, but would not have been surprised at, was that another post founded in this same region about the same time subsequently had to be abandoned due to a lack of water.[33]

The well-digging crew hit several dry holes before finding pure water after passing fifteen feet. In a dispatch to Major General Brooke at department headquarters, written some two and half weeks after they arrived, Arnold reported that they had "discovered a good water supply."[34] For the rest of its life as an active post, Fort Worth never had a water shortage. The original well furnished a reliable supply of safe drinking water in all seasons. For other purposes, water could be hauled in by "public wagon" from either the river or from the cold spring without having to go more than "one-eighth to one-half mile" from the post.[35]

The officers' and enlisted men's quarters were ready for occupancy by the middle of August. The men could feel justifiable pride at what they had accomplished in a mere nine weeks. Additional months of work lay ahead of them before Fort Worth would begin to take on the appearance of a real army post and even then the hasty and deficient construction would be painfully obvious. None of the buildings had foundations, despite the abundance of limestone right under their feet. Instead, their floors consisted of the hard-packed prairie, which turned into dust in the summer and mud in the winter, making it impossible to keep anything clean or dry. The walls and roofs, made of half finished timber, kept out neither the heat of summer nor the cold of winter, and even a light rain could produce misery. The arrangement of quarters was so poorly planned that the stable was put too close to the soldiers' barracks. The last word on the buildings came from a member of the garrison who said, "They were put up under a burning sun with little or no aid from the Government, by a weak and sickly command, unacclimated, and breathing the infectious malaria of the bottom-lands, where alone timber suitable for building can be obtained."[36]

There was a temporary air about Fort Worth that it never outgrew. This derived partly from its original designation as a secondary post. The lack of practical construction skills among its builders was another reason. But even if the notoriously penurious army had been willing to employ skilled labor, there was no place in the vicinity to hire a construction crew. By the time settlers with the necessary skills moved into the area, the fort was up and going.

Arnold himself had no interest in putting up permanent shelters at the site; if so inclined, he could have used the abundant limestone in the cliffs above the river as building material. But this would have required, at the very least, skilled supervision of his soldier-workers, and a great deal more back-breaking work before the post could be occupied. The orders of the day, it seemed, were "be quick" and "be cheap."[37]

Finally, the dilapidated state of Fort Worth can be traced directly back to General Worth's Orders No. 13. Worth directed Colonel Harney to "give the necessary orders" to his officers to construct a series of frontier forts according to the general's own plan. But Worth added this crucial proviso: "No permanent construction of quarters, etc. will be made until the dispositions herein ordered, shall be sanctioned by the superi-

or authority."[38] Whether he meant by "superior authority," his own headquarters or the war department in Washington is unclear, but either interpretation discouraged site officers like Ripley Arnold from investing too much labor and money in places that might be abandoned when the next orders came through. Worth's untimely death and the delay in assigning his permanent replacement complicated the issue, putting all long-term building projects in limbo.

Even after Company F moved into their new quarters, the place looked like a strong wind could blow it down. Two years later one officer described it as having a "very temporary character," and even at the end, the post commander, Hamilton W. Merrill, criticized what he called "the most temporary nature" of the public buildings at Fort Worth.[39]

4
CALL TO QUARTERS

What little is known about the layout of living quarters, stables and outbuildings at Fort Worth is derived from three official reports and the recollections of local old-timers recorded many years later. Two of those reports were by post quartermasters and the third was by army inspector Lieutenant Colonel William G. Freeman, who came through in 1853 shortly before the post was abandoned. Only Freeman left a rough sketch of the design.[1] Over the four years of Fort Worth's life as an active post the evolution of its buildings can be followed from these reports, which included surveys of all public buildings on the site. They show that it was in a state of transition from the beginning.[2]

The completed post covered several acres arranged around a central parade ground located "where Belknap Street now runs," and laid out on a rather "contracted" scale according to Lieutenant W. H. C. Whiting, the first official visitor to the fort. The lieutenant attributed the spartan layout to the fact that the fort was originally designed for just one company.[3]

The parade ground was 250 feet wide and a little less than 300 feet long, forming a rough quadrangle where the soldiers drilled and assembled. The geographic center of the post was the "tall flag staff" which stood on the parade ground about one block west of the present-day courthouse square. An 1877 description says the soldiers' quarters and the blacksmith's and wheelwright's workshops composed a double row of buildings on the north side of the parade ground "immediately on the bluff." Facing them on the south side were the officers' quarters. On the east were the stables, while the hospital and offices of the quartermaster and commissary supply were opposite on the west side. The "warehouses" for the quartermaster and commissary departments were farther west on a line with the officers' quarters. The sutler's store, when it was added, was "still [farther] west and north of these," about where West Weatherford and Taylor streets intersect today.[4]

Another early description dating from 1889 provides additional information that can be matched with the city street grid to pinpoint building locations. This shows the officers' row to be in the vicinity of present-day Belknap Street, west by southwest of where Belknap and Houston streets intersect.[5]

Separated from the other officers' quarters was the surgeon's house, which was on the east side of the parade ground, putting it uncomfortably close to the stables. Major Ripley Arnold's quarters were on the east end of officers' row, with the junior officers' cabins stretching out in a straight line to the west. The first soldiers' "shelter" was a little to the north, near the intersection of Houston and Bluff streets, and "under some trees." The stable covered a portion of the ground later taken up by the public square.[6]

For lack of any better points of reference, old-timers always descibed the layout of the fort in terms of buildings familiar to their contemporaries. Some of these references, like the old Leonard's Department Store, a landmark from the 1940s-1960s, can easily be pinpointed on modern street maps, but the earliest descriptions, which use such reference points as "the residence of our late fellow citizen G.W. Newman," are more problematical.[7]

The post was enclosed by a rope fence outlining the perimeter but otherwise providing a defensive barrier only against wandering livestock.[8] There was never a stockade or fortified structure on the site, contrary to the popular image of a frontier fort.

The first structures raised on the site were living quarters for the garrison. These consisted of three or four rough log-and-puncheon (or split log) cabins, weatherproofed by daubing and chinking mud and small pieces of wood into the cracks. They lacked floors but had chimneys of sticks held together with mud daubing. These rude accommodations were later described as "huts." Separate kitchens, also of split logs, were built at the same time. The quarters and kitchens were roofed with "rived boards [split off with an axe] and shingles," which were attached with wooden pins, nails being scarce on the frontier. The result did a poor job of keeping out rain. Doors were made from "slabs faced with a broad axe," hung on wooden hinges and fastened with a wooden latch. These huts, intended to shelter 120 men or slightly more than a full-strength company, served as the enlisted men's quarters for the next two years.[9]

Officers' quarters would have been the next priority for Arnold's work crews. Three sets of officers' quarters, made of rough-cut logs and roofed with shingles, were initially erected. Each had two rooms with a connecting passage or dogtrot and an attached kitchen. The kitchen extensions were roofed only with "rived boards," which were easier to prepare and put up than shingles. Attaching the kitchens to the living quarters was unusual, but it allowed the buildings to be thrown up more quickly. One set of these quarters, the cabin Arnold moved into,

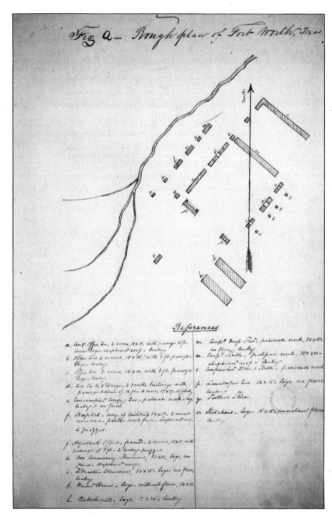

"Rough Plan of Fort Worth, Texas" by Lieutenant Colonel W. G. Freeman for his "Report of Inspection of the Eighth Military Department" in 1853. (Courtesy of the National Archives [RG 94].)

was a "substantial building," measuring fifty-two by seventeen and a half feet with a good stone chimney in each of the rooms.

The two junior officers' quarters were more modest. One of them was a framed structure measuring forty-one by sixteen feet, on the same floor plan as the commanding officer's cabin: two rooms with a connecting passageway. Like Arnold's cabin it also had a log kitchen attached to the rear and a pair of good stone chimneys. The whole was "sided with sawed clapboards." A simple description of the place, however, does not convey much of a sense of how habitable it was. There was some disagreement. Lieutenant Samuel Starr described it in May 1851 as a "good frame building," without further elaboration. Five months later, Lieutenant John Bold called it a "miserable frame building" and listed its chief flaws: the timber for the frames had been "got out by the enlisted men and put up green." The weather boarding which formed the sides was also green and "where put on has shrank so much as to admit winds and rain on all sides." The roof, which Bold described as being made of clapboards rather than shingles, also tended to "admit the rain freely."[10]

If the better of the junior officers' quarters left much to be desired, the other one was barely livable. It was a "temporary hut" on the familiar two-room floor plan but made of rough logs with the bark left on. Each room was fifteen feet square with a mud and stick chimney. A small kitchen, also of logs, was attached to the rear. There is a question whether these quarters had a clapboard or a shingled roof, but it did not do the job. Bold described his cabin as being "much dilapidated." By comparison the other cabin was almost luxurious. In the fall of 1851 it was occupied by two officers, Lieutenant Bold himself and Lieutenant Washington P. Street.[11]

Whatever their flaws, the officers' quarters were always more comfortable and more spacious than the enlisted men's barracks. At some Texas posts the officers' quarters could be identified by the wide "piazzas" on the front, but the officers assigned to Fort Worth enjoyed no such frills, largely because of the spartan construction methods adopted by Arnold. Except for greater privacy, the officers' quarters differed little from those of the men.[12]

Apparently, there was some delay building the officers' cabins. Two weeks after Samuel Starr arrived in the winter of 1849 and 1850, he was still living in a tent. He observed glumly to his wife, "I see but little prospect of getting into quarters for the present." Two weeks later he was finally able to move into one room of a two-room log cabin that he shared with the post surgeon.[13]

After living quarters, the next order of business for the Second Dragoons was to construct a stable. A dragoon had to take care of his mount, sometimes even before he took care of his own welfare. A horse—hard to replace and impossible to do without—was the most valuable piece of property the army entrusted to a man, and a deserter who took his horse with him could be assured of a harsher punishment when he was caught than a man who simply went over the hill. Indians

also were always on the lookout for unguarded horseflesh, considering it the greatest prize of all in their raids.

For these reasons, Arnold wasted no time getting his stables up. The first was a log building, a hundred by thirty feet, formed of split logs placed upright in the ground and covered over with a clapboard roof or rived boards. A small, attached room served as forage room, corn crib and company storeroom. That same structure was still standing two years later, although in an extreme "state of dilapidation."[14]

Like most of the buildings on the post, the stable leaked, but that was not the worst of it. It was too close to the living quarters of both officers and soldiers, so close, in fact, that when they closed their eyes at night they felt like they were sleeping in the same room with their horses. The reason for this was not a blunder on Arnold's part, but a well-intended effort to address the problem of securing their horses in the event of a surprise Indian attack. Others were not so impressed with the major's logic, however. Lieutenant Whiting, who was on a reconnaissance not an inspection trip, when he stopped in 1849, nonetheless felt obliged to criticize strongly this arrangement in his official report, noting that "however thorough the police may be, [it] cannot help but be offensive in summer." He suggested relocating the stables farther away but still "within a [rifle] shot from the barracks" and posting a picket at night would be "ample" security.[15] Apparently his suggestion was ignored because in 1853 the flies and the stench from the stables were still serious enough to provoke another round of criticism, this time in an official medical report.[16] That they had not been relocated shows again the low priority given to making any long-term improvements to an outpost never intended as permanent.

With men and beasts taken care of, the other buildings could be constructed with less urgency. These were the various structures required at a working post regardless of its size or long-term prospects. They included a hospital and dispensary complex, commissary and quartermaster storehouses, a guard-house, several workshops and a general-purpose office. Some were built of frame and some of log; all were rudimentary.

The hospital was the nicest and best finished of the original dozen or so structures, being sided with weather boards (one inch thick, placed vertically) and roofed with shingles. Inside it was "ceiled with inch boards." It measured thirty-four by seventeen feet, had a real floor (wooden planks) and "a good stone chimney." The combination of these features led Lieutenant Starr to describe the hospital in 1851 as "commodious," though his successor, Lieutenant Bold, noted it was just "tolerable tight" against the elements. The interior was divided into a main room and two smaller rooms, one used by the hospital steward and the other serving as a kitchen. Nearby was a dispensary, also of frame construction, which measured eleven feet square. It had no fireplace.

Other components of the post were added in the latter months of 1849, with scarcely any more care put into their construction. The first commissary (thirty-two by seventeen feet), where all the garrison's food supplies were kept, was built of rough-hewn logs and covered with a clapboard roof. It, like all the buildings, was prone to leak.[17]

The quartermaster storehouse, where all non-food supplies were kept—extra boots and uniforms, munitions, tools, harness gear—was also made of logs and roofed with clapboards. As a storeroom for valuable equipment, it was quite unsatisfactory, having a dirt floor and a roof described as "insecure against [the] rain." And at only twenty feet square, it was also inadequate for the garrison's needs.

A small frame house served as the adjutant's office and was probably one of the last original structures to be built. It had two rooms, each twelve feet square, with an eight-foot passageway connecting them. The siding was inch-thick planks placed in the ground vertically in the manner of Mexican "jacal" contruction. A "good stone chimney" provided warmth when the weather turned cold. It had the usual leaky roof. As the garrison grew in the next two years, this building was subsequently turned into additional officers' quarters.

A guardhouse used the same simple construction: rough logs and a clapboard roof. It consisted of two rooms, an outer guard room and an inner prison room—each twelve by fifteen feet—and echoed the floor plan of the jail at Fort Graham. The condition of the roof was not noted. By 1851 the original guardhouse needed an estimated $100 worth of repairs to keep it standing.

Workshops for the wheelwright and farrier were in a two-room log house with a ten-foot wide connecting dogtrot. Each man had a work space of fifteen square feet with a dirt floor and a leaky roof, the whole being characterized as "very hasty and incomplete structures."[18]

The flurry of construction under Ripley Arnold in the summer of 1849 provided only the bare necessities. In the three years that followed, that handful of buildings was supplemented, added on to, and in a few cases totally reconstructed. Every structure suffered from the same basic flaw: they were no sooner built than they began to require constant attention to keep them standing. Lieutenant Starr noted laconically in the spring of 1851, before any of the original structures had even reached their second birthday, that "most of the buildings require repairs, more or less." No amount of repairs however, could alter the fact that they were poorly constructed of inferior materials by unskilled laborers.

After four years, there were seventeen buildings on the site. Fifteen were of logs covered with pecan clapboard; the remaining two were wooden frame construction. Not a single stone building had been erected at the post. Even the stone chimneys and shingled roofs that had been added to a few structures were the work of unskilled labor.

What improvements were made in later years were due largely to the efforts of the Eighth Infantry soldiers who came in after the dragoons. Between the spring and fall of 1851 the number of officers' cabins increased to four. This was done by turning the former adjutant's office into living quarters. It had

the advantage of the "good stone chimney," but the usual roof problems.[19]

These four houses formed an officers' row that, despite the grand-sounding name, would have been hardly distinguishable from the rest of the post to the casual visitor. Lieutenant Bold reported in October 1851 that "the number of officers that can be accommodated at present is four." The commanding officer and the assistant surgeon each had his own cabin, the latter using his for both office and living quarters. That left two cabins for the use of the remaining officers. When Lieutenant Frederick Follett joined the command "from detached service" on October 13, 1851, a place had to be found for him, and with Captain Robert P. Maclay returning from court-martial duty in San Antonio on October 30, accommodations promised to get very tight.

In Lieutenant Bold's estimation, the existing officers' quarters required major repairs "to make them at all comfortable." He estimated repairs on the commanding officer's house alone would cost $296.75, and for the junior officers' quarters, $500. He had to settle for spending $19.75 out of his meager quartermaster's funds to put up muslin ceilings in three of the cabins and make roof repairs on all four. The muslin ceilings gave no protection against the incessant leaks but did help keep dust and debris from sifting down on the inhabitants. Additional expenditures would require higher authorization. He recommended constructing completely new quarters for four officers—two buildings of two rooms each with detached kitchens—and estimated the cost of each at $450.[20] Instead of new construction or even major repairs, Fort Worth's version of officers' row was reduced from four to three buildings in the next year when one of the older cabins proved unsalvageable. It was torn down and never replaced.

The architectural evolution of the post living quarters included wooden floors and casement windows, but like the other improvements, these were largely cosmetic. Window openings were covered by wood shutters that could be secured from within. Apparently, squared-up door and window frames could not be produced locally, so they had to be freighted in from the supply depot at San Antonio (as in the case of Fort Richardson). There is no indication that any of the cabins at Fort Worth ever had glass-paned windows. Glass panes were "not to be had," according to one pioneer.[21] Glass was expensive, besides being fragile, and would have had to be brought in from Shreveport or San Antonio. Window openings were probably covered with waxed paper, muslin or shutters.[22]

In 1853 the last inspection report at Fort Worth showed living accommodations little changed from those of 1849. The commanding officer's quarters still consisted of a two-room, hewn-log cabin with a dogtrot and a "leaky" clapboard roof. The 1849 log cabin for junior officers, fifteen feet by fifteen feet with an eight-foot dogtrot, still stood, still leaky. Two framed wooden houses made of green lumber had both been pulled down and replaced by another log building on the two-room floor plan (fourteen feet square), with an eight-foot wide passsageway between. Like the older structures, it leaked.[23]

For the enlisted men, most of the original "huts" were soon pulled down and replaced with a pair of larger barracks using the familiar log and clapboard construction. The expansion of the enlisted men's quarters marked the official transformation of Fort Worth from a one- to a two-company post.[24] The barracks were intended to house two companies, though even at that they were "rather limited in capacity." The larger of the two was ninety by sixteen feet, had a poor roof, mud chimneys and a dirt floor. Thirty feet were partitioned off for use as a company storeroom. The rest served as home for Company F, Eighth Infantry. A second, smaller barrack, sixty-four by sixteen feet, was constructed on the same plan, including mud chimneys and a dirt floor. Lieutenant Bold noted in his 1851 survey of the buildings that they did not just leak, they leaked badly.[25] Such conditions were not only demoralizing but contributed to an increased rate of sickness.

The smaller of the two barracks was occupied in the fall of 1851 by Company H of the Eighth Infantry. A small log cabin, "about 20 x 12 feet," stood behind Company H's barrack, which did double duty as the company storeroom and an orderly sergeant's quarters. This second generation of enlisted men's quarters had the benefit of kitchens, single log cabins measuring thirty-four by sixteen feet, behind each barrack. Each was little more than a fireplace and preparation area. But there were practical reasons for setting the kitchens off from the living quarters: flies and other critters attracted by uncovered food would be less bothersome, as would the excess heat generated by cooking fires. The arrangement lessened the chances of a disasterous conflagration, which was an ever present danger in the days of cooking over open fires.

These two barracks, first noted in 1851 reports, could house a total of fifty-seven men. If they followed the standard plan of other Texas forts, the men slept on double bunks, each four feet wide and covered with a straw-filled mattress.[26] Army-issue blankets could be strung around the walls in the winter to keep out the worst drafts, or alternately wetted down and hung in windows and doorways in the summer to provide a primitive form of evaporative cooling.

Not only were the barracks inadequate for the numbers of troops they housed, but they were "scarcely habitable," according to the post quartermaster. What Lieutenant Bold recommended was the construction of two new barracks in the form of "comfortable log or weather board buildings," capable of housing two companies of eighty-four men, kitchens included. The lieutenant estimated the cost of each complete unit (barrack and kitchen) at $1600. Ultimately, the need for new barracks became so critical that the army was forced to act. In its last two years, Fort Worth got decent housing for its enlisted men, the irony being that the construction was undertaken at the same time the army was making plans to shut Fort Worth down. In the final 1853 survey of the post there were three barracks at Fort Worth, only two of which were actually occupied. Both of these were built in 1852 and 1853 and were quite nice by frontier standards. They were "double buildings" (two rooms each) with the rooms measuring seventeen by seventeen feet connected by passageways of twelve feet. Both had wooden floors, and, best of all, were described as being dry. In August of 1853 they housed the members of Company B, Second Dragoons.

The third barrack, which stood unoccupied in 1853, was made of vertical-standing logs, had only dirt for a floor and leaked. It was probably one of the old barracks put up by the infantry soon after they arrived in the fall of 1849. By 1853 the garrison had diminished to the point where there was no longer a need for it, so it stood empty except when troops passed through in transit to other posts.

Sometime in the final two years, the original stable was reconstructed, still in the "palisade" form, but with another fifty feet added on.[27] A second "shed stable" was started in 1851 for the quartermaster's horses and mules. Like the original stable, it too was constructed of palisades, measuring 190 by fifteen feet. The work was done by the enlisted men and paid for out of existing quartermaster's funds, which helps explain why two years later it was still uncompleted. Toward the end of 1851 an estimated $100 was needed to complete the "work in progress" on the stable. When the garrison pulled out in late 1853 the quartermaster's stable—a large, sturdy structure—was still unfinished and became one of the prized structures grabbed by the local citizens as soon as the last soldier rode out the gate.

Although described as the finest building at the post, the hospital was still a victim of inadequate funds and a lack of urgency on the part of the builders, and reflected the same basic flaws of the other buildings. It had no examination or surgery rooms and no morgue. At larger posts, like Fort Concho, the morgue occupied a detached building close to the hospital, but at Fort Worth any deceased had to be buried quickly, without the benefit of autopsy or formal arrangements.[28]

Despite the best of intentions when it was started, two years later the hospital still stood half-finished with all work halted. This was hardly cause for alarm. As Lieutenant Starr observed after being at Fort Worth for only two weeks, "Things progress but slowly here."[29] The hospital was little used and the leisurely pace of construction reflected it. Lieutenant Bold described the place in 1851 as "a mere shell, without lathing, plastering or interior finish of any sort."[30] When the infantry came, they showed no more inclination to finish it than had the dragoons. In 1851 it needed $300 in repairs and finishing work, plus another $50 work on its kitchen area.

Finally, in October 1852, department headquarters authorized Major Hamilton Merrill, commander by that time, to expend a "certain [unspecified] sum" in repairing and completing it.[31] A few months later the structure stood as a minor monument to the folly of army construction: dragged out for three years while the post was occupied, it was finally rushed to completion just in time to be abandoned when the garrison departed.

Other structures went through a similar evolutionary process. Sometime after 1851, the old adjutant's log cabin was torn down and replaced by a frame building of two rooms, each eleven by eleven feet, joined by a seven-foot-wide passageway set off by "two leaky piazzas."

A new commissary storehouse, one hundred by twenty feet, was started in 1851 to replace the original log structure which, besides being too small, was "insecure against the rain." Construction halted in the fall of 1851, probably due to a shortage of funds. The cost of completing the structure at that point was estimated at $252.[32] Higher than anticipated costs had been incurred by employing "citizen labor" to do the work, a first for Fort Worth. Five men, hired for one month at a rate of fifty cents per day plus one ration each, provided the labor. They did only the skilled work, however. The heavy work of cutting, hauling, and preparing the lumber continued to be done by enlisted men. Before work was halted, the bill for the new storehouse amounted to just $7.50 for 6200 clapboards plus $40.50 for all other materials and labor.

In the next two years, an enlarged commissary was completed although at what cost is not known. In 1853 the building consisted of two storerooms totalling ninety by thirty-one feet. It was built of logs with a dirt floor and clapboard roof.[33]

Just two years after it was built the quartermaster's storeroom also needed extensive repairs. In 1851 Lieutenant Bold requested funds for a whole new "storage house and Quartermaster storeroom," estimating the costs at $677.50. A new quartermaster's storeroom was finally built, but with only slightly larger dimensions of thirty by fifteen. Construction was of logs with a dirt floor and a leaky roof.[34] A new, smaller guardhouse was put up in the same period, having a single twelve-by-twelve-foot room for prisoners. Neither the original nor its replacement was blessed with a wooden floor; the state of the roof was not recorded.[35]

Cooking and eating facilities improved over the years. Until 1851 the men had to eat in their quarters or outside on the shadeless parade ground. By 1853 they could dine in a company mess shed, thirty by fifteen feet, made of logs and having a dirt floor. As a shelter it left much to be desired, for the roof leaked when it rained and the floor turned into a swampy morass if the rains lasted very long. There were also five separate log kitchens, each fifteen by fifteen feet, standing behind the various barracks and officers' quarters. These included puncheon floors as well as porous roofs.

Perhaps the most popular addition for the men was the bake house, first noted in W. G. Freeman's 1853 report. This was probably the same building which had served as the combination company storeroom and orderly sergeant's quarters behind the Company H barrack in 1851. It was a simple enough job to convert it into a bakery by simply adding stone-and-mortar ovens. Baking in this facility was definitely a dry-weather activity, since the roof leaked as badly as that of any building on the post.

After 1851 one of the more dubious improvements to the post was the construction of three huts for laundresses (even though the occupants were unofficial members of the post) on the same row with the bakery, quartermaster's storeroom and mess shed. This was Fort Worth's version of what was known at larger posts as "suds row." They were put up by the soldiers just like the other buildings on the post. Each one-room cabin served as the place of work and probably living quarters for a washwoman. They did not need signs over the doorway; they were easily distinguished by the great, fire-blackened kettles standing out front ready for the next load of laundry. In at least one regard the laundresses were equal to the men; both had to put up with dirt floors and leaky roofs. Though there was nothing appealing about the huts, soldiers always seemed to spend an inordinate amount of time congregating in the area during their off-duty hours. There is virtually nothing in the official records about these little buildings or their occupants, but elsewhere in the West they had the reputation of being dens of assignation.[36]

The men were even happier to have a sutler's store on the post. The sutler's store, at the southwest corner of the grounds, was the nineteenth-century equivalent of a modern post exchange, where soldiers could buy utensils, trinkets, personal items, edibles, and spiritous refreshments, such as liquor and wine by the bottle, beer and ale by the glass. The store at Fort Worth does not show up in either of the 1851 quartermaster reports, leading to the conclusion that it, like the laundresses' huts, was built between 1851 and 1853.

Workshops of the blacksmith and carpenter (low priorities to begin with) were in serious need of replacement within two years after the originals went up. Although they were relatively minor facilities, the cost to replace them—estimated at $250 for labor and materials—was substantial. The final survey of the post in 1853 does not show such buildings present. The implication is not that the essential work of blacksmithing and carpentry were no longer being done at Fort Worth, but that they were now being done in the surrounding community.[37]

Most later sources agree, all the main buildings on the post were kept "neatly whitewashed," although there is no mention of this in any of the official inspection reports. A good coat of paint can cover up a multitude of flaws. Unfortunately, whitewash cannot keep out the rain or the winter winds or insect pests.[38]

None of the detailed descriptions of Fort Worth mention privies, leading to the conclusion that the men took care of nature's call according to the regulations for field service; they dug slit trenches or "sinks" as far away from living quarters as possible.

The ramshackle nature of the post was an unremitting source of embarrassment to its officers and an object of disapproval to visiting officers who came through on inspection tours. Among the most vocal critics was Second Lieutenant John Bold, Eighth Infantry, Company F, who took over as acting quartermaster late in 1851. He devoted a great deal of time in the next two years to making repairs insofar as his limited budget allowed and lobbying Washington for more funds to make additional repairs, but his reports show a thinly veiled contempt for his surroundings. In 1851 he described the officers' quarters, one of which must have been his own at the time, as "miserable." And his pungent descriptions of the other buildings at the post displayed a repititious "leaky motif." His commander at the end, Major H. W. Merrill, was more succinct and more diplomatic, but just as critical. In 1853 he called Fort Worth, "quite unsuitable for the service."[39]

Bold tried repeatedly to get something done. In his survey of the buildings in 1851 he recommended repairs and new construction totalling $6,626.25. In addition to new officers' quarters and barracks for enlisted men, he listed as "requirements" a new storage house and quartermaster storeroom and new blacksmith's and carpenter's shops. In essence, what he requested was construction of a new post. That was preposterous, of course, and the army never approved more than a fraction of recommended projects.[40]

Still the physical appearance of Fort Worth did not remain static for four years. From the summer of 1849 through the middle of 1853 the little outpost on the Trinity was constantly undergoing improvements and additions. These changes made Fort Worth more liveable and represented a significant improvement over the original buildings, but the results could never be confused with genteel accommodations. They were typical of the spartan ways of the U.S. Army. During the fiscal year beginning July 1, 1852, the government spent just $75 making "alterations and repairs" on Fort Worth. Most of that went into putting up a ceiling and patching the roof of the hospital.[41] The army got what it paid for. When Major H. W. Merrill was closing down Fort Worth in August, 1853, he advised his superiors that "the buildings here can be used another year," but he believed the place to be "of too temporary a nature to justify further expense or labor by making repairs."[42]

Others agreed. The quartermaster at Fort Concho argued in 1868 that the stone walls and chimneys marking the sites of abandoned posts like Belknap and Phantom Hill were monuments to waste. Temporary buildings, he thought, were sufficient on a frontier that was constantly shifting.[43]

5
FORT WORTH: AN ARTIST'S RECONSTRUCTION

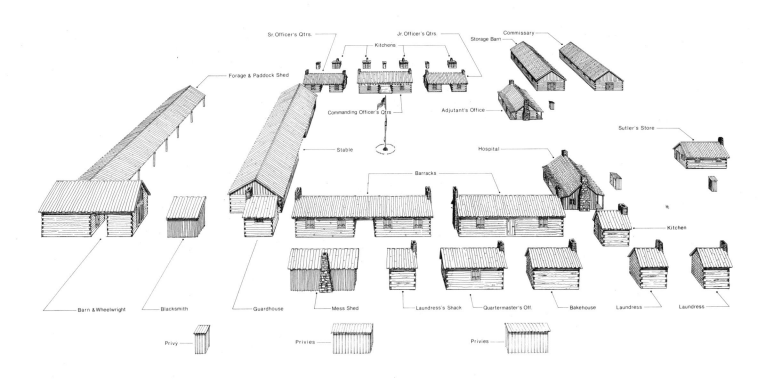

Sr. Officer's Qtrs.

Jr. Officer's Qtrs.

Commissary

Storage Barn

Kitchens

Forage & Paddock Shed

Commanding Officer's Qtrs

Adjutant's Office

Sutler's Store

Stable

Hospital

Barracks

Kitchen

Barn & Wheelwright

Blacksmith

Guardhouse

Mess Shed

Laundress's Shack

Quartermaster's Off.

Bakehouse

Laundress

Laundress

Privy

Privies

Privies

ARTIST'S NOTES

The idea for the drawings that follow came to me several years ago as a result of my particular interest in the original Fort Worth—the military post before there was a city. What may have originally sparked my interest was a bit of local folklore passed on to me by my late father, Frank B. Potter. The story goes that shortly after the establishment of the post, Major Ripley Arnold stood on the brink of the bluff gazing toward the northern horizon. One of his troopers, who was on guard duty, asked, "What are you looking at sir?"

"I'm not looking," Arnold is said to have replied, "I'm just listening to the footsteps of the oncoming thousands."

The statement has been attributed to others, including Robert E. Lee who was said to be visiting the fort at the time. This anecdote makes for a good story, but it cannot be true where Lee is concerned since research shows that Lee served as commandant at West Point from 1852 until 1855 when he was transferred to the Second Cavalry in Texas. No matter who said it, however, he was a keen prognosticator. Nearly 150 years later, hundreds of thousands have come to the banks of the Trinity where the lonely outpost once stood. And in the name of progress no vestige of the original fort remains. The only on-site recognition honoring the historic location is a bronze plaque on an irregular block of granite. This insignificant monument, which incorrectly refers to *Fort* Worth as *Camp* Worth, stands on the lawn of the old criminal courts building at the corner of Houston and Belknap streets. The location is approximately where the original fort flagpole stood.

With this in mind, I delved into the history and the architectural aspects of the early post. After some time, I set my mind on the vision of a full-scale replica to be located as near as possible to the original site. Many hours of research and drawing time and various presentations to the city and to influential individuals ensued. My ideas and drawings were well-received, but to date, nothing has happened. I have not given up on the project, or on a more recent proposal for a Fort Worth Cyclorama and Heritage Museum, complete with a large model of the fort along with various dioramas and displays commemorating our city's beginning. In the meantime, I reasoned, perhaps a book would be in order.

Much has been written about early Fort Worth, but very little material has addressed how it looked. Teaming with Rick Selcer, who has greatly enhanced the historical aspects of this subject, I endeavored to answer the question of appearance.

As is the case with most research projects, there are many questions regarding specific details. It should be noted that these drawings originate from the overall post layout available from the National Archives or the Department of the Army. Additional information is also available, though somewhat controversial. It is impossible to be sure whether this layout, for instance, represents the outpost as it was originally conceived, or as it actually existed at the time the post was abandoned. One thing is clear, however. The buildings fell down, were rebuilt, enlarged, resided, reroofed, and so on, throughout the entire life of the fort. Nothing in the records indicates architectural details such as the pitch of the roofs, locations of the windows and doors, their size or type, whether or not there were privies or slit trenches, how many buildings were whitewashed, or a uniform description of individual building sizes. Nor can we be certain where roads, paths, or trails were located, or of several other features. My task in executing these drawings, therefore, involved some artistic license in filling in the blanks.

Old Fort Worth, as was the case with nearly all Texas forts, did not include blockhouses or stockade walls. It did include a very tall flagstaff consisting of two long cottonwood poles, skinned and strapped together halfway up, and painted white. With Old Glory waving in the breeze, the flag staff could be seen from quite a distance.

Like most early Texas outposts, Fort Worth was a temporary proposition. Once civilization arrived and continued its western march, the fort's day was over. Thus, after only four years, Fort Worth was abandoned. Like the wildflowers of the field, however, what was left took root and grew into one of our nation's great cities.

—William B. Potter

Fort Worth as seen from the north. The Trinity River lies at the base of the bluffs.

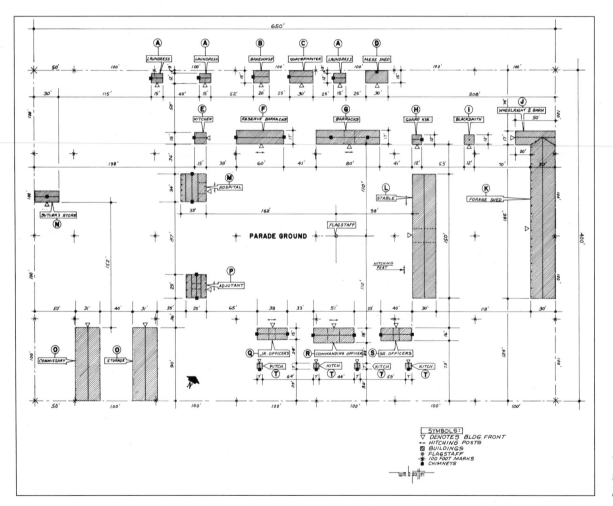

This Fort Worth site plan provides data that could be used if a full-scale replica is built.

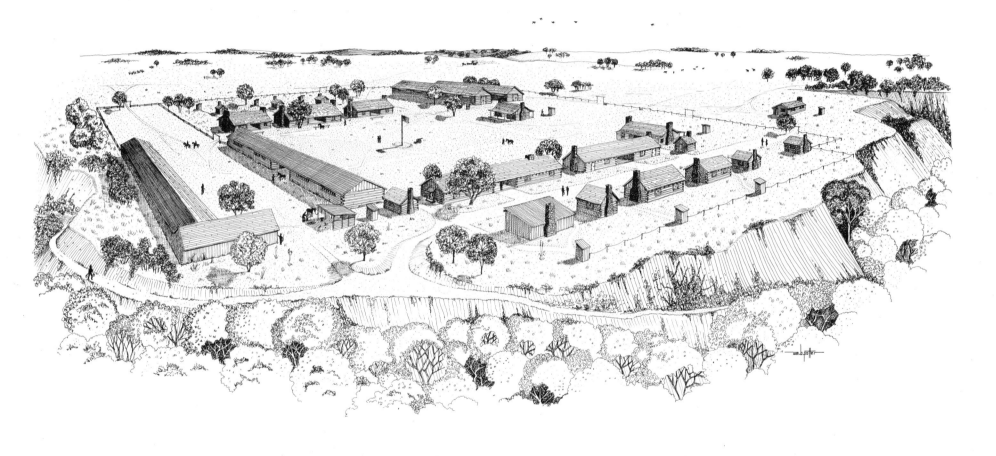

Clearing timber for use at the bluff-top site was an ongoing and hazardous process for members of the garrison.

"Silent Night, Lonely Night": weather extremes often made life miserable for the dragoons stationed at Fort Worth.

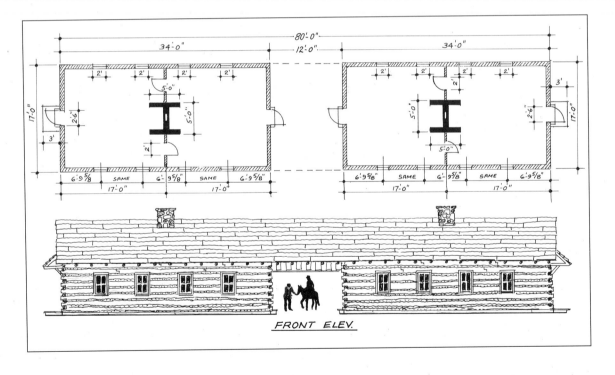

FRONT ELEV.

"Old Fort Worth": an overall view of the post from the west. Left to right, the forage shed, wheelwright, and barn are separated from the stable by a fenced area. At the upper left is a field of row crops. Opposite are two structures, the blacksmith shed and the guardhouse. In the same line bordering the parade ground lie the barracks, reserve barracks, and main post kitchen. Bordering the bluff are a double privy, the mess shed, laundress shack, quartermaster's quarters and office, bake house, and two additional laundress shacks. Across the parade ground (left to right) are the officers' and commanding officer's quarters, each with two small kitchens and privies behind. The two long buildings represent a storage barn and commissary. Across from the stable is the hospital in the foreground and the adjutant's office and quarters. Within a plank fence (lower right) is the sutler's store, privy and garden. The double-pole flagstaff is visible on the parade ground.

Enlisted men's barracks were constructed of hewn logs and topped with a clapboard roof. Daubing and chinking kept out the worst of the north Texas weather.

54

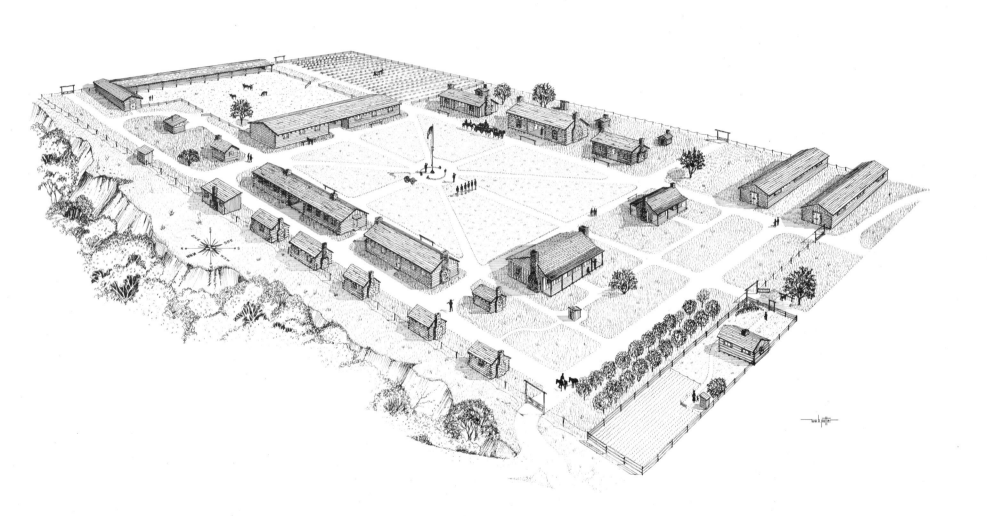

"Ghost Riders": long after Fort Worth was abandoned in 1853 its legacy remains in the name of the city and in the shape of a hand-made rocking chair said to have been given to Dr. Carroll M. Peak's wife as troops pulled out of the post for the last time.

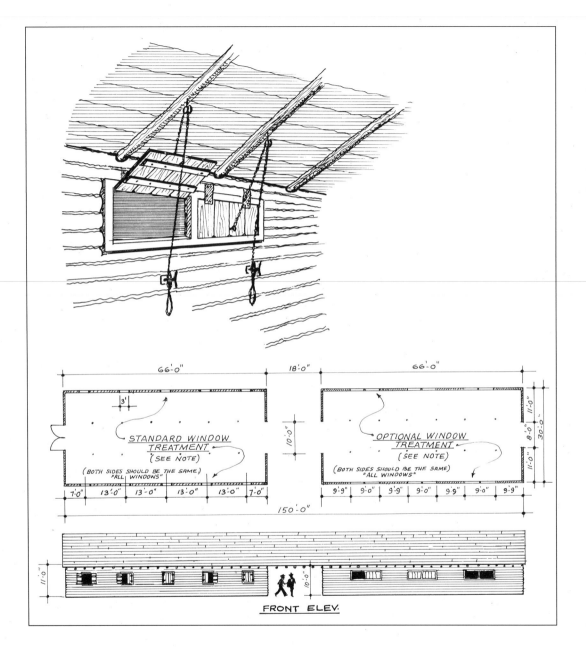

"Blue Mound Vista": A view from the south. Blue Mound, so called because of the "blue northers" that come roaring in from the north in winter, can be seen on the horizon beyond the prairie. A settler's wagon approaches the compound while troops drill on the parade ground. A lone trooper works with horse and plow in the field to the upper right.

The stable—like many of the buildings at Fort Worth—it was built of split logs and covered with a clapboard roof. Primary sources do not indicate how windows were hung or where they were located. It is unlikely, however, that glass panes were available on the frontier so the detail shown here is based on the assumption that shutters kept out the weather.

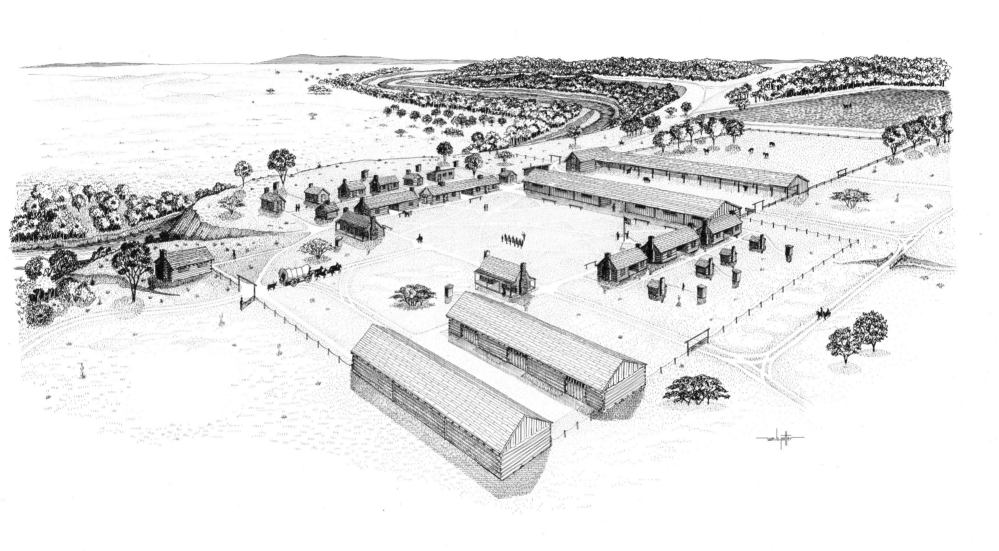

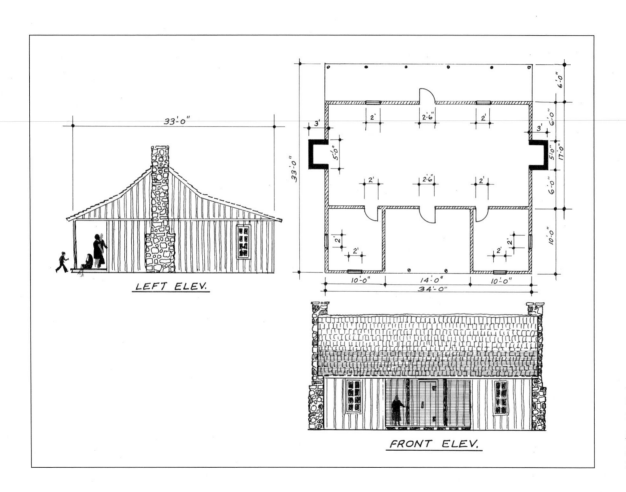

LEFT ELEV.

FRONT ELEV.

"Sick Call": Dr. Thomas H. Williams, with the assistance of an enlisted man, acted as the Fort Worth surgeon in the building on these facing pages from the autumn of 1849 until the post closed in 1853. Williams tended to diseases ranging from swamp fever (malaria) to dysentery and cholera.

Described in 1851 as "commodious" and the most comfortable building on the post, the hospital was constructed of upright planking covered by a shingle roof. It was finished with wood floors and the chimneys were made of native stone.

60

"Old Fort Worth": off-duty dragoons spend leisure time under a shade tree while others assemble on the parade ground for fatigue, guard mount and other details.

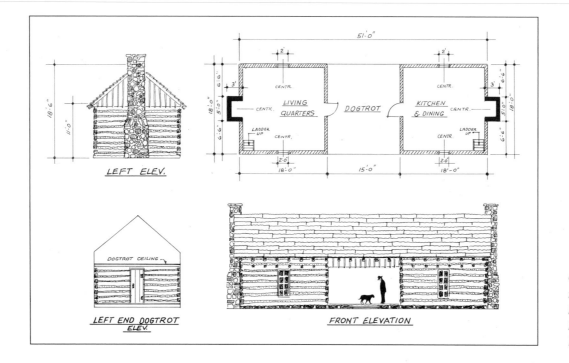

LEFT ELEV.

51'-0"

LIVING QUARTERS

DOGTROT

KITCHEN & DINING

CENTR.

LADDER UP

18'-0"

15'-0"

18'-0"

2'-0"

2'-0"

18'-6"

11'-0"

DOGTROT CEILING

LEFT END DOGTROT ELEV.

FRONT ELEVATION

Commanding Officer's Quarters, like most of the structures on the post, were built of hewn logs covered with a clapboard roof. The commander did have the luxury of wooden floors.

"Sunset at old Fort Worth": a view looking south southwest to a sunset beyond the confluence of the Clear and West Forks of the Trinity. The post garden, established by official orders in 1851, is at the lower left. By the time Fort Worth was abandoned in late 1853 an inspector could report, "A fine garden of eight acres is cultivated by the command."

"Low Water Crossing": a supply wagon, accompanied by protecting dragoons, flushes out a covey of Bob White quail as the column emerges from the river crossing.

"Retreat": an autumn sky is the backdrop to this view of the stable (left), officers' row, storage barn, and adjutant's quarters. The flag is being lowered while the bugler plays retreat. The mountain howitzer at the base of the flagstaff was the post's only artillery piece.

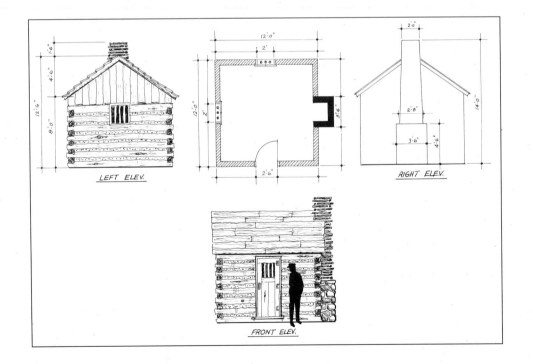

LEFT ELEV.

RIGHT ELEV.

FRONT ELEV.

The guardhouse was smaller that most Fort Worth structures, but like the others it had a leaky clapboard roof, dirt floor and rough-hewn log exterior.

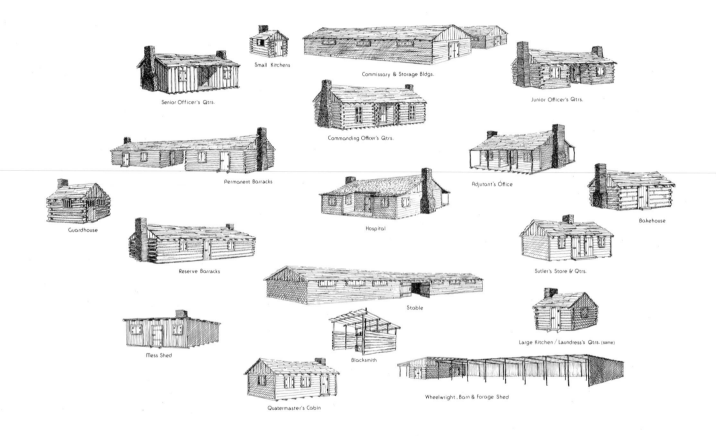

Small Kitchens

Commissary & Storage Bldgs.

Senior Officer's Qtrs.

Junior Officer's Qtrs.

Commanding Officer's Qtrs.

Permanent Barracks

Adjutant's Office

Bakehouse

Guardhouse

Hospital

Reserve Barracks

Sutler's Store & Qtrs.

Stable

Mess Shed

Large Kitchen / Laundress's Qtrs. (same)

Blacksmith

Quatermaster's Cabin

Wheelwright, Barn & Forage Shed

6
OFFICERS' CALL

With shelter in place, a dependable food supply for men and animals became the next order of business. For the handful of dragoons who first camped on the site, there was plenty of fresh game, especially on the prairies north of the river where plover, prairie chickens, and wild turkeys abounded. Wildlife, supplemented by the staples they brought with them, was adequate to fill their needs at first. But the men also knew that the game would soon desert the area.

At the end of July, Arnold requested that Fort Worth be officially designated a "double ration post," a classification usually reserved for posts in desolate regions, where especially hard labor was demanded or where the garrison spent a lot of time in the field. But the Twin Forks area was not particularly desolate, and the garrison had yet to take to the field. What Arnold had in mind were the demands of military hospitality. Worth was sixty miles from the nearest military post, and civilian settlements "where any accommodations could be had"

were also distant. Arnold reminded his superiors that "Many citizen gentlemen are travelling through this country who cannot always provide themselves with all that they need. . . . Gentility and necessity call loudly for our Hospitality." The largest class of important visitors were what the major called "transient officers" who had to be "entertained" by the commanding officer. Arnold's request was passed up the chain of command and approved by the adjutant general's office in early September.[1] Fort Worth retained the designation for the rest of its active life.

After settlers began moving into the area in growing numbers, the local market provided "plenty of milk, butter, fowls and eggs."[2] Civilians also supplied hay, corn, and fresh beef in abundance—for the right price. The farmers accepted the army's practice of bidding on contracts to supply these items and most deals were satisfactory to both sides. Early in 1851, Quartermaster Sam Starr paid three and three-quarters cents per pound for beef on the hoof; that figure rose to five cents per pound in the next two-and-a-half years. Starr got hay delivered and stacked for $3.19 per ton. When Lieutenant John Bold took over the quartermaster duties later that same year, his first hay contract cost $4 per ton. Corn was bought under contract on the open market for a price ranging from ninety cents to $1.15 per bushel.[3] Other locally purchased food supplies like milk and eggs did not require bidding for a contract.

The troopers' usual diet was plain and unvarying, consisting of flour, hardtack (the detested "hard bread" or "teeth dullers"), coffee, beans, sugar, bacon, and jerked beef, supplemented by "treats" like pickles, molasses or fresh beef. Fort Worth troopers were luckier than most when it came to fresh beef because the local herds were big and fat. While Starr served as quartermaster, the garrison (eighty-six enlisted men and three officers when at full strength) was issued fresh meat twice a week. The lieutenant calculated that each man could consume ten pounds of beef every month at a cost of $33.37. Officials in Washington felt the figure too high so the ration was cut to one issue every five days, each soldier receiving "two days issue each time."[4] Farther west, the garrisons seldom saw such luxury.

In the event their supply lines were ever cut, the men at Fort Worth did not have to worry about going hungry. On July 31, 1851, the garrison had 160 barrels of salt pork and 18,000 pounds of bacon, enough for fifteen months. They also had 190 barrels of flour and 20,000 pounds of "hard bread,"

enough for the next twelve months. The garrison's provisions were stored, however, in "rough log buildings" which did little to protect them from weather and rats.[5]

The quantity of supplies tells just half the story. Every item had to be hauled to Fort Worth by wagon at considerable expense. Lieutenant Starr emphatically reported in 1851 that he could not get flour except in small quantities, "and of *very* inferior quality," because there were no flour mills "in this section of the country." The situation was alleviated soon after when A.F. Leonard established a water-powered grist mill on the Trinity some seven or eight miles east of Fort Worth. "Leonard's Mill" not only served the "comfort, convenience and welfare" of citizens and soldiers, it also turned a tidy profit for its owner. Salt (more essential for preserving food than for cooking) was manufactured nearby in small quantities but it was of "inferior quality." As a result the garrison got its salt from New Orleans, paying $3 per bushel delivered. Beans could not be purchased at any price but Starr reported that "cow peas" made a satisfactory substitute and local farmers could supply them at $1 per bushel.[6]

The men welcomed variety in their diets from any source. Fresh produce, which added not just variety but essential vitamins, was recognized as beneficial, but the system had a hard time supplying it; fruit seems not to have been an option, though local farmers raised plenty of watermelons, mushmelons and peaches.[7] Vegetables were the most important food. But shipping fresh vegetables to distant outposts was impossible, and canned vegetables did not become part of government-issued rations until after the Civil War. Winter months were the worst, when fresh greens and fruits were unavailable in any form.

Early in 1851, authorities ordered every frontier post to "establish a system of kitchen gardens."[8] The difference between theory and practice could be measured in more than miles, though. Even on such a small post as Fort Worth, it was impossible to raise vegetables in sufficient quantities and variety to serve the garrison's needs. When he arrived in the winter of 1850, Lieutenant Sam Starr had observed, "the market affords plenty of milk, butter, fowls, eggs, but no vegetables."[9] Some local citizens were skeptical whether local conditions would even support raising melons, cantaloupe, squash, pumpkin, and sweet potatoes. The Carroll M. Peak family planted the first garden "about the fort." Their daughter, Clara Peak, recalled many years later, "They all told me I couldn't raise anything. But I tried it out and had as pretty a garden as you ever saw." Soon everyone was raising vegetables.[10]

In the meantime, the soldiers were put to gardening under direct orders from Washington. They laid out a small garden at the southeast corner of the parade ground near the blacksmith shop, and by September 1853 an inspector could report, "A fine garden of eight acres is cultivated by the command." By contrast, Fort McKavett on the San Saba River possessed a thirty-acre garden that furnished members of the Eighth Infantry who garrisoned the post with a "steady supply" of fresh produce. On the other hand, Fort Worth was much better off than Fort Griffin on the upper Brazos where the soil was so poor that the garden could not sustain the garrison and the men suffered greatly.[11]

Though the garrison at Fort Worth was never short of food due to the richness of the surrounding country, such staples as coffee, rice, sugar, beans, and even potatoes still had to be hauled in over lengthy and exposed supply routes. Other non-essential items had to be freighted in. Vinegar and candles, for example, were not to be had "except by importation." Tallow was available locally, but only in small quantities from scattered homesteads. "Hard soap" could not be bought from the community, though "soft soap"—made up of three-fourths water, which made a tolerable substitute—could be bought at eighty cents a pound.[12]

Bringing in stores was the job of the U.S. Army's inefficient, underfunded and overextended quartermaster department. It was a difficult and expensive operation for a department that was severely strained to meet even the minimal demands of peacetime. Supplies had to be purchased and collected at river and coastal depots, then transported over great distances by ox- or mule-drawn wagon. The quartermaster department contracted with civilian teamsters who furnished their own wagons while the army furnished escorts on demand. By 1850 the cost of such escorts had gotten so expensive that General Brooke ordered them cut-back.[13] The lifeline for distant posts like Fort Worth suddenly got more tenuous.

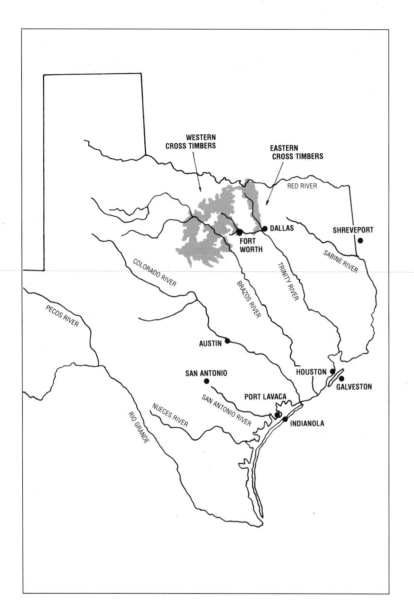

Fort Worth was served by three routes stretching east and south to depots in Shreveport, Houston, and Austin, all of which drew their supplies out of New Orleans. The nearest of these, Austin, was 186 miles away, Shreveport was 240 miles, and Houston, 250 miles from Fort Worth. In "wet season" the Texas roads became impassable, holding up deliveries for days or even weeks at a time. During one period in 1851 it took a month to get supplies from the Gulf port of Indianola to San Antonio due to the rains and bad roads.[14]

Goods were transported at standard rates according to weight and distance. The fee charged by civilian teamsters from Houston to Fort Worth was $3 per hundred pounds. That same hundred pounds transported from San Antonio to Fort Worth cost $2.75, which does not seem like much until the numbers are multiplied. For what it took to keep as many as 100 men in food and supplies, the weight quickly added up to some serious tonnage, and that meant major expense.[15] Most quartermaster officers considered the rates exorbitant and damned the "paper-collared Comanches" who charged them.

In addition to clothing, subsistence, and medical supplies, the quartermaster department also had to supply horses and mules, relying on civilian contractors for this job, too. It cost $27,735.70 just to supply animals to the U.S. Army in Texas in fiscal year 1850-51.[16] Some of those horses were "re-mounts" and were delivered to the Second Dragoons at Fort Worth. Every post return filed by Major Arnold included the number of horses on hand and the number of remounts needed. He always needed two or three, and sometimes as many as a dozen.

In the beginning Fort Worth received its supplies from Austin via Fort Graham, with Austin being supplied from any one of several Gulf ports. The road linking Fort Graham to Austin was "much travelled" by supply trains, mail couriers, and groups of soldiers shuttling back and forth to North Texas, and as early as 1849, there was already an "excellent road" between Graham and Worth, "skirting the western edge of the Cross Timbers."[17] It was the same road that Arnold and his dragoons had followed on their first trip north, having been opened originally to serve Johnson's Station and the other small communities in the neighborhood. The Austin-to-Fort-Worth road was well-marked and as safe as any in Texas, and with Fort Graham only fifty-six miles from Fort Worth and 130 miles from Austin, it provided a convenient stop between the two points. Despite the shortest distance and the stopover at Fort Graham, the Austin road was not the favorite among the freighters because of the terrain. It crossed eight major streams along the way: the Brazos, the north, middle, and south Bosque, the Leon, the Lampasas, the San Gabriel, and the Brushy. Most of these were considered "vexatious crossings," the worst being the Brazos because it had to be crossed by ferry at one of two points (Fort Graham or Waco Village) during all but the driest seasons. A loaded supply train might make only ten miles a day if the weather was good, and that averaged out to nearly three weeks in transit from Austin to Fort Worth. Double that for the time required to get special orders from the garrison at Fort Worth filled.

The Shreveport road was even less popular than the Austin route, also for reasons of terrain. The road, for most of the 240 miles, was "good" in the winter months and "very good" in the summer. Of the three routes, it was safest from marauding Indians, and for part of the way the surface was even "turn-piked."[18] But there were difficult water crossings at four different points. The first, going east, was Mountain Creek, a "very bad little stream" with a "bad bottom" and rapid current. Then travellers had to cross another three miles of inhospitable bottom land before reaching the Trinity River at Dallas where they caught the first ferry. A few miles farther on they came to the East Fork of the Trinity and another ferry crossing, then finally the Sabine River and yet another ferry. Numerous small streams along the way were insignificant except after heavy rains, whereupon they became treacherous.

By 1851 most of Fort Worth's supplies were coming up from Houston, following the route of the Trinity River northward to Fort Worth via Parker's Bluff, Porter's Bluff, or Pine Bluff. Despite being the longest of the three routes at 250 miles, the Houston Road had one big advantage; it crossed only one significant stream, the Navasota, and that could be easily forded. This made the Houston Road "much the best route on which to forward supplies to this post [Fort Worth]."[19]

Because of the great distances and difficult terrain

involved with the other routes, a suggestion was made in 1851 to develop a new supply route via the Red River. Robert's Landing was only 120 miles north over an existing road, and that distance could be reduced to 105 miles if a more direct route were built. Another point in its favor: there was plenty of water for wagon teams along the way. At least one officer believed this was "the most favorable [route] from which to draw supplies for Forts Worth and Graham."[20] The Red River tended to be navigable for just six to eight months out of the year, however, and this was not enough for army needs.

Contractors used by the army in North Texas included such men as "Uncle Press" Farmer (also one-time post sutler at Fort Worth), John White, and Billy Walsh.[21] White drove his ox teams regularly between Fort Worth, Houston and Galveston, once being gone six months and given up by the local community as dead—probably killed by Indians. But he turned up alive, explaining only that he had been delayed. Some said the bullwhackers and mule skinners were too tough to kill. Billy Walsh held a major government contract in the early 1850s to freight supplies overland to isolated posts. Walsh's teams were a familiar sight at Fort Worth and Fort Graham, among others on the frontier.[22]

By 1853 the surrounding country was sufficiently settled that the garrison could buy all the bacon, flour, and beans they needed locally and save on the cost of hauling them in. The savings were considerable. A barrel of flour cost $15 when delivered from an army depot, for instance. The same amount bought locally cost only $8, the chief difference being that local suppliers sold it in sacks rather than barrels. Thanks to the post garden, local purchasing, and tough negotiating on contracts, it cost just twenty-two cents per ration to feed a soldier at Fort Worth. Seven cents of that amount was incurred by transportation costs.[23]

Once the basics were taken care of—food, water, shelter—the men of Company F could return to full-time soldiering. But the garrison was constantly short-handed. Fort Worth was intended for a single company of dragoons, which, according to 1848 U.S. Army regulations, meant fifty privates under the command of a captain, two lieutenants, four or five sergeants, and four corporals. Adding a bugler, farrier, quartermaster, and adjutant could bring the total up to sixty-six men. In fact, however, one or two commissioned officers and thirty to forty men per company was the average on the frontier.[24]

Company F, Second Dragoons, barely made the average. At the end of June, Major Arnold was fifteen enlisted men and two lieutenants short of his authorized strength. At the end of August, he was sixteen men short and still had no lieutenants. September found him eighteen men short, including three men who had been "discharged on Surgeon's certificate for disability."[25] Manpower shortage at Fort Worth was a chronic problem. Sickness, the army's penny-pinching ways, and an archaic replacement system were to blame. Arnold complained initially to Colonel Harney at regimental headquarters. When that produced no results, he wrote directly to

Washington. At the end of one of his first dispatches from the post, dated June 15, he appended the company roster, specifically to demonstrate his desperate manpower situation. He noted that he had "but twenty-five Privates for Duty—building Post, Scouting, etc.," listing them by name. Allowing his frustration to show, he wrote, "This is *not* a mere morning Report but the Roll of my entire Company. . . ." "I am building a new Post at this place," he continued, ". . . and my company is so small that I cannot keep up my Scouting Parties."[26]

On September 1, Arnold wrote again to plead for additional troops. "I would beg again to call attention to the strength of my Company. Twenty-one Privates for Duty out of which take [my] Hospital Steward and Hospital Cook and I have nineteen men at this extreme Frontier Post for Building, Scouting, Escorting, etc." Arnold was deadly serious. "In case of difficulty with the Indians on this frontier I should be in rather a feeble condition."[27]

He did not know it at the time but help was on the way. In October Captain Robert P. Maclay marched in at the head of Company F, Eighth Infantry to join Arnold's dragoons in the garrison. Then in December, Lieutenant Samuel H. Starr brought in eighteen new men from Second Dragoon headquarters as replacements for Arnold's depleted company. Starr replaced Lieutenant Charles H. Tyler, who had never actually reported for duty since being put on the company rolls, though his second lieutenant's commission had come through on April 25. When advised that Tyler had been "transferred" from Company F and replaced by Starr, Arnold commented with more than a hint of sarcasm, "It was the first intimation I had that Lieut. Tyler even belonged to the Company."[28]

Maclay and Starr were welcome and long overdue additions to the officers' ranks. Robert Plunket Maclay, born in Pennsylvania in 1820, entered West Point in 1836 and graduated with his class four years later, just in time to catch the end of the Second Seminole War. He fought with the Eighth Infantry under Zachary Taylor in the Mexican War, being wounded at Resaca de la Palma. After the war he returned to Texas with his regiment to take up duties on the frontier. When he came to Fort Worth in the fall of 1849, he had been a captain less than six months. His health, which was never good, was not likely to improve on the North Texas plains.[29]

Samuel Henry Starr of New York was a seventeen-year veteran in 1849. He first entered the U.S. Army as a private in 1832, rising to the rank of sergeant by 1846 while serving in the artillery and engineers. In June 1848, the thirty-seven-year-old sergeant transferred to the Second Dragoons and accepted an officer's commission as second lieutenant. He had a wife, Eliza, and a daughter, Kate, but he left them behind in Austin when he came north to Fort Worth. He had been assigned to Major Arnold's company since August 1 per Orders No. 23, but due to delays in meeting his fresh recruits from Carlisle Barracks, Pennsylvania, he did not make the acquaintance of his commanding officer until four months later. It was not an auspicious start for his new posting.

Second Lieutenant Starr was a man of great initiative and native intelligence. He was also a demanding officer, not above using physical force to get a point across to his men, a tendency that perhaps reflected his own rise from the lowest ranks. He also retained an enlisted man's contempt for gold-braided officers. Starr's career in 1849 seemed destined to include many more years of frontier service before retirement finally rescued him.[30]

The additions brought the post's strength up to slightly more than 100 men and officers in two companies, still an inadequate number to carry out their given mission, but at least capable of performing the normal duties of a frontier garrison.

Arnold could not know how close he had come to not getting his reinforcements. General Brooke had agonized over how best to use the limited forces available to him in the Eighth Department. His most urgent needs that fall were at Fredericksburg (Fort Martin Scott) versus Forts Graham and Worth. Ultimately deciding on the latter, he wrote the War Department to explain his decision to "reinforce certain points on the Northwest Frontier of the Eighth Department instead of Fredericksburg."[31]

A handful of replacements did not begin to solve the problem of chronically understrength regiments in Texas. Brooke had already asked the War Department that his Dragoon companies be filled up "to the maximum." Finally, in 1850, some long-term relief came through. On June 17 Congress expand-ed the regular army to 14,000 men and officers. On the local level, where it really mattered, this meant company strength was increased to eighty-six men and officers.[32]

The number of soldiers at Fort Worth hovered around 100 for the rest of its existence. The 1850 U.S. Census, tallied that second summer on the Trinity, showed 113 military personnel, counting women and children.[33] With dragoons and infantry both at the post now, Major Arnold, as senior officer, commanded the combined forces.

Besides sheer numbers, Arnold had specific openings in his command that desperately needed to be filled. At the head of the list were a bugler and a "subaltern." Subaltern was the old-fashioned term, borrowed from the British army, for a staff officer, usually a second lieutenant fresh out of West Point. Arnold needed a subaltern or two to perform the vital functions of adjutant and quartermaster. These were the two most important positions on any commander's staff. It was the adjutant's job to take care of all official paperwork and correspondence. He filed reports, collected statistics, kept records, and personally saw to it that orders were delivered to subordinates.

Arguably the most important person at the fort was not the commanding officer but the quartermaster, whose duties were usually combined with those of a commissary supply officer. It was his job to see that the men were kept supplied with basic necessities, and that all necessary supplies were ordered in sufficient quantity, delivered on schedule, and distributed to the men, as well as keeping records of everything received and handed out. He also hired civilian laborers, signed supply contracts, assigned living quarters by rank, supervised construction of new quarters when needed, and saw to the general upkeep of the post. Many of the duties were trivial, but the job was essential. In the fiscal year 1853-1854, Brevet Major Merrill, acting as both commanding officer and quartermaster, disbursed $6,861 in quartermaster funds at Fort Worth, including $36 for postage.[34]

At one point, Quartermaster Sam Starr needed to know precisely what quantity of "jerked beef" constituted a single ration. The query provoked a veritable flurry of official correspondence between Fort Worth, San Antonio and Washington before he got his answer—five ounces.[35] One quartermaster complained that the job required "the patience of Job (without his boils), the meekness of Moses, and the resources of Rothschild."[36]

For the first four months, Major Arnold performed all the duties of adjutant, quartermaster, and commissary supply officer, in addition to being post commander. The lack of subordinates to share the load proved a severe test of his administrative skills and made a difficult job even tougher. In his dispatch of June 15, to Adjutant General Roger Jones, Arnold reiterated his need for more men and pleaded "that I might at least have a Subaltern officer." His frustration was normal at distant posts. In 1853 when Colonel Joseph K. F. Mansfield inspected army posts in New Mexico he found eleven of twenty-one places he visited to be under the command of a single commissioned officer, with four of those eleven commanders also functioning as quartermaster and commissary supply officer.[37]

Arnold eventually got the subaltern he had been asking for when Second Lieutenant John Bold, Eighth U.S. Infantry, arrived in October 1849. There had not been a single lieutenant on the post until he came through the gate with Captain Maclay and the rest of Company F, Eighth Infantry. Even after Bold's arrival, the combined companies of infantry and dragoons at Fort Worth were missing a total of four lieutenants—three dragoon and one infantry. Although Bold was infantry, as long as he was at Fort Worth he was under Arnold's command.

The twenty-three-year-old Bold promptly assumed the duties of commissary and "Post Treasurer." Arnold continued to act as his own quartermaster until Sam Starr joined the garrison in December. Starr took over the duties of quartermaster from the major, plus the duties of commissary from Lieutenant Bold. Ripley Arnold had a working staff.[38]

Even when junior officers were assigned to the post, there was no stability. For three years Major Arnold was forced to watch his subordinates come and go on "detached service" or reassignments to other commands. Some men were carried on the rolls for record-keeping reasons, but never joined the garrison. The names of Lieutenants William Steele of the dragoons and Thomas G. Picher of the infantry appear on Fort Worth's post returns for a year although Arnold never saw them.

Finally, on November 20, 1850, First Lieutenant

Washington P. Street came to Fort Worth, joining Sam Starr to make the first time in nearly two years that Company F of the Dragoons could count its full complement of junior officers. Arnold, Maclay, Bold and Starr had divided the duties among themselves up to that point, with most of the responsibility falling on just three of the men because Captain Maclay was rarely on the post.

Arnold had some difficulty delegating responsibility even after he acquired junior officers. The major preferred to do things himself, especially when he was far more knowledgeable than the staff officer. Arnold had been a quartermaster in his early years before being promoted to post commander so there were instances when he got involved in the quartermaster's duties when he was not welcome. This resulted in a tiff on one memorable occasion between Ripley Arnold and Sam Starr over just whose responsibility it was to hire teamsters, muleteers, and the like. Bypassing the normal chain of command, Arnold hired his own teamsters "in opposition to the wishes and judgment of his Quartermaster." The frustrated Lieutenant Starr complained directly to San Antonio that he had "no confidence" in the men employed by Arnold, and, therefore, Starr refused to pay them out of his allocated funds.[39] The problem was resolved, but Arnold's meticulous attention to minutiae combined with his stubbornness caused him trouble on more than one occasion while he was at Fort Worth.

After Arnold turned over the post in August 1852, his replacement, Brevet Major Hamilton W. Merrill, lodged the same complaint as his predecessor with Second Dragoon headquarters: "The services of a Subaltern are greatly required with the Company and at the Post for Staff duties."[40] In the meantime, Merrill, again following Arnold's lead, assumed the duties of "Assistant Acting Quartermaster" and "Assistant Acting Commissary Supply." The next month Brevet Second Lieutenant Daniel Beall showed up, but Merrill was still without First Lieutenants Arthur D. Tree ("detached service") and Jonas P. Holliday ("reported sick"). The following month, Holliday returned from sick leave, but Beall was reassigned to Fort Mason.[41]

It is not known whether Arnold considered having a subaltern or a bugler more important. Arnold mentioned both specifically in his first dispatch from the Twin Forks. The bugler, usually a teenager, was the only musician assigned to dragoon companies. Although Confederate General Richard Ewell would later complain that the army needed "more shooters and fewer tooters," the bugler was always considered an essential member of any troop because commands were issued by, and the day divided by, a set of simple bugle calls which were familiar to every recruit and shavetail in the army. In his dispatch of June 15, Arnold requested another bugler because, "The Boy I have is sickly and his time will expire in November next."[42]

As Arnold feared, bugler Thomas Noland was discharged on November 23, 1849, "for expiration of service" and there was no replacement at hand. Six months later Company F still did not have a bugler. Arnold wrote to regimental headquarters practically pleading: "Buglers [are] required."[43] Fortunately, the garrison had not had to do without a bugler for all that time. When Company F of the Eighth Infantry marched into Fort Worth in October 1849, they brought their own bugler with them who thereafter did double duty for both the infantry and the dragoons. Arnold's pleas for a bugler for the dragoons finally got a response. In December 1850, there were two buglers with the dragoons at Fort Worth. In the next month that number was down to a single "tooter," but the problem was never completely solved. In January 1852, bugler James Moffatt was on loan from Company G to Company F at Fort Worth, "awaiting orders of his transfer" to Arnold's command. Those orders did not come through until the spring.[44]

The garrison at Fort Worth was always stretched thin. Arnold and his successors duly noted in monthly post returns the number of replacements they needed, with little hope of having their requests filled. Company F, Second Dragoons, was a skeleton command, as the major pointed out to his superiors on numerous occasions, and the situation was further complicated when members of the Eighth Infantry marched in. August 1850 found Arnold requesting the equivalent of two additional companies—forty infantrymen and thirty-five dragoons. In 1851 the totals for "Recruits Required" ranged from eleven to sixty men.[45]

On May 2, 1852, Arnold added a personal note to the monthly muster rolls that hinted at his exasperation: "I would respectfully call attention to the fact that I have Forty-two [enlisted] men in 'F' Co., four of whom have been detached for more than two years."[46] Arnold didn't need just bodies, he wanted "drilled recruits." This was his first request in his June 15th dispatch from Fort Worth. He was so concerned that they be properly *drilled* that he underlined the word and disparaged the last recruits sent out from the cavalry depot. They had arrived the previous November, and, "with one exception, had not even been drilled at the Carbine Manual or Sabre Exercises, or at least knew nothing of either."[47]

When the first additions to the little garrison arrived in the fall and winter of 1849, the new men did not do much to relieve Arnold's anxiety. They were a poor lot, indifferently trained and few in number. It was an oft-repeated pattern. Replacements typically arrived at their new garrisons fresh from Carlisle Barracks, Pennsylvania (dragoons), or Governor's Island, New York (infantry), as unfinished works. Supposedly, they had been instructed in such basic soldierly skills as close-order drill, care and use of weapons, and combat tactics at their "school of instruction," but the truth was that they arrived half-trained. It was left to the post commander, or his designated junior officers, to complete the instruction necessary to turn raw recruits into capable soldiers. It was a problem recognized by General-in-Chief of the Army Winfield Scott, who at one point complained about the generally poor training and quality of recruits.[48]

Ripley Arnold, having been a line officer in both the

Seminole and Mexican wars and therefore familiar with standard drill and tactical maneuvers, decided to take their training into his own hands. In January 1850, he wrote directly to the War Department asking them to send him a copy of the then-current 1841 U.S. Cavalry Tactics manual,[49] a basic guide to close-order drill, not a field manual such as the army uses today. It told him how to put his troops in formation and maneuver those formations, but nothing about the "art of war," tactical evolution, or, specifically, Indian fighting. That sort of knowledge had to come from hard experience. Arnold's experience included no training in either cavalry tactics or drill. His class at West Point graduated the year *before* horses were introduced and mounted drill was added to the curriculum at the U.S. Military Academy.[50]

Arnold put his men through the standard regulation drills, including the manual at arms, marching, and sword exercise, both mounted and dismounted. Before he was through, he probably had the best drilled company on the frontier, although they never attained Arnold's standards of excellence. On August 31, 1849, he reported the "instruction" of his men as "good," their military appearance just "fair." At the end of February 1850, however, after six months of training under his tutelage, he was able to report both their "instruction" and "military appearance" were "good."[51]

Unlike the situation at some posts, Arnold never "subordinated military instruction to the labours of the axe, saw and hammer." This was the criticism voiced by the army's inspec-

tor of Fort McKavett in 1853. While McKavett's neatly laid out stone buildings were snug and smart looking, the infantry companies garrisoned there were "sloppy" and "disorderly" on the parade ground.[52] Arnold kept his military priorities straight at Fort Worth, but the physical appearance of the post reflected his emphasis on soldiers over quarters.

When Major Hamilton Merrill, leading Company B of the Dragoons, replaced Arnold as post commander in late 1852, he apparently continued the high standards set by his predecessor. The 1853 inspection report noted that, "In the saddle [they] acquitted themselves very handsomely, marching with accuracy by twos, fours and with company front, at a walk, trot and gallop." Dismounted, they were not quite as impressive, but Lieutenant Colonel Freeman cited them nonetheless for showing "a fair degree of proficiency." He watched them drill on the broad parade ground "as skirmishers" (traditional dismounted tactics against Indian opponents). Then they mounted up again and put on a truly thrilling show "leaping the bar and ditch with great spirit and perfect mastery of their horses." Freeman concluded this part of his report admiringly, noting that "much attention [has] been given to this part of their instruction."[53]

The men displayed the same pride in their arms, equipment, and horses that they did in their drills. The dragoons' horses, sixty in number at this time, were all "serviceable," to use army parlance, and more than that, they were "in finer condition than those of any mounted troops in Texas." Their uniforms, though not new, were in good repair and generally well fitted. Their arms, inspected by Lieutenant Colonel Freeman on review, were clean, this being the single most important element in any official inspection. And their equipment was commendably neat and well preserved.[54]

But none of this work was the sort of stuff to make newspaper headlines. Both officers and men spent their time at Fort Worth in tedious routine rather than planning and conducting Indian campaigns. Arnold drilled his men and sent out his patrols, or "scouts," but the effort hardly seemed worthwhile. He commanded a garrison with little sense of purpose or mission. Coming from Old World cultures and eastern cities, the men cared little for the beauty of the country they were living in, nor for its bright economic future. They could not see it as R. B. Marcy did when he visited North Texas in 1853 and was struck by what a "rich and beautiful section" it was.[55]

There were two ways to escape the tedium—desertion and discharge, perennial afflictions of every frontier garrison that cost the army more losses than sickness or combat. Men whose term of service was up, or men who simply chose to take "French leave," drained morale and efficiency of the command. Men deserted for many reasons, including low pay, homesickness, boredom and mistreatment by their officers. On the frontier, a man could go over the hill and disappear forever. After 1849, the California gold fields acted as a magnet drawing hopeful young men from all over the country. Even a garrison more than a thousand miles from the bonan-

za was not immune to the siren call of the precious metal. But the leading cause of desertion from posts like Fort Worth was what one western traveler called "intolerable ennui"—the overwhelming sense of loneliness and dreariness that took hold of men stuck in garrison duty on the far frontier.[56]

To the credit of its officers, Fort Worth was never plagued by desertions like some other Texas posts (Fort Phantom Hill, for example), but it had its share.[57] At the end of August 1850, Arnold reported five deserters from his company. One of them, Samuel Sprague of New York, was a corporal with less than one year's service. He took off on August 7, the same day as Privates Andrew I. Harrison and William Lindsey (there is no evidence they went together). All three took U.S. Army mules to speed their flight and Colt revolvers for self-defense. Just three days earlier Privates William Dixon and Hugh Doyle had also gone AWOL, making their getaway on "dragoon horses" and likewise armed with government-issue Colts. Like Corporal Lindsey, the three privates were all from the east coast, suggesting that homesickness and culture shock may have been the deciding factors in their decisions to run.[58]

Dixon and Lindsey both had histories of being malcontents, having been non-commissioned officers earlier before being demoted. Dixon was reduced from first sergeant on April 21, 1849, while the company was still at Fort Graham. This did not prevent him from riding with Major Arnold to establish Fort Worth six weeks later. By January 1850, he was back in the major's good graces, having been appointed hospital steward at Fort Worth. Lindsey had been promoted to corporal on May 12, 1850, but he was listed as a private when he deserted on August 7. Harrison had also ridden with Arnold on that historic occasion, but neither duty nor sense of history slowed him down. There is no record that any of the five were ever apprehended.

The army tended to be as upset over the loss of expensive government property as over the loss of the men, and the vigor with which deserters were pursued sometimes depended upon the value of the property taken. In the case of this fivesome, replacing a "public mule" cost $70, a "dragoon horse," $85. Colt revolvers were valued at $7.50 each.[59]

On August 11, Lieutenant John Bold rode out at the head of a search party in pursuit of the deserters. He was back at Fort Worth on September 5. The record is not clear whether the search was successful, but there were seven men confined in the guardhouse in September, including four dragoons. In November 1850, three more deserters took off, this time two troopers and an infantryman. A month later the guardhouse was empty, suggesting that the latest group may have gotten away scot-free.[60]

The post complement of soldiers was also depleted by discharge for a variety of reasons. Men often opted to leave when their enlistment ran out, but there were also administrative causes and broken health. The latter was usually described on the rolls as "Surgeon's Certificate of Primary [or] Ordinary Disability." Disease, accidents and injuries took their toll on the frontier. A rarer category came under the general heading "discharged by Special Orders of the War Department." These might be men who had lied to get into the service, had a criminal past, or had proven to be chronic troublemakers.

Men who served their full enlistment and retired honorably were a heavy loss to the units because their experience and knowledge were not easily replaced. This was particularly true of non-commissioned officers. First Sergeant Jacob Dearing and Sergeant Levi McWilliams were both discharged at Fort Worth on June 11, 1850. Dearing had ridden as Major Arnold's second in command when Company F founded Fort Worth the previous summer, while McWilliams was a veteran soldier. Alphonso Freeman, a dependable private who had been in the dragoons since June 1845 was discharged on June 6, 1850.[61]

Pay was partly to blame for the loss of men: before 1854 there was no provision for paying veteran troops on a higher scale commensurate with their experience. A trooper made $7 a month for infantry and $8 for dragoons regardless of experience. One way of keeping men was to offer a bonus or "bounty" for re-enlisting for another five-year hitch. Typically, the bounty consisted of three-months' pay in one lump sum.[62] The offer did little to keep men in the service, however. On May 31, 1851, eighteen members of Company F, Second Dragoons, were discharged at Fort Worth, two for "certificate of disability" and sixteen for "expiration of service," leaving Arnold with only thirty-seven men on the active roll, and of that number, three were sick, six more were confined in the guardhouse for minor offenses, and, on the previous day, Private John Robinson had deserted.[63]

One of the best ways to keep the ranks filled was with aggressive recruiting from the civilian community. Records show that in February 1851, headquarters appointed Lieutenant Washington Street recruiting officer for the Eighth Infantry at Fort Worth. To meet his expenditures he was allowed $30 in discretionary funds with the proviso, "It is distinctly understood that this amount is to be expended exclusively on recruiting for the Eighth Infantry." His first expenditure was a bounty paid to Private John O'Kieffe to re-enlist for his third five-year hitch.[64] But his recruiting record wasn't so successful. Few western youths who grew up on horseback volunteered for the infantry.

The dragoons had more success luring adventuresome Texas boys—young men who hoped to "see the elephant"—into the ranks. Company B, Second Dragoons (the last unit at Fort Worth) signed on five local men in 1853, just before abandoning the fort: Raleigh O. Kearney, Patrick Tracey, James B. Cooke, Henry H. Jones, and Peter Miltonburger all called Tarrant County home before joining. There were eight others on the company roll who hailed from Texas, but the Lone Star State wasn't fertile recruiting ground compared to the great eastern cities where overcrowding, unemployment and poverty were powerful motives for enlisting.[65]

7

GUARD MOUNTING

June 17, 1851, was a red-letter day in the life of Fort Worth. On that date Ripley Arnold turned over command to Brevet Lieutenant Colonel James Bomford of the Eighth Infantry pursuant to Orders No. 46, issued at San Antonio on May 15, 1851. Bomford brought Companies F and H with him from Fort Gates to take up residence on the Trinity while Arnold led Company F, Second Dragoons, back to Fort Graham, which had been their home two years before. For the first time, Fort Worth became solely an infantry post. During the two years prior, it had housed either dragoons or combined dragoons and infantry. Among other changes brought about by the transfer, the numbers in the garrison increased dramatically. Arnold carried fewer than fifty men with him; Bomford brought in ninety-one infantrymen. Private Peter Keough of the dragoons remained behind to take charge of "public property," chiefly supplies, and Private Christian Bowman was left in the care of Dr. Thomas Williams because

he was too sick to travel. The reasons for the change can only be speculated on, but surely Arnold's loss of eighteen men the previous month due to "disability" or "expiration of service" had something to do with it. His weakened command could not adequately man the garrison. A more likely reason, however, was the campaign against the Comanches and their allies being conducted at this time by Lieutenant Colonel William Hardee of the Second Dragoons south of the Nueces River. Being at Fort Graham put Arnold and his company closer to Hardee in the event they were needed.[1]

Whatever the reasons, Arnold and the dragoons were not gone long from Fort Worth. In January 1852, they returned to relieve Bomford and the infantry pursuant to Orders No. 95 issued at San Antonio on December 15. The formal transfer from Bomford to Arnold was effected on January 11. The last of the doughboys, members of Company H, had pulled out the day before, headed for Fort Mason, leaving two of their number behind in Fort Worth's hospital. Their places were taken by Companies F and I of the dragoons, and the status quo was restored on the Trinity. At the end of the month, eleven men of the Fifth Infantry Regiment joined them from Fort Belknap. For the rest of its active life, Fort Worth was never without some dragoons in its garrison.[2]

Regardless of whether they were infantry or dragoons, officers and soldiers alike found that garrison life consisted of long days filled with the routine duties of stable and mess. No man relished garrison duty on the frontier; it had to be endured. The unappealing nature of it was summed up by Secretary of War C.M. Conrad in his Annual Report of 1852: "They [garrison troops] are exposed to all the hardships and dangers of war without its excitement to stimulate, or its hopes of honorable distinction to sustain them."[3]

By tradition, the day began with reveille at either 5:00, 6:00, or 6:30 A.M. depending on the season (5:00 A.M. in the summer). The morning gun was fired at the first note of reveille. At 7:30, the sickly reported to the assistant surgeon for "Doctor's Call." This was followed by assembly for roll call and breakfast at 8:00. After morning mess, duty assignments—"guard mounting" and "fatigue"—were at 9:00. Meanwhile, those who were not sick, on work details or other special assignments, spent the morning drilling. Dinner was at noon, followed by more fatigue duty for the balance of the afternoon. "Recall from fatigue" occurred about 5:00 P.M., and at sunset retreat was sounded, followed by the firing of the evening gun.[4]

The "Officer of the Day"—usually Lieutenant Starr or Major Arnold—oversaw all the activities. An enlisted man was chosen each morning from the guard mount to serve as orderly to the commanding officer. It was a much favored duty because the work was far lighter than sentinel or fatigue. All else being equal, the honor went to the "cleanest soldier of the detail."[5]

The day ended, also according to tradition, with "tattoo" followed by "assembly" for final roll call, then "retreat." "Call to quarters," at 8:30 was followed by "taps," the signal for extinguishing all lights. After that, soldiers were not allowed to leave the barracks except to take a turn at night guard duty or to answer the nature's call.

The day was not all work. What one dragoon called "a short period of leisure and joyousness" was allowed between retreat and taps, which turned the barrack room into a "scene of revelry and glee." Musical instruments came out and card players gathered around a tallow candle to "thumb over" a filthy, well-worn deck. Readers went off on their own, perhaps armed with a copy of *Robinson Crusoe* or *The Life of Colonel Gardner*.[6]

Inspections by the post commander were held once a week, usually on Sunday mornings so that the soldiers could have the rest of the day at leisure. Saturdays were usually set aside as clean-up days, with the whole command carrying out a general police of the garrison from inside out. On a war footing or on alert, this traditional routine was shelved for the duration of the threat, which is one reason soldiers enjoyed an occasional war scare or expedition into the field; it broke up the monotony of garrison life. From morning to night, seven days a week, it was a grueling schedule when observed strictly. The U.S. Army, however, was like any other structured organization: while some officers went strictly by the book, others allowed more leeway. The difference showed in inspection reports and desertion rates.

In an era when few men carried timepieces, the soldiers depended on a distinct series of bugle calls to divide their day. Without a bugler, military life lost much of its order and rhythm, which accounts for Arnold's plea for a bugler in those first months.

The principal peacetime duties of frontier garrisons like Fort Worth were escorting and patrolling. Escort duty meant accompanying mail coaches, freight wagons, and emigrant trains across the empty plains between forts. But since Fort Worth was not on any mail or trade routes, and California-bound immigrants passed far to the south, the troopers were never called upon to ride escort.

Patrolling, or "scouting," was the most important activity for the little garrison on the Trinity, as it was for almost every post on the army's defense line. Lieutenant W. H. C. Whiting regarded the eight posts he visited in central Texas in 1849—which included Fort Worth—as primarily "starting points and resting places for the scouts."[7] Fort Worth's troopers were expected to patrol over a distance of 120 miles to the north

and west. Even if Company F had been at its full authorized strength of officers and men, there still would have been too few to have effectively patrolled half this distance from the fort. When the Eighth Infantry Regiment was assigned to Fort Worth, the command could cover even less area because the garrison was on foot. So they did the best they could, grateful that the north Texas frontier was peaceful and that their sector was not any larger.

By orders of General Brooke in July 1849, scouts were to be sent out monthly, remaining in the field up to fifteen days. Subsequent instructions recommended that these movements take the form of short daily marches to conserve horse flesh. If the enemy was sighted, troopers were to make "a vigorous pursuit" with the object of "recovering stolen property and punish the offenders." If the chase turned into a long affair, the soldiers were to advise the nearest post, requisition supplies and, if necessary, reinforcements. The strength of the troop was to be governed by the probable number of Indians they were chasing. "Diligence" was recommended at all times.[8]

A September, 1850, circular to the commanding officers at Forts Crogham, Gates, Graham and Worth advised them to "order such scouts to be made below present frontier line as may be considered best for the prevention of [Indian] depredations." With this in mind, in October 1950, Major Arnold began sending weekly scouts all the way up to the Red River, eighty-five miles north of his post. He maintained this punishing pace of operations for the next three months, though his men encountered no war parties. The principal result of this diligence did not make the frontier any safer but it did force more men on sick call because of their exposure to the elements and the lack of medical treatment while in the field. Many men returned from patrols sick, increasing the demands on the post's lone surgeon. In 1851 such extended scouts were cut back considerably.[9]

Scouting was at best monotonous; pursuing Indian raiders was both the most dreaded and most eagerly anticipated. It could mean long weeks in the saddle, constantly under threat of ambush, with no promise of success. On the other hand, it also meant the chance to put into practice all that they had learned in countless hours of drill on the parade ground. None of Uncle Sam's finest ever expected to lose a stand-up battle to the Indians, so chasing down and bringing a raiding party to battle could be a great adventure, a chance to "see the elephant." The troopers and infantrymen assigned to Fort Worth never got the chance to see the elephant, coming close only one time—in the summer of 1851.

When not on scouting duty, the men were put to work painting, cleaning grounds, quarters and stables, gardening, caring for the horses and mules, laying in supplies of hay and corn, or doing routine repairs to equipment and quarters. "Stable guard," usually made up of three men, was a top priority at a dragoon post and was divided into four-hour watches. One lucky soldier took a group of horses two to three hundred yards from the post to graze on prairie grasses while the others mucked out stables and looked after the other animals.[10]

Other special duties required of enlisted men at every garrison included hospital steward, hospital cook, company and adjutant's clerk, baker, quartermaster sergeant, orderly, teamster, herder, company tailor, wood chopper, and blacksmith. All chores were carried out under the eye of the sergeant of the guard. The most onerous, if not the most dangerous, duty at the post was cutting timber in the river bottoms during the summer months. The rise in accidents and in sickness during the summer months could be directly related to this work. Timber cutting wound down in the fall and winter, a welcome relief to the men even if it also meant a long spell of cold and rainy weather, which brought its own share of health problems.

Another much despised duty was "procuring vegetables" (gardening), something that had to be done every day when they were in season. The men enjoyed fresh vegetables and anything to break the monotony of regular army rations, but gardening was hardly a labor of love.

For the soldiers posted at Fort Worth, it was a lonely and unexciting place, not exactly "God-forsaken," but certainly no Eden. When the men were off duty they had to entertain themselves without the benefit of a nearby town or even recreational facilities on the post. As Sam Starr discovered, "going to town" meant a sixty-to-seventy-mile round trip to Dallas. That required a three-day pass which kept most men from even trying, plus it was only a fair-weather trip. When Starr went, it was usually to attend to official business in his capacity as quartermaster and commissary subsistence officer. He made the trip there in a single day, then "tarrying at Dallas a day," before returning on the third day. Such a journey required a good horse and a strong backside.[11]

For entertainment and relaxation, the men were left to their own devices, with predictable results: they engaged in a little hell-raising whenever they could get away with it. There is a reasonable assumption, based on a wealth of reports from other frontier posts, that the soldiers—officers and men alike—used liquor to raise their spirits. According to an officer who was at Fort Worth, the garrison celebrated Christmas 1850 with one long party lasting from December 25th through January 1st. Lieutenant Starr, who had just left his wife behind at Austin, wrote her that he had a "very merry time" those six days, adding that "I got sick from the effects of the merry making and was compelled to take medicine." Reading between the lines of Starr's correspondence with his wife in the months that followed, he seemed to be "sick" quite often, which required frequent dosings with his special "medicine." When he wrote his wife on July 4, 1850, he informed her that he had just gotten up from a big dinner, "and my ideas are not the clearest." One of the things he did on his occasional trips to Dallas was attend meetings of the "Sons of Temperance," a forerunner of today's Alcoholics Anonymous. Taken individually, these references by Starr mean little, but

taken *en toto*, they paint a picture of another army officer in a lonely frontier posting who sometimes drowned his problems in the bottle.[12]

Sam Starr's flirtations with the bottle never got out of hand, but the same could not be said for a lot of officers. The history of the nineteenth century army is full of examples of officers posted on the frontier who fought losing battles with alcohol while trying to escape frustration and boredom. Henry H. Sibley, Ripley Arnold's extremely bright and audacious classmate at West Point and subsequent brother officer in the Second Dragoons, got too chummy with whiskey during his U.S. Army service in Texas in the 1850s.[13] Starr himself had personal friends among the dragoon officer corps who succumbed to alcoholism. One of those, a Lieutenant Neill, drank so hard he suffered from the delirium tremens and eventually shot himself. Starr learned of his fate while stationed at Fort Worth.[14]

Encouraged by the example of their officers, the troopers also imbibed frequently and heavily. Percival Lowe, a soldier in the Second Dragoons who served in Kansas, wrote that his comrades on the frontier "learned to quench thirst, subdue hunger, and otherwise obliterate their misery with whiskey."[15] They drank not just off duty but on duty as well, and for soldiers locked in the guardhouse, drunkenness invariably proved to be one of the factors behind their incarceration. The army inspector who visited Fort Lancaster, Texas, in 1856 found seventy-six prisoners in the post guardhouse, fifteen of

Samuel H. Starr in civilian clothes during the antebellum period. Lieutenant Starr's letters to his wife, Eliza, during his first three months at Fort Worth are the best source of information on military life at the post. (Courtesy of the Center for American History, University of Texas at Austin.)

them confined for drunkenness. He concluded grimly, "I presume the great error is in enlisting confirmed drunkards who desire nothing better than to get drunk and lay in the guardhouse."[16]

He might have also pointed out the stark desolation of the place—Fort Lancaster's nearest neighbor was Fort Davis, 158 dusty miles to the west. Loneliness and isolation from civilized society were powerful incentives to drunkenness. One historian has called intemperance, "the greatest and most persistent discipline problem" at western posts such as Lancaster and Worth.[17]

The dragoons especially had a well-deserved reputation for hard fighting and hard drinking; on occasion they had a hard time choosing between the two. This sad state of affairs was not news in several frontier counties of Texas. Many citizens were convinced that the dragoons were generally worthless as soldiers, at the very least, far inferior to the mounted rangers. In July 1852, the residents of Navarro, McClellan, Ellis, Bell and Williamson counties wrote Governor Peter H. Bell complaining of shocking levels of drunkenness among the troops who were supposed to be protecting them. The charge soon became public knowledge, causing some dragoon officers to deny it vehemently and others to inquire of their superiors if it were indeed true.[18]

Whiskey was traditionally supplied by either government-appointed sutlers or independent whiskey peddlers. Until 1830 the government provided it as part of a soldier's daily ration. After Congress changed that practice, the men had to purchase their liquor, and private suppliers leaped to fill the void left by the government's retreat.

Strictly speaking, sutlers were forbidden to sell what the army euphemistically called "ardent spirits" (hard liquor), but the prohibition was widely disregarded in the belief that if the sutlers did not supply the need, someone else from the civilian community would, and at least Uncle Sam had some control over the sutlers. As a result, the army looked the other way in allowing its post commanders to issue liquor-selling permits to sutlers.[19]

Even though the sutlers worked for the government, alcohol was hard to regulate when any wayfarer might leave a bottle or two behind when he left, and local citizens could freely buy and sell spirits to each other, "off the reservation." Trying to keep temptation as far as possible from his men, Arnold prohibited liquor sales any closer to the post than Henry Daggett's store at Live Oak Point—but distance was only a minor hindrance for any soldier doggedly intent on getting drunk. In June 1851, Major Arnold personally set out to find one of his AWOL troopers. He apprehended Private John Connigland three quarters of a mile away "in a state of intoxication."[20]

Connigland's case was hardly unusual. A month earlier Private Joseph Murphy refused to report to work detail one morning. He was found by a Corporal Zonkowsky "over at the Sutler's Store . . . drunk and unable to perform any kind of duty." No one accused the sutler of complicity in the affair but no one was surprised either.[21]

Murphy and Connigland paid for their crimes by spending six weeks in the guardhouse followed by court martial proceedings before Ripley Arnold who sat as presiding officer. Both were found guilty and their pay was docked for a period of months. Murphy and Connigland, however, were also returned to the ranks. If every man who got drunk had been drummed out of the regiment, many frontier garrisons would have been quickly decimated. Wise commanders dealt with alcohol abuse in a variety of ways, including banishing liquor from the post. But restricting sales and harsh corporal punishment did little to solve the problem, and chronic abuse led to carelessness, insubordination, and belligerence. The post commandant at Fort Griffin complained in his medical report during this time that, "Fully one-half of the surgical cases occuring in times of peace are produced through whiskey supplied to the troops."[22] Whether the garrison at Fort Worth was more immune than other frontier units to the lure of liquor and its spiritual relatives is unknown. Most of the members of Company B, Second Dragoons, who occupied the post at the end, however, were members of the temperance society, a source of pride to the commanding officer.[23]

The sutler was far more than the local liquor merchant. His store was the social center of the post, especially on payday when the men purchased such luxuries as tobacco and sweets in addition to spirits. Like every other frontier post in the nineteenth century, Fort Worth had sutlers, although little is known of their names and activities. It is generally accepted that "Uncle Press Farmer" was the first sutler. His activities can be derived from the experiences of other frontier posts. The sutlers worked under contract to the U.S. Army, receiving their positions directly from the secretary of war, and the competition was always fierce. They paid a fee or tax for the license to operate on army property, but operated only at the pleasure of the post commander. A change of commanders or a simple falling out often meant the old sutler was out and a new sutler was in. To keep their concession they were expected to maintain sufficient quantity and quality in their stock, charge reasonable prices, stay open only during specified hours, and not sell liquor to "drunken enlisted men and Citizens."[24]

The process was very political and very lucrative. Sutlers were allowed to pocket all the profits they made, which could be considerable on an isolated post like Fort Worth where they enjoyed a virtual monopoly for the business of a hundred or more men. The government protected the sutler's interests by not allowing any other "frontier merchant" to sell stock within a mile of the post.[25] Years later during Ulysses Grant's second term as president the inherent abuse in the system produced the Belknap Scandal in which at least one post sutler/trader paid the secretary of war $6,000 a year for his concession.[26]

While the contract sutler enjoyed a virtual monopoly, nothing in the law prevented other traders from setting up shop off post to serve the local community, soldiers and civilians alike. A sutler forced off the post could quickly become a competitor by setting up shop in the nearest town. Some frontier officers despised the sutlers as parasites, but no commander at Fort Worth ever reported any trouble with the local contract suppliers. At their best, they provided a welcome link to civilization. At their worst they were a pox on military life.

According to some local accounts, Press Farmer got the first contract in return for relinquishing his claim to the property on which the post was located. That same lore also calls him the first permanent civilian resident and the first merchant of the little town that grew up around the fort.[27] If the latter is true, it may be because he lost his concession and was forced to relocate his store off the reservation. In any event, the shadowy Press Farmer went into the history books as one of the pioneer fathers of Fort Worth, an honor most sutlers never enjoyed. He was followed in the sutler's store by Alex Young, a man about whom nothing is known. How many other sutlers Fort Worth had during its four years is impossible to know.

Apart from the assumption that imbibing was a popular pastime, there is only the sketchiest record of what the garrison at Fort Worth did for social activities. Occasional events must have filled their time—amateur theatricals, for example, as well as literary society parties, special occasion dinners, and dances.

Letter writing and keeping a journal also provided some

relaxation, while serving the very practical benefit of keeping soldiers in touch with distant friends and family. Some officers wrote to their wives daily, not so much to share news but because it made them feel like they were talking face-to-face with their loved ones. Under such circumstances it made little difference whether the letters were delivered in a timely fashion or even at all.

For young officers who had recently spent four years of their lives in the stimulating, scholarly atmosphere of the United States Military Academy, the move to the frontier was a shock to the intellect. When the opportunity came along to further polish the intellectual faculties they had first developed at West Point, they leaped at it. In 1850, Fort Worth happened to be blessed by the presence of a "French gentleman" who taught his native language as well as various fine arts to all comers. Adolphus Gouhenaught took out a land patent near the fort and built a home for himself and his sister. Among his ardent pupils were Major and Mrs. Arnold and their two oldest daughters, as well as all the post's junior officers. By all reports Gouhenaught was not only an excellent teacher but a true Renaissance gentleman. "He teaches the language after a plan very simple, requiring very little effort of the memory," marvelled Sam Starr, who called Gouhenaught "a universal genius [who] teaches music, drawing, dancing, everything."[28] If he was all he was advertised, Fort Worth must have had the most cultured officers of any Texas post in 1850. What was important about Monsieur Gouhenaught was that

the soldiers learned to take advantage of every talent they had in their small circle to relieve boredom and loneliness.

Many soldiers acquired pets, although not always of the normal canine or feline variety. Goats and pigs also filled the bill, but the owner had to be careful his companion did not wind up in somebody's cooking pot. Since Fort Worth was still in fairly desolate country, wild creatures were a familiar sight in the neighborhood during the early years. A wild animal might make an unlikely pet, but they helped while away the hours and provided welcome companionship during the long stretches of idleness. Sam Starr made a wonderful pet out of a "beautiful fawn [which] follows me wherever I go, and is wonderfully tame." Unfortunately, the "little rascal," as Starr called it, also had a habit of chewing up his clothes and on one occasion, a "new quilt cover" which his wife had made for him.[29]

The only women enlisted men saw regularly—besides Mrs. Arnold and Mrs. Starr—were laundresses, but there is little information on these familiar residents of every post. Laundresses were considered regular support personnel of any post, getting their room and board at army expense and approved for inclusion on company rosters. Also by regulation, no more than four were allowed per company. They took care of a detestable domestic chore, receiving a fixed wage of seventy cents per month for doing the enlisted men's laundry plus a dollar per month for the officers'.[30] At some posts the laundresses were the wives of enlisted men, but there is no record that this was true of Fort Worth. At other posts, particularly in the deep South, laundresses were often negro slaves, owned by officers and non-commissioned officers, who washed for whomever paid them. When the laundresses were single women, black or white, they were often prostitutes, or at least their social status was on the same level. The color, marital status, even the names of the women who labored daily over the wash kettles at Fort Worth have been lost to history.

At Fort Worth, the officers, naturally, were in the best position to secure female companionship for social occasions. During Christmas week of 1850, in the general spirit of merry-making, they decided to organize an officers' dance. At the time there were not more than half a dozen officers on the post, so they may have also invited some of the local citizens, including farmers' daughters from all over the area. That entailed taking one of the post's wagons to pick up the lady visitors. One girl turned out to be "six feet high," which probably meant she towered over most of the gentlemen. But the officers were the most surprised to find that their dates had no footwear for dancing: "they were shoeless!" The quandry was solved when "They purchased a lot of Boy's Brogans and shod the girls." There were no laces for the shoes, however, so the rustic damsels had to dance in "their stiff cowhide shoes" with graceless abandon. Both officers and their guests remembered that dance for a long time.[31]

In the matter of entertainments or simple pleasures, the officers always had it better than the men. Rank had its privileges and even at Fort Worth where no more than three or four officers was the norm, they exercised their license as much as possible. After the post aquired a full complement of officers, mealtimes were made more companionable by organizing a "Bachelors' mess" where news was shared and different officers performed to the amusement of their fellows.

Officers were also allowed to have "servants," or slaves, to take care of normal housekeeping chores. After he brought Mrs. Arnold and the children to Fort Worth, Major Arnold employed four or five servants for his family. Even someone living on a lowly lieutenant's pay like Sam Starr could afford two servants—when he could find them. Unless a man brought his slaves with him, however, he was dependant upon luck to find help. Starr was able to "make a bargain" with Middleton Tate Johnson to secure two servants—a nurse and a cook-housekeeper—for his wife, but because of the expense and the scarcity of hired labor on the frontier, he himself had to do without.[32] Sometimes enlisted men were employed by the officers as personal servants, and these men were known in army vernacular as "strikers." Such men performed regular domestic chores such as cooking and cleaning, for which they might receive up to five dollars a month, plus private sleeping quarters, better food, and limited field duty. It was considered a plum for soldiers with time on their hands who had the right disposition.

Being so far from wives and families could work cruel tricks on a man's mind, making him despondent, anxious, short-tempered, and even paranoid. Ripley Arnold got so lonely for his wife and four children that he sent for them and set them up on the post as soon as he could construct suitable living quarters. Most junior officers preferred to leave their wives behind in Austin or San Antonio where life was more hospitable, but such noble self-sacrifice could change as quickly as the winds on the North Texas plains. Sam Starr left Eliza in Austin with their young daughter Kate when he came north to the Trinity in the winter of 1849. Before five weeks had passed, he missed her terribly and implored her to "write soon." Not long after, he wrote about "getting a house suitable for my family by March [1850]," then as the loneliness grew worse he asked her how she felt about living in one room of a double cabin with him. When several weeks had gone by and still she had not written to him, paranoia began to set in.

> I hope you have not eloped with any one—and carried Kate off with you for that would be too bad. It is fashionable now, I believe, for officer's ladies to elope for a Mrs. Major Miller of the army has eloped it appears. So go, but leave Kate—do.[33]

When he began receiving letters from her, the desperation passed. He was overjoyed that summer to learn that she had given birth to a daughter, probably conceived not long before he left for Fort Worth in the fall, "and that you are both doing well." He began making plans to come see her as soon as he could get a pass and to bring the servants he had bought from Tate Johnson, but there is little doubt that he would much preferred to have been at her side full time than stuck in one room of a leaky officer's cabin on the Trinity River.[34]

Lieutenant Starr finally had his wife and daughters with him in Fort Worth by the summer of 1850. Four or five months was long enough to depend on the mails and an occasional visit to Austin to keep a relationship going. But they had hardly settled down on officers' row when the army moved him again. In 1852 he was reassigned to Fort Gates where his wife and children again joined him after some delay. The feelings of loneliness, doubt, and melancholy that he felt coming to a strange place far from home and family were not unique with the Lieutenant.

For the enlisted men, the situation was even worse. Any chance of having their families nearby was greatly reduced. The frontier army was largely made up of bachelors, so women like Kate Arnold functioned as a combination hostess, nurse, and regimental mother to the men in the ranks. Everyone, not just husbands, was thankful for their presence.

Without women's companionship on any regular basis, the soldiers had to find other leisure pursuits. Unlike most larger garrisons, Fort Worth lacked both a post band and a lending library. It was doubtful that the library was missed, but music was another matter. Not having a post band was a sure sign of just how isolated the little garrison on the Trinity was. It could also be detrimental to the morale of a unit in the same way that poor food and irregular mail service were.

Said Lieutenant Colonel W. G. Freeman on his inspection trip through Texas in 1853, "The presence of a regimental band tends greatly to enliven a post and render the men contented."[35] According to 1841 regulations, a portion of the post general fund could be used to maintain a small musical ensemble and to purchase their instruments. Sixteen bandsmen from enlisted ranks were authorized for the regiment by 1847 regulations. Those men, however, were on duty at regimental headquarters in Austin. Fort Worth would have to do without.[36]

Neither was there a local church in the beginning, although in the next year two ministers of the gospel moved into the area and began holding services in private homes. Depending on size and conditions, some frontier forts had a resident chaplain (who was to give "satisfaction") and were designated "Chaplain Posts."[37] Fort Worth never had such a distinction and a willing officer had to read the service on Sundays.

The first real preachers at the fort were itinerant and held services in return for room and board. In April 1850, John Allen Freeman, who had earlier organized the Lonesome Dove Church north of Fort Worth, was asked by Major Arnold to preach a sermon to the men. He accepted and the garrison was properly churched for at least one Sunday.[38] It was several years before the first true church was constructed. In the early years religion was not much of the social glue it was to become after the town was established. The all-male garrison needed more than Sunday sermons and somebody to get folks married and buried properly. The gentler entertainments of choir music and church socials were missing.

A local wedding was an event to celebrate in grand style, however, and the soldiers provided an enthusiastic congregation for the happy couple. On July 13, 1851, James Ventioner, Jr., married Millie Farmer, the daughter of Elijah Farmer, at the fort. While neither of the principals was connected to the military, the soldiers were invited and had a high time.[39]

The most popular form of public entertainment in which both soldiers and civilians joined were "big barbecues." They were a lot more frequent than weddings and did not require dressing up. A large steer was slaughtered and cooked slowly over an open fire. Then "fixins" were prepared which might include pies and cakes made with sorghum syrup for sweetening. When everyone had eaten, those who still had the energy could take part in sporting contests. Mrs. Carroll M. Peak, wife of Dr. Peak, recalled attending her first community barbecue in 1859, but they were "the fort's chief form of amusement" long before she and her husband arrived in 1852.[40]

The best part of garrison life at Fort Worth was that, in the words of Sam Starr, "living is cheap." This fact could make up for a lot of sacrifices in luxury and entertainment. The army provided basic room and board, and for additional variety, fresh food such as eggs and dairy products could be purchased on the local market for a modest sum. Even on the notoriously low pay, a man could put a little money aside. Or alternately, he could spend a little more to improve his living conditions. The Arnolds entertained travelers and local guests frequently and, apparently, willingly. At one point, however, Arnold complained to his superiors, "I think that I may safely assert that the Commanding Officer of the Post will be obliged to entertain more Persons than the Commanding Officer of any Atlantic station." Despite his grumbling, he kept a retinue of four or five servants to care for six family members, while spending only $29 out of pocket every month for housekeeping expenses.[41]

Living quarters were only a problem when there were more officers than there were quarters. When that happened, additional cabins could be constructed, but that took time, and there was no guarantee the results would be snug and dry. That was a long-term solution anyway. When the number of officers exceeded the available living quarters temporarily, the customary solution was to invoke the ranking system. This system, whereby the highest ranking officers got first pick of the available quarters with the junior officers getting what was left according to their rank, was known as "ranking out." This practice tended to cause the greatest dislocation and hard feelings when new officers arrived. Then depending on their rank one or more officers might be bumped, leaving the low man doubled up with another comrade, or, in the worst scenario, transferred to a tent. This arrangement was most distressing when married officers and their wives had spent months fixing up their assigned quarters and making them homey, only to be forced out on short notice as soon as a new officer arrived on post.

When Sam Starr got to Fort Worth, he spent the first few weeks that winter of 1849-1850 living on the parade ground in a drafty tent. Subsequently, he moved into officers' row, sharing one room of a two-room cabin with Dr. Thomas H. Williams. Williams at that time was in the process of constructing his own cabin on the post, so Starr planned to bring his family up and take over the cabin just as soon as the doctor moved out. In the meantime, he informed his wife, "I think that we can live comfortably in one room till the Doctor evacuates his."[42] By "we" he meant his wife, himself, and their young daughter—three people in a room no more than fifteen feet square. Meanwhile, the doctor was ensconced in his room at the other end of the eight-foot dogtrot. It was an awkwardly cozy arrangement, but one considered normal because privacy was one of the first things a soldier gave up.

Without military action or town life, the men looked forward with more-than-normal eagerness to the regular mail delivery and supply trains—their only links to the outside world. The mail couriers brought letters from home and newspapers, which might be old but were still cherished and re-read until they were worn out or every word was memorized. Until the spring of 1850 mail service to posts in North Texas was irregular and unpredictable. Then on May 19, regimental headquarters in San Antonio issued Special Orders No. 26 "establishing a weekly express between the Posts in the Eighth

Military Department." The garrison did not get the good news until May 30, but there was rejoicing in all ranks. No longer would they have to pray for the infrequent courier bringing news from civilization or wait weeks for their own letters to go out. Riders were dispatched weekly to Fort Graham to pick up the mail which was brought up from Austin.[43]

Fort Worth's first official post office was Austin, 200 miles south. After a few months that was changed to Waco, which served both Fort Graham and Fort Worth. This was some 120 miles closer, but still a long trip to the mail box for the soldiers on the Trinity. The wear and tear of those frequent trips were killing on men and horses alike, neither of which the major could spare. In January 1850, Arnold requested that in the future their mail be directed to Dallas, which he noted was only thirty-five miles distant, but Waco was still the official post office in 1853 when Fort Worth was abandoned.[44]

Even with improved mail service, it still took up to eight days for an ordinary dispatch from Fort Worth to reach department headquarters in San Antonio, and anywhere from four to six weeks by military post to reach Washington.[45] Civilian mail could take even longer because it received lower priority.

As increasing numbers of settlers began to make homes in the area, the government began mail delivery for civilians. In 1851, Johnson's Station was designated as Tarrant County's first (civil) post office, no small consideration if the Twin Forks region was ever to develop.

Military mail travelled either by "express wagon" or "dra-goon express" on their weekly runs. These trips were considerd "extra duty" for the volunteer troopers, who operated under the auspices of the post quartermaster. The riders were also expected to carry verbal messages back and forth between lonely officers and their families who had been left behind in the relative comfort and safety of Austin. Sometimes these messages got garbled and had to be untangled in the next written communication, but that was accepted as part of the system. In addition to the regular postal service, senior officers could sometimes be prevailed upon to carry letters in their personal baggage. This was a courtesy few commanders begrudged.

The journey between Fort Worth and Austin was long and arduous, although the carriers were seldom in danger for their lives. The Indians only twice interfered with mail delivery on the Texas frontier, both times in the spring of 1850 when they caught solitary mail riders in the open between isolated posts — neither of them Fort Worth. On those two occasions troops proved unable to catch the marauders, but rangers were able to track them down, much to the army's embarrassment.[46] Otherwise, the Indians left the mail riders alone. They may have been intimidated by the normally well-armed and alert soldiers, unmotivated by the prospect of filching the white man's mail, or, after March 1853, uninterested in stealing the army's choice of transportation. Orders No. 17 out of Corpus Christi on March 8 directed that henceforward, "all express service be done with mules in the Eighth Department."[47] The soldiers were to save their valuable horses for scouting and field operations, not routine runs between posts. Besides saving horseflesh, that simple order may have saved the lives of a few mail couriers since Plains Indians had nothing but contempt for the dependable army mule.

More troublesome than the Indians were mail carriers who took advantage of their position of trust to desert. Normally, the riders were carefully chosen, not only for their bravery and riding ability, but for their trustworthiness. Since they were absent from their posts for days at a time and completely on their own, the temptation for a homesick or disgruntled soldier to ditch the mail and keep right on going was great. Twice it proved to be too great for local troopers. In January 1850, the "express man from Fort Graham" enroute to Austin deserted, "carrying with him all the mail." Fort Worth did not get the news until a few days after the fact, whereupon Sam Starr promptly sat down and wrote a letter to his wife Eliza explaining why she had not heard from him in a while. He was not too concerned about the theft or the desertion. "I regret this," he wrote, "only as you may think I have been careless in writing to you, as [my last letter] contained nothing of importance."[48]

On December 11, 1853, Private Peter Miltonburger, only six months in the army, was on "detached service" as a mail rider to Waco. He too got as far as Fort Graham, then went "over the hill," taking with him his Colt revolver, musketoon, saber, and "Public mule." There is no record of Private Miltonburger ever being caught, or the mail he was carrying being delivered.[49]

The growth of the garrison at Fort Worth and its surrounding community was an increasing strain on the tenuous postal lifeline. It was imperative to keep it open, not only for official communication but for the morale of the garrison. Sometimes mail service was held up for reasons that had nothing to do with Indians, desertions, or other dramatic happenings. In August 1853, Major Merrill complained to headquarters that he was unable to prepay the postage on his letters because he had no stamps.[50] Among numerous shortages in men and materiel that the army had to deal with at distant posts, it probably never figured on postage stamps.

Ranking in importance with mail and supplies, an even bigger event on the calendar was payday. Enlisted men were paid on December 31, April 30, June 30, August 31, and October 31. The system, however, did not always work according to plan, particularly on the frontier. Arnold's men labored to put up Fort Worth that summer of 1849 although they had not been paid since December 31, 1848. The paymaster finally caught up with them at the end of August. But there was no place to spend the money; the new post did not have a sutler's store yet.[51]

The paymaster's job was dangerous and unglamorous, demanding men of iron constitution, steel nerves, and rock-solid integrity. Beginning in the summer of 1850, the payroll was delivered to the Trinity thanks to the heroic and generally unrecognized efforts of Major Albert Sidney Johnston, one of two paymasters for the Lone Star State. Early on, the money had to come from New Orleans to Austin before being disbursed to the scattered garrisons. Fort Worth did not become part of his route until 1851 or 1852 when he also included stops at Forts Graham, Belknap, and Phantom Hill.[52] The long intervals between paydays cut down on logistical problems and simplified the army's bookkeeping. On the Texas frontier a monthly schedule would have been physically impossible since it took Major Johnston thirty-five days to make his rounds, covering 730 miles in the process. Even so, the interval was cut down in 1854 to a standard two months between paydays, but that reform came too late to affect Fort Worth.

The pay wagon was a mule-drawn ambulance—a box-like, four-wheel conveyance with a canvas top and no springs. Whenever it rolled through the gate with its precious cargo, the men greeted the major like a long lost friend. Johnston was accompanied only by a clerk, a black driver and black cook, plus an escort of between four and twelve dragoons. He carried as much as $40,000 with him on his rounds to pay soldiers' wages, replenish quartermasters' funds and fulfill contracts at the various posts. No payroll was ever highjacked while Johnston was paymaster, but his driver once absconded with $3,000. Johnston replaced the stolen funds out of his own pocket.[53]

The rolling payroll travelled twenty to thirty miles per day across the Texas plains between posts and often served as unofficial courier service, performing errands and delivering personal items for residents of the posts. Johnston was the most popular officer in the army as far as the troops were concerned, especially because he always got through and delivered the money.[54]

8
ADJUTANT'S CALL

The commander of a frontier army post—often lacking junior officers and isolated from distant headquarters—had to shoulder the burden of command alone. Brevet Major Ripley A. Arnold, a strict disciplinarian, led by example, setting high standards for himself and his men. Meticulous and responsible, he bore the burden as a West Pointer should. He was considered overbearing by some of his men and by local settlers who felt he was too hard-nosed in carrying out policy, especially in letting contracts and laying claim to local resources.[1]

Despite his youth, Arnold's steady performance and undeniable courage won rapid promotion in the antebellum army. He was barely twenty-one when he graduated from West Point, and in the years that followed he maintained a youthful intensity and passion in his convictions that occasionally got in the way of his better judgement. Unlike many officers in the frontier army, he was not a heavy drinker nor a war-loving Indian fighter. He disliked drunkenness and he treated the Indians who came under his jurisdiction with fairness. Duty and honor were the only things about which he could be called obsessive. He knew right from wrong, refusing to back down when convinced he was right; "compromise" and "concede" were not part of his vocabulary.

His sense of honor, however, did not prevent him from dabbling on the side in land speculation and horse racing, with questionable judgement to be sure. Many officers in the nineteenth century army maintained outside business interests to supplement their meager incomes; Ripley Arnold was simply more shrewd and perhaps less circumspect in his outside dealings and it caused him trouble that may have contributed to his untimely death at Fort Graham.[2]

Arnold had few personal friends, not only because of his prickly personality, but because the constant moving and distant postings on the frontier put him in places where he had few social equals and little time for socializing. He was stiff and stand-offish, a stickler for rules but not so much as to be labelled a martinet by those under his command. He never let military formality get in the way of being a good host to those who passed through Fort Worth. Most soldiers in his command would probably have agreed with the assessment of Sam Starr after his first two weeks at Fort Worth: "I like Major Arnold, so far, well."[3]

Arnold punished infractions of the rules promptly and sometimes harshly when they impaired a soldier's ability to perform his duties, while with less serious infractions he could display a certain imaginative flair. Once when an enlisted man stole a pig from William Little, a settler who lived on the north side of the river, Arnold personally investigated the incident. After discovering the remains of a half-eaten pig in a soldiers' quarters, Arnold identified the guilty party and ordered punishment to fit the crime. The greasy evidence was hung around the soldier's neck, then he was tied to a post in front of the barracks with his hands above his head and his feet barely touching the ground, and left hanging there all day under a hot July sun. There were no reports of any further pork rustlings while Ripley Arnold was in command.[4]

It is fair to say, Arnold fit the picture painted by Private Samuel Chamberlain of the harsh and sometimes tyrannical dragoon officer. He had no compunction about ordering a man who was too drunk to report for his regular fatigue detail "bucked" for two straight days. This was the punishment assigned to Private Joseph Murphy in May, 1851, after he was

discovered in a drunken state hanging around the sutler's store. Bucking, which was usually combined with "gagging," was a despised form of military punishment wherein a soldier was seated on the ground with his knees drawn up to his chest, his hands tied together in front of his knees, and a pole inserted between knees and elbows. He was left in this excruciating position until the commanding officer decided he had been punished enough. After his bucking, Murphy was confined in the guardhouse from May 8 until July 21 when he was formally court-martialed at Fort Graham in front of Major Arnold, Major Henry H. Sibley, Lieutenant Sam Starr, and two others. Arnold was just as quick to place his officers under arrest "in none too gentlemanly way" when roused to anger by a breach of military discipline.[5]

Yet Arnold could also temper his actions with a degree of mercy. In the case of Private Murphy, in consideration of the "severe" punishment already inflicted and the time already spent in confinement, his sentence was "remitted" and he was returned to duty. When Private William Griffin, also charged with "drunkenness on duty" at Fort Worth, came before Arnold's court, he, too, was shown leniency, being sentenced to forfeit five dollars of his monthly pay for three months, "on account of the long confinement of the Prisoner previous to Trial."[6]

Arnold's ideas on punishment were not excessively harsh for that day. A range of brutal punishments, which enjoyed the sanctity of long use, could be inflicted at a commander's whim, and without the benefit of court-martial. These included, in addition to bucking (and gagging), tying men up by their thumbs and leaving them dangling that way for hours; or ordering miscreants to "march parade" while carrying a full pack or heavy log. Other punishments in the repertory of frontier post commanders included confinement in stocks, "riding the wooden horse," and solitary confinement in the guardhouse on bread and water. Commanders at Texas posts had a special torture for habitual drunkards: the soldier was forced to wear a "barrel jacket" (an old flour barrel with holes cut out for the head and arms) for up to a week at a time.[7]

But these punishments were minor compared to what deserters got: flogging and branding. This long, drawn-out ordeal consisted of fifty lashes across the bare back with the cat-o'-nine-tails, then while the prisoner was still insensate, he was branded on the left hip with a one-and-a-half-inch "D." Finally, his head was shaved and he was drummed out of the service in front of the assembled garrison.[8]

The brutal martinet was a familiar type at isolated posts across the West, and Lieutenant Starr was court-martialed for striking an enlisted man on parade after being transferred from Fort Worth.[9] The excessive brutality of some officers brought about a small but welcome reform in 1853. By General Orders No. 3, issued from the adjutant general's office on January 27, 1853, the common practice of "bucking" soldiers was prohibited. The order was received in Fort Worth on March 5 and duly noted in the Post Returns. By this time

Hamilton Merrill was in charge at Fort Worth, and by his own account, he did not have any discipline problems.[10]

Being so far from the watchful eye of headquarters, it would have been easy to have let the traditional spit-and-polish routines of military life lapse. But this was not the way of either Ripley Arnold or Hamilton Merrill. When Lieutenant Colonel Freeman inspected Fort Worth in 1853 he commended the garrison on its excellent discipline and "police" (cleanliness), noting approvingly that the guardhouse did not contain a single prisoner. He was "gratified," even amazed to find this "saddest of all places in a garrison" empty. Fort Worth, the twenty-first stop on his tour, was the "solitary exception" in that regard. Major Merrill proudly informed the colonel that he rarely had occasion to confine any of his men and attributed this good record to their teetotaling ways.[11]

Like discipline, the health of the garrison was always a concern to the commanding officers at Fort Worth and to their superiors. A healthy command was a more efficient and happier one. In the beginning, the men of Company F considered themselves lucky to have gotten out of Camp Worth at San Antonio a jump ahead of the cholera epidemic that took the lives of General Worth and many other friends and comrades in the spring of 1849. But the troopers were scarcely better off in the first months at their new encampment. "Fever" and "ague," as they were then called, were common ailments afflicting anyone who lived near the Trinity River. Lieutenant W. H. C. Whiting, referred to "the pestilent region of the

Trinity," and compared it unfavorably to the more healthful country bordering the Brazos. Fort Worth was Whiting's last stop on his 1849 swing through the central part of the state, and he found it to be the unhealthiest post on the frontier. Forts Martin Scott, Croghan, Gates, and Graham were all variously described as being "healthy" or "fit," but these terms were notably missing from his description of Fort Worth. Elsewhere in his report he made it clear he did not approve of the location of Fort Worth in any respect.[12]

The conditions were partly natural and partly man-made. When Sam Starr arrived late in 1849, he remarked that "mosquitoes are plenty," in a letter to his wife.[13] Unbeknownst to Starr, or anyone else at the time, he had just diagnosed the cause of the most serious outbreaks—malaria and yellow fever—that would plague the garrison during warm seasons for the next four years. Malaria was usually known among southerners as "swamp fever," and was believed to be caused by poisonous air that emanated from swamps. Its symptoms were intermittent paroxysms of chills, fever, and profuse sweating. In treating it, medical officers were aided by *Mitchell's Treatise Upon Malarious Fevers*, a copy of which was kept on hand at most frontier posts.

Yellow fever, also known as yellow jack and black vomit, was another mosquito-borne disease which struck the intestinal tract, causing hemorrhages, jaundice, and uncontrollable vomiting. One contemporary visitor to Texas described the effects of yellow fever in vivid language:

Men in the vigor and prime of life, and health, one day, and the next a disfigured, repulsive corpse! Where neither age, caste or disposition is spared; but when with one fell swoop the young man in his prime. . . is cut down like grain before the scythe in harvest time. Spare me from that fell and loathsome disease![14]

Cholera was another matter, and its origins were less mysterious to the ordinary person: it came from "bad" water, although nobody understood how bacteria worked at this early date. Two earlier epidemics had already hit Texas, the first in 1833 at Victoria and Brazoria, and the second in December 1848 at Port Lavaca. Ominously, the second outbreak was caused by soldiers coming back from the Mexican War, which was also the case with the third outbreak at Indianola among troops of the Eighth Infantry in February 1848. When they moved inland to San Antonio, they carried the disease with them. Other units coming through the Texas ports were soon exposed.[15] Some of the men of the Second Dragoons were probably already coming down with it when they first arrived, which helps to explain the excessively long sick lists of the next few months. Post surgeon Thomas H. Williams, from his nearly four years of observing soldiers come and go at Fort Worth, wondered if a great many of the illnesses reported to him did not originate "prior to the arrival of the patients at this post."[16] Such musings represented a shrewd medical prognosis by the doctor, but of course were complete-

104

ly unprovable from the limited background information available to him. His job was to treat the problems in his command as they arose, not delve into the medical histories of every trooper who came through Fort Worth. He missed the worst period of sickness at Fort Worth because he did not arrive until the fall of 1849.

The word soon got around in Texas that communities using chiefly cistern water, as opposed to well water, were practically exempt from the ravages of cholera.[17] Since both the civilian and military populations at Fort Worth relied primarily on well water for all their needs, the relative absence of cholera among Fort Worthers is noteworthy.

In addition to cholera and malaria, typhoid fever—also caused by contaminated water—was another chronic problem. Drawing drinking water from shallow wells and creeks, which was the common practice, was always dangerous. The water from such sources, which was used by both the garrison and civilians, was never pure, making typhoid outbreaks "common and frequently fatal" in those early years.[18] Death from typhoid fever was no easier than death from cholera, but the latter was never a problem at Fort Worth.

In June 1849, twelve members of the company, including two non-commissioned officers and ten enlisted men, reported sick. Eleven men reported sick in August and twenty-one in September, until the sick season peaked in October with an alarming twenty-seven privates and four NCOs from both dragoons and infantry reporting sick. In November, as cooler weather arrived and lingering effects of the cholera faded, the numbers were down to twelve enlisted men on the sick roll; by December, the numbers of sick in the garrison were a manageable half dozen. None of these men died, though several were given discharges due to "physical disability."[19]

The post hospital's first official patient when it opened in August was Private William Yolbel. Yolbel was one of the original dragoons who had accompanied Major Arnold when the post was established. The exact nature of the ailment was not specified, but he had been sick since June. Before the end of August he had plenty of company on sick call.[20]

To combat sickness and disease, frontier garrisons had to rely on whatever medical personnel the army could provide, and at many posts the training and professionalism of the medical officer was just short of appalling. Many surgeons had not graduated from genuine medical schools and underwent only the most cursory certification by the army before being assigned. James Hildreth, a First Regiment dragoon decried the competence of the medical officers: "They seem to think the life and health of the poor despised soldier of but little consequence; and as long as they can keep up an appearance of doing their duty they care not to inquire the result." Some surgeons even referred to their charges as "the sick, lame, and lazy." A soldier who reported for morning doctor's call with a slight indisposition might, after a few days of treatment, become truly ill, even to the point of death. "Gross mal-practice" was what Hildreth called it.[21]

Initially, the Fort Worth garrison relied on the services of a civilian "contract physician" whose chief qualifications were being available and willing to relocate to a god-forsaken frontier post.[22] That man was J. M. Standifer, a thirty-four-year-old Georgian who lived nearby with his wife Elizabeth and three children. Dr. Standifer arrived at Fort Worth in June and was carried on the post returns until October 1849. His job description simply read, "employed to act as an Assistant Surgeon for this Post." Standifer requisitioned the first medical and hospital stores for Fort Worth, "for one Company Dragoons stationed at this post." The supplies had to be sent from New York and did not arrive for four months. Standifer's brief stay at Fort Worth must have been pleasant enough. The Standifer children, ages eight, five, and three in 1849, played with Major Arnold's children about the post.[23]

Standifer was replaced by Dr. Thomas H. Williams, just twenty-three at the time of the 1850 census and a regular army assistant surgeon. Williams was already a veteran of several Texas postings. After an arduous ocean voyage from New York, he had landed in Texas at Port Lavaca on May 30, 1849, heading a detachment of Eighth Infantry recruits. From the coast, he went to San Antonio, Austin, then Buffalo on the lower Trinity River. While at Buffalo, he received Orders No. 62, telling him to report to "the post on the West Fork of the Trinity . . . relieving the citizen Surgeon now employed at the latter place, and who will be discharged." On October 6,

Williams reported to Major Arnold and forwarded a dispatch to San Antonio, notifying headquarters that he had "arrived at this place and relieved Dr. Standiford [sic]."[24]

Williams, a trained physician, was the only officer to serve without interruption at Worth until it was abandoned in August 1853. He never took leave during that time and received only one cursory performance review by his superiors. That came when Army Inspector W. G. Freeman visited the post in September 1853. Freeman missed Williams by a few days, however, because as the post was being closed, the assistant surgeon had been transferred to another station, leaving Fort Worth without a medical officer for the last month of its existence. Dr. Williams also took with him all the hospital records, and packed up all the stores and medicines for forwarding to the "medical purveyor" of the Eighth Military Department. Under the circumstances, Lieutenant Colonel Freeman was unable to fairly evaluate the medical facilities or the professional competence of the post surgeon.[25]

The record shows that Williams was one of the best medical officers in the U.S. Army. He kept up with advances in his field by having regular issues of the *American Journal of Medical Sciences*, and the *Medico Chirurgical Review* shipped to him from the East. He also conducted tests on the local environment to try to prevent medical problems, forwarding mud and water specimens from the river to the "Superintendent of the Observatory" for analysis. Like his counterparts, Williams was also expected to make regular "meteorological observations" for the War Department. The resulting "meteorological registers" were filed at San Antonio each month. Ironically the surgeon's sick reports were only filed quarterly.[26]

Getting medical supplies to the Trinity proved a never-ending challenge. Williams did not receive a fully equipped "Medicine Pannier Chest," which contained all the surgical instruments he might need, until April 1852. He had to file his annual medical requisitions in July, and hope they were delivered in sufficient quantities and in timely fashion. This was not always the case. On April 18, 1853, he complained to headquarters that his supplies for the year commencing July 1, 1852, for which he had received an invoice in September, were still lost somewhere between New York and Fort Worth. A week later they finally arrived. It is no wonder that he requested a leave of absence from the surgeon general of the army on January 4, 1853. It was denied.[27]

Williams was one of only twenty-one surgeons and fifty-nine assistant surgeons serving the army's fifteen regiments. And Fort Worth was only one of more than eighty posts scattered across the nation in this period, so the garrison was fortunate to have any sort of trained medical professional present full-time. Williams was aided by volunteer enlisted men who served as "hospital stewards" and "nurses" without benefit of extra pay. The steward was usually a man who had been a pharmacist, chemist, or medical student in private life. In rank they were considered equal to ordnance sergeants. Being a nurse required no special training or previous experience. For

their "noble" services hospital stewards and nurses received better housing accommodations and lighter duty than their fellows. A few years after Fort Worth had closed, hospital stewards and nurses were rewarded with extra-duty pay.[28]

At Fort Worth, the first soldier "attached to the Hospital Department" was Private John Saw who took up his duties on December 1, 1849. He was followed by Privates Christian Bohrmann and William Dixon. The latter took over on January 30, 1850, and deserted just six months and five days later. None of the enlisted men tended to stay with the hospital department long, though whether they were rotated as policy or requested transfer back to "the line" is unclear.[29]

Despite the odds, conditions had improved dramatically since that first summer three years earlier. In its last months, the garrison's sick list averaged five men daily, about seven percent of the total command, a rate quite in keeping with other posts and commendable by the standards of the day. Major Merrill told Lieutenant Colonel Freeman with only slight disingenuousness, that he considered the local climate "temperate and healthful."[30] This would have been news to the dragoons who were there in the summer of 1849.

For most of that period, fevers "of an intermittent type" were the prevailing cause of sickness among the garrison, as opposed to epidemics or chronic diseases.[31] "Intermittent fever," probably, was poorly understood but greatly feared. For fevers of any sort, conventional wisdom prescribed a treatment of a purgative dose of calomel, rhubarb, and aloes, or alternatively a compound extract of colocynth, to be followed by castor oil or "Rochelle salts," both of these being cathartics. The purpose was "to cleanse the alimentary canal and excite the functions of the liver." Quinine was also prescribed to check the paroxysms that normally accompanied malarial fever, and to prevent "intermittent" fever from turning into "recurring" fever. In April of 1850, Williams received a supply of unspecified "vaccine virus." What use he made of it is unknown. As grim as treatment with purgatives and cathartics sounds, it was sufficient to prevent any fatalities among the 1,037 cases of fever handled by Dr. Williams up to 1852.[32]

Fort Worth boasted an admirable record during its four years as an army post in terms of deaths from injury or disease. In the first three years under Assistant Surgeon Williams' doctoring, the garrison suffered only nine deaths, which he was careful to distinguish from his unblemished record in treating fevers. None of the fatalities was attributable to combat. Unfortunately, the records are incomplete for 1853, but there is no reason to suspect a rash of deaths among the garrison at the end. Among the nine deaths between October 1849 and the end of 1852, two were the result of typhoid fever, one from chronic diarrhea, one from "phthisis pulmonalis," one from "obesity of the heart," one from "melaena," one from "oedematous laryngitis," one from chronic dysentery, and one from "scorbutus" (scurvy).[33] Dr. Williams and post commanders Arnold, Maclay and Merrill could take pride in that record.

Like other frontier garrisons, they were far removed from real hospitals and medicines. Once a man fell ill, unless he had a strong constitution, his chances of recovery were not good. Injuries might prove fatal if infection set in or they did not heal properly.

The sort of low-grade sickness that kept the hospital busy sapped the effectiveness of the garrison and made life miserable for the men. The principal causes, as identified by Dr. Williams, were a less-than-ideal climate, specifically "extreme heat and moisture," unwholesome food and dissolute habits among the soldiers. None of these could be readily ameliorated by Williams, and he seemed resigned to a certain level of mortality as a constant at a frontier post. More than anything, including the soldiers' "dissolute habits," he deplored the heavy labor "in the [river] bottom every summer and fall, getting out timber for building purposes." The lightest showers were sufficient to convert the bottoms into "soft mud," observed Lieutenant Whiting, "and when the water subsides, it leaves to the sun a mass of rotted vegetable matter and half-dried mud."[34] In short, the area below the bluff became a breeding ground for disease.

In addition to less-than-pure water supplies, insect pests, and a mud flat below the bluff, the garrison had to contend with north Texas' notoriously fickle weather. Mother Nature was no friend of the soldiers when she shifted from scorching summers, when the temperature might soar as high as 111 degrees, to wet and bitterly cold winters, when the temperature might plunge as much as thirty degrees in an hour.[35] Fortunately, such weather extremes were rare.[36]

While spared from the worst epidemics of the day, Fort Worth's troopers suffered from the usual assortment of gastrointestinal ailments that afflicted men living under adverse conditions. Scurvy was the most common, but any number of ailments could be attributed to a poor diet. A steady regimen of beans, hardtack and bacon for months on end could play tricks with the digestive system of even the hardiest soldier. The worst culprit was the notorious and much detested, practically inedible hardtack. And the fresh bread which the soldiers baked from army-provided ingredients was not much better. Several years later, the post surgeon at Fort Griffin reported, "There is no doubt that many cases of diarrhea and diseases of the digestive system are produced by the bad quality of the bread."[37] It was predictable: soldiers created their own menus and cooked their own victuals, leading to stomach problems.

A certain amount of sickness was a part of the status quo at every frontier post and commanders could take pride when they reported a sickness rate lower than the average. When Lieutenant Colonel Robert E. Lee served at Camp Cooper, Texas, in the midst of a typically sultry summer ("The hot weather seems to have set in permanently," he wrote), for instance, he reported with the positive news that illness was "on the decrease."[38] Harsh living conditions, poor hygiene, and the lack of medical knowledge combined to ensure that a certain percentage of the garrison was always unavailable for duty. A half a dozen men on sick call on any given day was considered normal at a frontier post of company strength or greater.

9
FORM RANKS

Fort Worth post returns—like those of other frontier forts—are exhaustive. Whether the subject is sick call, courts martial or equipment, everything—man, animal and piece of armament or equipment—is set forth in detail, largely because the Washington bureaucracy was obsessed with keeping accurate records on the state of readiness at each of hundreds of posts. The quartermaster, commissary and ordnance inventories were all carefully scrutinized—even if they were at the end of a long supply line—and Major Ripley Arnold paid close attention to such things.

Equipment issued to soldiers was divided into arms, clothing, and accoutrements, the latter including cartridge boxes, saber belts, holsters, and the like. Troops at Fort Worth, regardless of branch of service, drew their arms from Ordnance Depot at San Antonio, and other items, including saddles and "horse furniture," from the Quartermaster Depot at the same place. Requisitioning supplies was a trying process involving lots of time and paperwork. Foul-ups, delays and shortages were normal.

When Company F first arrived on the Trinity, Arnold described their "military appearance" as "fair." He made additional notations about their arms and accoutrements—"tolerable"—and their clothing—"bad." He was particularly concerned about the latter because in his previous report at the end of April he had noted that uniforms for his men were "bad and scarce." Apparently he had received nothing in the way of replacement clothing by the time Arnold moved his company north. That the men were outfitted in tattered and raggedy uniforms would have sorely vexed the fastidious officer. Sometime in the next two months the supply wagons arrived with new uniforms; however, in his report of August 31 he described the men's clothing as "good." But their military appearance only "tolerable," their arms and accoutrements "old and bad."[1]

Dragoon clothing, like everything in a soldier's life, was strictly regulated, but regulations were observed more in the breach than in fact. There were different uniforms for field, fatigue, and dress. On the frontier a dress uniform was superfluous; Arnold's men would have spent practically all their time in either field or fatigue uniforms, both known in military vernacular as "undress." For fatigue and field service, dress consisted of a shell jacket and pants (known as "overalls" or "pantaloons"), made from either blue wool or white cotton depending on the climate and season, and a tall cloth forage cap. The cold weather uniform consisted of a dark blue jacket and blue-gray trousers. All trousers—reinforced in the seat and inside of the legs—were high-waisted, supported by suspenders. Enlisted men were issued "stable frocks," or knee length dusters, made of "coarse, inexpensive, undyed material" for use when grooming their horses. Both jacket and trousers sported distinctive yellow trim on cuffs, shoulder straps, collars, and leg stripes. Headgear also had a distinctive band of the same bright color, yellow being the branch color of the Second Dragoons. Since most of Arnold's men had served in the recent Mexican War, combat service gave them the privilege of wearing a red stripe on their coat sleeves, an innovation dating to 1836. Ankle-high boots of black leather, made to fit either foot, completed the basic uniform.[2]

Officers' dress uniforms consisted of dark blue, double-breasted frock coats and trousers of either dark blue or blue-gray color, depending on rank, plus insignia of rank. As a captain, Ripley Arnold would have worn the blue-gray pants, but as a brevet major, he was considered field grade so he could wear the more distinguished looking dark blue pants. His official rank was captain, so he wore double gold bars on his shoulders. In summer the frock coat could be exchanged for a white cotton or linen shell jacket but only "during the extreme heat of the season."

Another sign of an officers' position was a sash—yellow for non-commissioned officers and orange for commissioned officers. After 1847, for ceremonial occasions, field grade officers, even brevet majors, complemented everything with a plumed, cocked hat—an affectation of an American army obsessed with Napoleon and Napoleonic pomp.[3]

The dragoon uniform, whether dress or undress, officer or enlisted man, tended to be elaborate and ostentatious—another throw-back to the showy attire of Europe's grandest armies. The officers' version had cords, braids, plumes and gilt accessories. The official dragoon plate, which adorned hats, buckles and flags also reflected the Old World motif: it was a Napoleonic silver eagle on a gilt star. Arnold and his fellow dragoon officers could only be out of dress uniform for "ordinary stable duty, marches, or active service." But the uniform described in regulations bore little resemblance to what the men actually wore on the frontier. Few of the fancy uniforms and adornments would ever be on display away from main encampments and big cities. Garrison commanders saved their finery—and that of their men—for visits by army inspectors.

Even a spit-and-polish officer like Ripley Arnold would not have insisted that they strictly follow uniform regulations for their normal duties. Clothing on the frontier—unauthorized, colorful shirts and wide-brimmed hats, for example—often reflected the soldiers' tastes. Modern experts agree, the dragoons were the eccentric individualists of the army and the Second Dragoons were the most eccentric of all. This drew the ire of the departmental commander in 1849. Major General Brooke sent out a circular in November reminding post commanders of the requirements listed in the *General Regulations of the Army*, "prescribing the mode of wearing the hair and beard by officers and soldiers." He noted that these regulations were "in some instances being entirely disregarded" and such a "principle of disobedience" would no longer be tolerated.[4]

To survive as a commander in the Second Dragoons, an officer had to have an extra measure of tolerance for the unconventional. In good conscience Ripley Arnold could record his men's appearance on the muster roll as "fair," knowing the standards were different on the Trinity than at Carlisle Barracks. Yet in the face of common sense and much evidence to the contrary, one highly respected expert on nineteenth-century military uniforms and arms says, "Full dress had its uses on the frontier in impressing visiting Indians, and it was often worn."[5] There is only one report of a dress parade at Fort Worth, and on that occasion in 1853 the inspecting officer addressed his attention to the drill and weapons of the troopers, not their uniforms.[6]

Uniforms of the U. S. dragoons and infantry as they appeared in Horstman's Official Uniform Regulations Book *of 1851. Each plate was hand-colored after being engraved. They were personally approved by General Roger Jones, Adjutant General of the Army at the time. (Courtesy of the Frontier Army Museum, Fort Leavenworth, Kansas.)*

United States military uniforms underwent a major change in 1851. The new attire consisted of a frock coat of dark blue cloth, sky blue pants for regimental officers and enlisted men, and a tall, conical hat, raked forward, replacing the soft forage cap. It was soon discovered that the frock coat was devilishly uncomfortable for mounted men; late in 1851 the shell jacket was reinstated for dragoons. In the interest of economy, it was decided one basic uniform pattern should serve for full dress, fatigue, garrison, and field duty—in both summer and winter. Gone was the former requirement to switch seasonally between dark blues and whites. Bowing to popular demand, the army also authorized the broad-brimmed "Andrews hat"—known later as the campaign hat—for members of the Second Dragoons stationed in Texas. The men had been wearing this style of soft felt hat in place of the official forage cap ever since the Mexican War, as pleased about defying regulations as they were with the more practical design. They owed the thanks for their new hatwear to Colonel William Harney who as regimental commander of the Second Dragoons personally placed the requisition with the War Department. Orange became the color of service of the dragoons in the new regulations.[7]

The troopers at Fort Worth may have never seen the 1851-style uniforms (the Quartermaster Department was anxious to clear out its stock of old uniforms before issuing the newer style). When Company B pulled out in 1853, they were outfitted in fatigue clothing of the "old pattern," though some of the men still retained their old sky-blue dress jackets. In their last review the only uniforms they had to parade in were their fatigues, but those, it was noted, were in "good order and generally well fitted."[8]

On the frontier, however, adoption of new uniforms—which were suited better for parade grounds than battlefields—lagged far behind their production and distribution.

Like the dragoons, infantry dress tended to bear little relation to the uniform regulations handed down by bureaucrats in Washington, D.C. Most infantrymen arrived in Texas wearing some variation on the uniform decreed by 1847 regulations. The Mexican War attire for regulars was distinguished by sky- or Saxony-blue pants and kersey jackets for enlisted men, the same color trousers but with dark blue, double-breasted frock coats for officers. Officers also wore red silk or worsted sashes as a mark of rank. Both ranks wore the dark blue, wool forage cap. These regulations were modified in 1851, requiring dark blue frock coats for all ranks, and replacing the soft forage cap with a tall shako-style cap having a lacquered leather visor. In the new uniform regulations, sky blue for facings, patches and detail work was the designated color for infantry.[9]

Infantrymen on the frontier tended to customize their uniforms to fit local conditions, personal tastes, and current fads. Some soldiers called the results their "prairie outfits," which might consist of the old, 1839-style wool forage cap or broad-brimmed felt hat, a soft-collar flannel shirt of dark blue or checkered material, and perhaps a neckerchief.[10] All that was kept of the regulation uniform was the sky-blue trousers. A single black waist belt, buckled with a brass plate in front, replaced the whitened, criss-cross leather belts of the Mexican War. The waist belt held a variety of cap pouches, cartridge boxes, and weapons. When permitted to do so by officers, the infantryman travelled light, carrying a wooden canteen and a canvas haversack.

The commanding officer of the post set the tone, and in Arnold's case he had final say in matters of dress for both the dragoons and infantry at Fort Worth. At the end of 1850, bowing to reality, Arnold issued orders that soldiers need not wear the full, regulation uniform. The men welcomed this relaxation of the rules, but some of his junior officers were not so sure. When a new shipment of uniforms arrived for the infantry, Lieutenant Washington Street wrote to San Antonio headquarters to inquire whether he should issue them. The reply assured him that Arnold was well within his authority setting dress code and not to bother issuing the new clothing.[11]

The firearms of infantry and dragoons were substantially the same. Foot soldiers carried a regulation .69 caliber Model 1842 percussion musket with bayonet; many also equipped themselves with a long hunting knife and a non-regulation five- or six-shot revolver. Dragoons carried a carbine, two pistols, and a saber—all regulation. Although in theory the saber was the dragoon's primary weapon, they were treated with disdain. Neither infantry nor dragoon had much respect for any

Regimental colors of the Eighth U.S. Infantry, carried through the Mexican War and later retired to West Point. Made of blue silk, the heraldry contains a bald eagle clutching an olive branch and a bunch of arrows, surrounded by twenty-eight stars and a scroll identifying the regiment—all in red, white, green, brown, and gold. (Courtesy of the United States Military Academy, West Point, New York.)

edged weapon bigger than a Bowie knife. Infantrymen often left their bayonets with the baggage train, in fact. As one infantry sergeant once explained to an easterner: "There is no such thing as hand-to-hand combat with the Indians."[12]

There is good reason to believe Arnold's troopers did not carry sabers along when they came north to establish Fort Worth. There is no official record of sabers among the men, although other weapons and accoutrements are prominently mentioned. Still, sabers were regulation equipment and at $7 each, the army did not want them lost or discarded. When Company B, Second Dragoons, replaced Company F at Fort Worth in August 1852, they carried the standard U.S. Model 1840 heavy dragoon saber, commonly known as "old wrist-breaker" by those who had to wield it.[13]

The dragoons' secondary weapon according to the tactics manual was the pistol. Arnold's men may have used either the old Model 1836 single-shot flintlock pistol, usually carried in a pair of saddle holsters and therefore known as "horse pistols," or the Model 1842 smoothbore single-shot percussion pistol. In December 1849, the Model 1848 Colt revolver was first supplied to the dragoons. It gradually came to replace the outdated flintlock and percussion pistols, but in the meantime it was sometimes carried in tandem. In 1850, the dragoons were called upon to participate in field-testing the new Colt Revolving Pistol, also known as the Walker Colt.[14] This six-shot, percussion-fired weapon was a tremendous improvement over the old horse pistols. Arnold received a circular from headquarters on November 11, 1850, asking him to report upon "the advantages or disadvantages of revolver Pistols." His official recommendation is unknown, but it is known that the cavalrymen had fallen in love with the Colt when they first saw it during the Mexican War. The intimidating pistol weighed more than four-and-a-half pounds, had a nine-inch barrel, and fired a .44 caliber bullet. Though it would be some time before the army officially sanctioned the handgun, members of Company B at Fort Worth in 1853 all proudly carried Colt's pistol.[15]

The dragoon's most effective weapon, whether mounted or on foot, was the single-shot rifle. Arnold's men originally carried the Hall breechloading carbine (several models were available by this date, including both smoothbore and rifled). The basic design had been introduced in 1836 specifically for the Second Dragoons. It was improved on until 1843. With its short, twenty-one inch barrel, these weapons were of limited range and accuracy but superior to sabers and pistols.[16]

When Company B of the Second Dragoons replaced Arnold's Company F at Fort Worth, they carried the newer Springfield cavalry musketoon. Designated the Model 1847 cavalry musketoon, it was issued in limited quantities before 1853. They were so slow getting into service, in fact, that the Second Dragoons formally requested the War Department to speed up issuing them in June 1850. After less than a year of service at Fort Worth, Company B's musketoons were considered "unserviceable." When the troops were inspected on

September 7, 1853, three out of every four of the weapons "had some smaller parts missing or broken," but their sabers and Colt pistols were in satisfactory shape.[17]

Each dragoon at Fort Worth carried $39.50 worth of weapons, along with an unspecified amount for his accoutrements, powder and ball. Add an $85 horse and a full uniform from flannel drawers (thirty-three cents each) to greatcoat ($7.62 each), and a fully armed and equipped trooper cost Uncle Sam more than $150 in 1849—ample cause for docking a soldier a month's pay for losing or misusing his equipment. In August 1849, Major General Brooke warned his troops sternly: "The utmost responsibility and care," he wrote, were to be exercised in the use of army arms equipment. "They are to be used expressly and only for the service intended, *viz*, in scouting parties and pursuit of Indians."[18] Such mundane matters as uniforms and equipment occupied much more of Ripley Arnold's time than did concerns about Indians. He had to balance his perfectionist tendencies against the realities of the frontier and occasional visits by army inspectors.

By the end of October 1849, Arnold had upgraded his command's military appearance from "tolerable" to "fair," and their clothing to "good." However, their arms and accoutrements were still "bad" and with little chance of improving any time soon. With the arrival of winter, men and equipment both suffered from the harsh conditions. At the end of December 1849, Arnold emphasized the deplorable state of their arms and accoutrements by adding "and unserviceable" to the previous notation "bad." The situation improved in the early part of 1850, however, when the major described everything as "good" in his February report. That evaluation held steady for the rest of 1850, and for as long as Arnold was in command.[19]

10
ASSEMBLY

At first, the post on the Trinity had few near neighbors, the closest settlement being Johnson's Station. The first white settler of record was twenty-two-year-old Kentuckian Ed Terrell, who arrived in November 1843 and built a log cabin on the bluff and, the following spring, a trading post near Live Oak Point. Terrell did not stay long because of the Indian threat, but his trading post remained and was turned into a general store and community center in 1849 by Henry Daggett. That little store was a lonely mercantile outpost for some time, but its new owner managed to carry on a "lucrative trade" with the Indians and the settlers who lived "in and around the post."[1]

The presence of the U.S. Army was the determining factor in the population growth that followed. Tarrant County was organized in December 1849 and only two years later civil law arrived when Judge John H. Reagan gavelled the first district court into session in Henry Daggett's store. Daggett's store also served as the polling place for the first county elections.[2]

Farms and plowed fields soon dotted the landscape. Lieutenant W. H. C. Whiting reported in 1849 that squatters' houses were numerous on the prairie after crossing Hickory Creek, some thirty miles south of Fort Worth, and that settlements were "rapidly increasing" throughout the lower Cross Timbers.[3] This was confirmed by Lieutenant Sam Starr, who wrote his wife in early 1850 that, "There are numerous settlers all around." An early history of the city says within two or three years "some half dozen families gathered" around the little fort. This number may have been reached even earlier. When the Holloway family arrived from Missouri in December of 1849, "there were about a half dozen log cabins here besides the soldiers' quarters." In the years that followed, the closest families lived north and west of the military reservation. Relieved of the Indian threat and with farming uppermost on their minds, most new settlers preferred to spread out around the county rather than bunch up near the fort. The 1850 U.S.

Census shows 689 settlers (not counting slaves) scattered across Tarrant County.[4]

For those living closest to the post there was a sense of security knowing that the soldiers were nearby and protecting civilian lives and property. According to local lore, the soldiers and settlers created a warning system to summon the garrison at the appearance of Indians. One musket shot would bring five troopers (minimal danger); two shots meant "send ten troopers"; three shots in rapid succession indicated serious danger—send fifteen soldiers.[5]

All reports of new settlers—including traders, merchants and businessmen—would have been good news for a state government that was anxious to fill its empty lands and for the few hardy pioneers who had hung on in North Texas waiting for the army to secure the territory. Isolated communities like Alton, Birdville and Whiterock were still at risk, but they no longer thought they were the last line of civilization.

Trooper and civilian depended on each other. When Ripley Arnold first moved his command to the Trinity in the summer of 1849, he brought a soldier who served as farrier and blacksmith.[6] That soon changed and the work was turned over to settlers living nearby. Contract workers were employed in various support services: wheelwright, farrier, and blacksmith, for instance. Other civilians worked as needed on repair and construction. Although not carried on the rolls as army regulations required, civilians must have been employed at Fort Worth in the first year and a half of its existence. The ear-liest record of civilians working at Fort Worth for wages is in August 1851. Four men were hired that month by Lieutenant and Assistant Quartermaster John Bold: a guide and inter-preter, two muleteers, and a wheelwright. The guide-inter-preter and the wheelwright were each paid $40 a month plus one ration daily; the muleteers received $20 a month plus a daily ration.[7] Post returns continued to show civilians working at Fort Worth under the auspices of the quartermaster's depart-ment until it was abandoned in 1853.

At some point the post ran its own herd of beef in addition to or instead of purchasing meat locally. Soldiers could not be transformed into cowboys readily so they called on the settlers for help. To manage a herd of 100 cattle, three herdsmen were hired at $20 per month each, plus a per diem ration estimated at nineteen cents per man. The total of $77.10 each month came out of quartermaster and commissary supply funds.[8]

The guide-interpreter held the most essential position of the civilian employees, leading monthly scout parties and act-ing as liaison with local Indians. Even old Indian fighters like Ripley Arnold and Hamilton Merrill did not speak the local dialects or know local customs, and they were unfamiliar with the country they guarded. The civilian guide was of such importance that a "Special Order" (No. 42) from General Brooke's headquarters read in part:

An experienced Indian interpreter and guide will be employed at each post on the Frontier District, whose duties in addition to interpreting the Indian . . . language, will be to give information, from time to time, of the movements or designs of the Indians. None but men of intelligence will be employed.[9]

Other civilian personnel (all under the jurisdiction of the post quartermaster who determined their pay and allowances) received a single ration per day and a wage varying from $20 per month for muleteers to $45 for farriers and blacksmiths. Unskilled workers were hired only when major building repairs were needed and the commanding officer did not want to use enlisted men. In October 1851, Lieutenant Colonel James Bomford of the Eighth Infantry, commanding, authorized five day-laborers to shore up some of the sagging buildings at fifty cents per worker per day plus rations.[10]

Civilians with skills that guaranteed regular employment at the fort built homes nearby and brought in their families, thus contributing to the beginnings of a village on the bluffs. By the spring of 1851, local pioneers working under contract provided tallow for candles and soap, beef for the troopers, and hay for the garrison's horses. The arrangements tended to be quite profitable for the locals, and encouraged further settlement near the fort. A. F. Leonard and Henry Daggett held the first beef contract and went into a partnership in a general store on the bluff. This was the same Leonard who built the area's first commercial grist mill in the eastern part of the county. Daggett branched out into real estate.[11] Daggett and

Leonard—unlike many unremembered and unsung pioneers —not only benefitted from the protection Fort Worth provided, they actually made money on the garrison's presence.

Unfortunately, there was a darker side to most towns that sprang up around frontier military posts. Wherever a large body of mostly single men gathered, whores, saloonkeepers, and gamblers swarmed to the area to set up "hog ranches" (as the red-light district was politely known). When the noted landscape architect and conservationist Frederick Law Olmsted visited Fort Duncan, Texas, in 1855, for example, he noted that the chief occupation of the citizens of nearby Eagle Pass was "selling liquor and gambling," with the soldiers as their principal customers.[12] There is no record, however, that such problems plagued the garrison at Fort Worth. Apparently, there was only enough business to support one saloon—the First and Last Chance Saloon run by Captain Ed Terrell (the same man who started a trading post in the area in 1843). He opened for business in 1849, "in a tent near the camp."[13]

The working relationship between fort and settlers produced occasional friction. In one instance, Major Arnold refused to pay landowners for the timber his men removed and found himself operating in the gray area between eminent domain and legal ownership. He had signed supply contracts with local citizens based on shaky legal grounds. One of the timber agreements was negotiated with an unnamed "gentleman" who had "located his head right upon the half section occupied by the post." By the terms of his accord with Arnold, the army would pay the gentleman "at the same rate as was paid at Fort Graham," but it was contingent upon his ability to prove up his title. Such proof was not easily secured, however, under the state's land laws, as the post quartermaster noted in May 1851: "Of course nothing has been paid him."[14]

Local settlers came to resent Arnold taking whatever he needed, and wood cutting seemed to be the sorest point between civilians and the army. The war department took a firm stand. The May 1851 quartermaster's report also stated: "No claim for fuel has yet been made, nor will any be admitted until the claimant shall produce a clear title to the land."[15]

The problem was inherited by Arnold's successor and was still not resolved when the last dragoon rode out of Fort Worth in 1853. They left behind "a disputed tract of land" for which not a cent had been paid in rent or for the "timber and fuel cut" during the previous four years.[16] The partnership of civilian and military did have a positive side. The army had secured the region and, on leaving, had left behind real estate with standing buildings, pure water wells, gardens, and fences.

In spite of minor disputes, garrison and community relations were good but not particularly close. As long as there was a serious Indian threat, the community appreciated the army's presence, but as that threat faded, so did fondness for the garrison. Although Fort Worth troopers did contribute to the local economy, the men raised or hauled in much of their own food, performed most of their own labor, and demanded army authorized prices for everything they bought on the local mar-

ket. In March 1851, Arnold received orders that his troops were to cut their own hay if the local contract price went above $10 per ton, cutting off a lucrative source of income for local farmers.[17]

The garrison was largely a man's world and never included many dependents, though Major Arnold was able to create a genuine home life at Fort Worth. His family lived in a "hewed log cedar house upon the hill" and reached out to the civilian community surrounding the fort.[18] When they departed they left behind many friends of all ages. According to Mrs. Margaret Holloway who spent some of her early childhood years on the post, her only two playmates were the Arnold girls, "Kate and Sophie"*[sic]*.[19]

When Arnold had come north in the spring of 1849 he left his twenty-five-year-old wife, Kate, and three small children (the youngest just a few months old) at San Antonio. According to local lore, he soon moved them to Johnson's Station where they would be closer but not subject to the rigors of life on a new and unfinished military post. Before the year was out, however, he brought them to a modest, hastily built log cabin at Fort Worth.

When Mrs. Arnold—described by Sam Starr as "a sociable little woman and pleasant"—joined her husband, she became the first white woman at Fort Worth.[20] According to some sources, she only stayed from spring through fall every year, returning to Washington, D.C., for the winters. Yet based on the time and difficulties entailed in traveling such a great distance, that seems highly unlikely.[21] A fourth child was born to the Arnolds in the latter part of 1850, but Willis Arnold died soon after. When the government census takers came through Tarrant County that summer, they listed only three Arnold children—the youngest, Sophia, just one year old. Before the end of 1850 Sophia died. Apparently both youngsters were victims of a cholera outbreak. Indeed, post medical records show an unusual number of soldiers on sick call in September and October but provide no clue as to the cause of the illnesses.[22]

Willis and Sophia Arnold were interred on a tree-shrouded plot of ground about a mile from the fort, the earliest occupants of the community's first cemetery (later known as Pioneer Rest). Two side-by-side cairns, topped with heavy limestone slabs dug out of the cliffs, mark the spot. The twin tombstones were unadorned except for the names of the two children, their parents, and the year.

Kate Arnold and her children had few counterparts. Few women would have welcomed a move to Fort Worth. One officer's wife, who saw much of the Southwest while following her husband, wrote of 1851 Texas: "With the exception of San Antonio, all other posts in Texas and New Mexico are wretched in the extreme."[23] Male comradery and hard work substituted for loved ones left behind. When the army abandoned Fort Worth in 1853, there were only seven women—civilian or military—in the community, and when Dr. Carroll M. Peak and his bride arrived from Dallas in early 1853, Mrs. Peak became number eight.[2]

Limestone slabs mark the graves of the two Arnold children buried at Fort Worth in 1850. To the rear, a large granite stone marks the site of Ripley Arnold's grave, installed in modern times to replace the original headstone.

11
TO HORSE

Had Fort Worth's garrison ever faced a genuine threat of Indian depredations, their mission might have been more meaningful. In fact, the soldiers rarely saw hostile Indians. To be sure, Texas had problems with Indian raids during the years Fort Worth was an active post, but it was more imagined than real. There was no danger of massive tribal uprisings. Instead, the principal Indian menace to Texans came from roving bands of Comanches and Apaches who struck unexpectedly, then melted away.

Texas was home to two highly different groups of Indians. The first was composed of small, nonaggressive tribes of East Texas: Delawares, Keechis, Anadarkos, Ionis, Caddos, Tonkawas, and Wacos—sometimes known as the "allied bands."[1] The warlike Plains Indians of West Texas—principally the Comanches and Lipan Apaches—made up the second. The allied bands had been driven out of their homes in the Piney Woods following the Cherokee War of 1838 and had

resettled on the upper Brazos, just "a few days march" from the future site of Fort Worth. From there they ranged between the Brazos and Trinity rivers, doing little harm but scaring away potential settlers by their mere presence. In 1841, when Simon B. Farrar was planning a move to North Texas "for the purpose of stock raising," he chose Ellis County rather than the upper Trinity (present-day Tarrant County) because he thought it "safe from Indian raids and depredations."[2]

Time and experience would prove the agricultural Indians more a nuisance than a serious threat to settlement. By 1847, according to reports of the U.S. Government's Indian commissioners in Texas, the total number of Anadarkos, Ionis and Caddos had been severely reduced and they had so intermarried that they were identified by officials as one people. They huddled together in small semi-permanent villages and seldom roamed far from their log-and-grass huts. They survived on what meager crops they could raise and, in later years, government handouts of meat, corn and salt. One military inspector described them as "perfectly harmless."[3] Frontier settlers might have argued the point.

By contrast, the Apaches and Comanches roamed at will over the vast areas of West Texas, occasionally raiding settlements in the central and eastern parts of the state. Both tribes were relentless foes, the latter being the more dangerous because of their greater numbers and love of war.

While the Comanches loved to make war, they were even more interested in plunder, and their record of mayhem against their more peaceful Texas neighbors reflected this. They rarely attacked unless they had overwhelming superiority, and they avoided military strongpoints like Fort Worth. Their method was to raid stock and carry off women and children into captivity. Writing in 1856, Colonel J. K. F. Mansfield described their techniques: "They keep out of sight and commit depredations and murders at times when least expected."[4] They made war on whites and on other Indian tribes with equal ferocity.

Texas Apaches were primarily Lipans and probably numbered no more than 500 in small bands scattered from the Edwards Plateau south into Mexico. Like the Comanches they were nomadic and warlike, but the men also practiced farming when they were on their home grounds. Their raiding parties, which seldom consisted of more than five to fifteen warriors, were no threat to vigilant and well-armed white settlements.[5]

Fort Worth was literally on the boundary between the Plains Indians and the passive eastern tribes. The garrison had to keep an eye on its peace-loving neighbors nearby, while at the same time watching for incursions across the frontier line by the Comanches or Apaches. Fort Worth was well to the east of their normal range: the "Comanche Trail" skirted the headwaters of the Colorado and Brazos rivers, and the Comanches' favored territory was the staked plains; Apache territory was "principally west of the Pecos River and bordering on Mexico and New Mexico."[6] Generally, neither group descended the Trinity as far as the Twin Forks.

In the 1840s an uneasy truce had been arranged between the Comanches and whites following the devastating Comanche raid in 1840 when 1,000 warriors raided all the way to the Gulf Coast. It was the last major Indian engagement within Texas borders. Afterwards, peaceful trade was encouraged under the enlightened leadership of Sam Houston as president of the Republic of Texas. Peace conferences were held at several places to end hostilities, sometimes with Houston's personal participation, resulting in a series of treaties pledging friendship and cooperation on both sides. One of those was the Bird's Fort Treaty, signed in 1843 in present-day eastern Tarrant County, which established a vague boundary between white settlements and Indian lands on the northwest frontier. But there was no guarantee that boundary would be respected by either side, which is why first rangers, then federal troops were stationed in the area. Another treaty, signed at Comanche Peak in 1846, persuaded the Comanches to move farther west and to acknowledge the sovereignty of the United States over them.[7] It, too, seemed to be more truce than lasting treaty.

In the same period the Lipans proved more amenable to negotiations. The tribe made treaties with the Texans in 1838 and 1845 and with the United States in 1846. As a result many withdrew to the Pecos region and directed their raids southward into Mexico.

A new Indian threat swept through the state in 1848 and 1849, spurring construction of Worth's chain of federal forts. The Rio Grande country was hardest hit, with every community clamoring for the army to locate a fort nearby. North Texas was not immune to the widespread panic. In mid-1849, a settler named Maloney of Denton County called for a punitive expedition against local Indians to recover what he claimed were large numbers of horses "stolen from our citizens." A party of home guard was to assemble at Hickory Creek (twenty-five miles from Fort Worth) on July 14, 1849, to chase down the hostiles. Cooler heads would prevail. Texas Governor George Wood, who worried about the clash, wrote to General George M. Brooke to clarify the situation. Major Arnold reported to the department commander that rumors about Indians stealing large numbers of horses in his quarter were "false," and the Denton home guard was persuaded not to start a conflict in North Texas.[8]

Initially nervous at his new post, Arnold remained steadfast. A little more than two weeks after he arrived he expressed a mood of cautious optimism in a dispatch to General Brooke in San Antonio: "I am hopeful that our presence here will deter the Indians, from whom we have as yet had no trouble."[9] The situation, however, remained tense. In August, Brooke "requisitioned" three companies of "mounted volunteers" from the governor of Texas to assist the army, and the following month every army post in the state was put on alert. Commanders across the state were kept up to date on the latest Indian depredations and warned to stay alert. Meanwhile, Arnold continued to report no Indian problems in his sector.[10]

The situation was so tense in January 1850 that General Brooke wrote gloomily to his superiors in Washington: "I cannot perceive the avoidance of a general [Indian] war." The legislature of the state was alarmed enough that in January and again in September they passed strong resolutions calling on the federal government to place "adequate armed forces" on the borderlands to protect the lives and property of citizens.[11]

Neither of these views accurately reflected the situation in North Texas. On the northwestern frontier, the dragoons at Fort Worth could only watch and wait. Arnold saw no looming threat to his own command and so advised his superiors in a notation added to his regular report in May 1850: "Indians peaceable in my vicinity." He said he had been visited "in recent months" by parties of "Wacos, Tonis, Anadarkos, and Tahwacarros [sic]," but none of them represented a threat to the post. They were friendly, he noted, being principally "engaged at their corn patches."[12]

That same month, as reports circulated of a virtual state of war south of him, Arnold wrote a letter to headquarters seeking clarification of his own position, specifically, "whether Fort Worth might be considered in Indian country." The fact of his uncertainty was a clear indication of how quiet things were in his sector. The reply Arnold received on June 1 was not much help. He was advised to maintain vigilance and continue forwarding information on Indian activities to San Antonio. At this time he had just thirty-nine dragoons and thirty-three infantry "present for duty" to cover the 130 or more miles between Fort Graham and the Red River.[13] Nine days later another letter arrived advising Arnold of new Indian depredations farther south and repeating the earlier instructions to maintain "increased vigilance."[14] A few months later a circular went out from headquarters in San Antonio advising all post commanders that an unnamed party of Indians, probably Comanches, had carried off the two daughters of a Mr. Thomas on October 1, and ordered "a vigorous pursuit" if the raiders were seen.[15] Arnold's patrols saw no war parties.

After an initial onslaught, Comanche raids in central Texas shifted south and west, closer to tribal sanctuaries in Mexico. The Comanches were at least partially deterred by the Fort Martin Scott Treaty of 1850, named for the place where it was signed, seventy miles north of Fredericksburg on the Guadalupe River. It was negotiated by Indian Commissioner John H. Rollins, representing the federal government, and delegates from six central Texas tribes. Although not specifically signed by the Comanches, it eased tensions all along the frontier because thirty-five important chiefs and warriors affixed their names to it, agreeing to give up horse stealing, not make war on other peaceable tribes, and "forever to remain at peace with the United States." By drawing closer to the whites, the treaty Indians isolated the Comanches and denied them potential allies.

The Fort Martin Scott Treaty was a major step in pacifying the northwestern frontier. The army wanted to be sure that both Indians and whites refrained from any provocative actions that might nullify it. All garrison commanders in Texas, including Ripley Arnold, received a copy of the agreement along with specific orders to "carry out the spirit of the accompanying Treaty with the Indians of Texas."[16] While the sedentary tribes kept the peace for the most part, Lieutenant W. H. C. Whiting did report a few disturbances in 1849. "Occasionally a horse or beef is stolen, but murders are of rare occurrence," he wrote.[17] In his 1852 medical report Fort Worth surgeon Williams said there were no Indians "living nearer the post than the upper Brazos River."[18] Those were innocuous and mild mannered, more interested in receiving handouts than in making war. Whiting confirms what Arnold reported about Indian visits to his post: rather than threatening the garrison, the tribes who regularly visited had nothing on their minds more dangerous than trade.

To get the the Plains Indians to cooperate, however, would take more forceful persuasion. In June 1850, General Brooke ordered Lieutenant Colonel William Hardee to "conduct a vigorous campaign against the Savages," using every "disposable" dragoon at Forts Mcintosh, Inge, Merrill, and Lincoln. The following spring, Hardee led a force of 200 Second Dragoon troopers into Indian country on the Llano and upper Brazos rivers. Their mission was not to start a war but "to negotiate and secure intelligence."[19] The expedition was a success. No pitched battles were fought, but the Lipans and Comanches were chased out of the area and Hardee conducted the first careful count of Indians on the frontier.

The thirty-nine men and officers of Company F, Second Dragoons, at Fort Worth were not included in Brooke's orders in June of 1850, and with just forty men and eighty-one serviceable horses on post the next May, they did not participate in Hardee's campaign. But Major Arnold received orders from headquarters in Austin to "be in readiness to render assistance to Bvt. Lt. Col. Hardee."[20] That was as close as the garrison at Fort Worth ever got to an actual Indian campaign.

Fort Worth pioneers like George L. Harris and John Peter Smith later recalled sizeable Indian encampments near the post. Smith described Caddo, Waco and "Ionian [sic] bands whose camp fires dotted the prairies at night in every direction around Fort Worth." Similarly, Harris remembered that as a boy "the Indians came here a great deal," setting up their "wigwams" west of the fort on Arlington Heights or north of the river on Marine Creek. On one occasion they apparently came en masse, because he stood on the bluff and counted some "150 or 200

wigwams of the Caddo Indians" set up on Marine Creek. When they moved on, the Caddos left behind some of their tepees. Harris and three of his friends set them on fire. The blaze raged out of control burning off a large area of prairie.[21]

Other early residents agreed both that the Indians came to the fort frequently and that they were unfailingly friendly. John James Woody, whose father Sam Woody came from eastern Tennesee in 1850 and owned farms in Tarrant and Wise counties, remembered the Indians as being "very amicable." They liked to trade horses with the elder Woody and had genuine respect for him. According to another account, "The most amicable relations were preserved with the Indians, who were frequent visitors, and during the four years occupancy of this post by the U.S. troops, scarcely a single interruption to the most perfect concord occurred."[22]

This did not mean the Indians were trustworthy or pacified, but that they were intimidated by the soldiers in their midst. Woody recalled that the same Indians who traded horses with his father during the day had a different attitude after dark. "Often on moonlight nights, they would creep back down through that county and steal horses and cattle." Lieutenant Whiting also reported that while the old men and chiefs came to the fort "in good faith and amity" to trade fresh game for the products of white civilization, the young men were likely to be on the warpath elsewhere. But their raids were always directed against settlements in the "lower country." Tarrant County was "remarkably free of disturbance."[23]

This tended to create some animosity between troops on the upper and lower posts on the frontier line. After an 1851 raid by Lipan Apaches "about San Antonio and the lower Rio Grande," the mounted rifles at Fort Inge believed that troops at Forts Worth and Graham were in cahoots with the hostiles, allowing them to use the country between the Brazos and Trinity rivers as a sanctuary. Lieutenant Dabney Maury of the mounted rifles even expressed the unfounded and preposterous opinion that "Whenever [the Apaches] were about to make a raid down our way, they would tell the Dragoons they had war with the Rifles and gravely bid them good-by."[24]

Much of the widespread fear of Indians can be attributed to a lack of information. There was a common misconception among Texans that their state was overrun with bloodthirsty savages who, should they ever find common cause, would rise up and slaughter every white man they could lay hands on. Not until the summer of 1851, when the U.S. Army made an impromptu census of Indians in the state, did the actual numbers become known. Veteran Indian Agent Robert S. Neighbors had estimated in his report of 1849 to General Worth that there were 29,575 Indians living in Texas, including 5,915 warriors. Neighbors added a disclaimer that it was "very difficult to get the actual numbers [because] he had to rely on figures given him by the chiefs of the various tribes." The U.S. Census of 1850, probably basing its numbers on Major Neighbors' report, counted 29,000 American Indians in Texas. In 1851, a more careful accounting by Captain William J. Hardee showed 3,952 Native Americans of all tribes, sexes, and ages, living "on the borders of Texas," including some 921 warriors.[25] The overwhelming majority of the 3,952 Indians were peaceable, and the total number was declining steadily due to death and migration to Mexico, New Mexico and Oklahoma. Hardee estimated some 700 Comanches in north Texas, but only 140 of that number were warriors.[26]

Major Hamilton Merrill observed from Fort Worth in 1853 that most of the allied bands had migrated out of the state in the previous two years, pushed by aggressively expanding white settlement. Those that remained lived "much in fear of being removed" to the north side of the Red River where others had already resettled. Only two sizable groups still made their homes in the northern part of the state—one under José María encamped on the Brazos about thirty-five miles northwest of Fort Graham, and the other on the Clear Fork of the Brazos between Fort Belknap and Fort Phantom Hill. They were mostly Caddos and Ionis, quietly raising corn and hunting. Neither group numbered more than 150, and neither was close enough to Fort Worth to be Merrill's responsibility.[27]

The question of how many Indians there were in Texas greatly affected frontier policy. The administrations in Washington and Austin wanted to know in order to set Indian policy. The army needed to know in order to determine how many and what size garrisons to maintain. The army already had more posts in Texas (nineteen) than in any other state or territory, although they were all undermanned.

In the spring of 1851 Brevet Colonel Samuel Cooper conducted his own inspection of Indian country up the Brazos River from Fort Graham, accompanied by Major Henry Hopkins Sibley, commander at Graham. The colonel was most interested in gathering information on the Comanches. He concluded there were not more than 2,000 warriors in the state, "and they cannot concentrate at any one time for hostile purposes one-fourth of that number." He added that the largest number of Comanches known to have visited any army post "at one time" was seventy warriors.[28]

When Lieutenant Colonel W. G. Freeman visited Fort Worth on his inspection tour in September 1853, he asked Major Merrill how many Indians he thought resided in the state. Merrill's expertise came partly from being commander of a frontier post, but more from the fact that, as Freeman's report stated, "He has served a number of years in Texas and has had excellent opportunities of observation and information." It was Merrill, at the head of Company B, Second Dragoons, who had commanded the escort for Commissioner Rollins to the Indian council in 1850 that produced the historic Fort Martin Scott Treaty. Now, Merrill's informed guess was that there were no more than 1,570 Indians living in Texas, "of whom 250 are warriors." Another 680 lived across the Red River and frequently crossed into the state, "making a total [native population] of 2,250 men, women and children." Just a few weeks before, Merrill had provided the same conservative figures to the superintendent of Indian affairs in

Texas, apparently without citing the transient population. The most important number, he told Major R.S. Neighbours, were the 250 "capable of bearing arms." He further guessed that the Comanches and Lipans together constituted perhaps 1,100 of the total.[29] This was little more than half the Indians counted by Hardee just three years before. It seems likely that these optimistic reports, coupled with the years of routine returns from the advanced posts on the Texas frontier, played a significant part in the army's belated decision to shut down several posts in the state in the mid-1850s.

Freeman's inspection revealed a great deal more about the true Indian situation in Texas than numbers alone. Starting at the Indianola depot on the coast and working his way north through fifteen forts, camps and depots, on the Rio Grande, Nueces, Colorado and other rivers and streams, he did not see any Indians until he got to Fort Mason on the Llano River in central Texas. He found Tonkawas, and they had only come "to beg."[30]

When Freeman reached Fort Worth on September 7, he reported, "No Indians have visited the post since last autumn, except a small party of Caddoes and Ionies." He received this intelligence from Major Merrill.[31] While the Indians may not have paid any formal visits to Fort Worth in nearly a year, they were still operating in the vicinity, stealing livestock, while pleading friendship. Just four months earlier, Merrill hired a local civilian for the new job of "secret agent and guide." The pay was the same—$40 a month plus a daily ration—as he had been paying the fort's guide-interpreter (who was still on the payroll), but the new man's job was to "trace and recover" stolen animals from the Indians.[32]

Freeman did not know a lot about Indian tribal organization. In his report from Fort Worth he identified well-known Anadarko leader José María as "chief" of the Caddos and Ionis, a mistake any Texas homesteader could have corrected.[33] Like the Caddos and Ionis, José María's people called the Brazos River country (present-day Parker County) home, but they were a distinct tribe from the others. Settlers in north Texas looked on Maria's people as allies against the Comanches. The chief himself, because of his great dignity and wisdom, was often regarded as a spokesman for all the peaceable tribes of the region, but it was not an official position in the tribal hierarchies. The Anadarkos, who sometimes traded at Fort Worth, did not number more than 250 men, women, and children at this time.

The most dangerous tribe in North Texas was the Wichitas, whom Lieutenant Whiting described in 1850 as "a wild tribe with which as yet no relations have been established."[34] The Wichitas were members of the Caddoan linguistic family, which meant they were closely related to the Tawakonis, the Wacos, the Keechis, the Anadarkos, and the Ionis. Most of the Wichitas normally stayed north of the Red River, but they roamed as far south as the Twin Forks, raiding in small parties like the Comanches, then retreating to their sanctuaries across the river.[35] Their terrifying appearance, caused by heavy tattooing of both males and females, made them even more fearsome than most other Indians. They were never strong enough to challenge the garrison at Fort Worth openly. In 1853 Merrill estimated they numbered no more than 150, counting both warriors and their families.[36] The Wichitas tended to give Fort Worth wide latitude, preferring to terrorize isolated farms and small parties of unwary travelers. If Fort Worth served any useful purpose as a bulwark against Indian depredations, it was to keep the Wichitas honest by penning them north of the Red River.

In the summer of 1852, Jesse Stern, special agent of the Indian Bureau, succeeded for the first time in establishing an understanding with the Wichitas, which put an end to their depredations for a time. Thanks to Stern's efforts, a number of stolen mules and horses were returned and the chief of the Wichitas promised his people would commit no more "outrages." Subsequently, Stern reported in late 1852 that the "whole line of frontier" under his supervision was free of Indian aggression.[37]

If we can believe an oft-quoted local source, the troops at Fort Worth faced an Indian attack only once during four years of standing guard on the Trinity. That came in 1850 and, not surprisingly, involved Comanches. The story comes from Howard W. Peak, early Fort Worth resident and notorious raconteur, and was never reported in any official dispatches from the post. Nor was Peak himself a part of the story, admitting he got it from "an old file of my father." Nonetheless, it deserves re-telling because Peak was a genuine Fort Worth pioneer and one of the major sources for the city's early history.

According to the family story, Chief Jim Ned commanded a band of Comanches who resided in the area west of Fort Worth known as Palo Pinto (Spanish for "painted woods"). In the spring of 1850 the chief decided to "wipe the fort out of existence" because it protected the white settlers pushing onto Indian lands and also because Major Arnold's scouts had killed one of his favorite men. Some 200 Indians in war paint headed for Fort Worth in two groups, one under Ned and the other under a younger chief named Feathertail. On the way they were discovered by "an adventurous fur trapper" named Cockerell, who promptly galloped to the fort to warn the garrison. Instead of adopting a defensive posture, the troopers, led by Cockerell, mounted up and set out behind Major Arnold, Captain Maclay, and Lieutenant Street to intercept the war party.[38]

They came upon Chief Ned's group camped out and sound asleep, slipped up on them, killed thirty-seven Indians and severely wounded another fifteen. The injured Comanches were executed on the spot because there were not enough men for a guard detail and not enough time to march them back to the fort before continuing the pursuit. Chief Jim Ned escaped, riding away to join Feathertail's group. Not a trooper was wounded in the melee.

This was just the opening round. The dragoons set out after the second band under Feathertail. They chased them back to Palo Pinto and prepared to launch a surprise attack on the Comanche village. But before they could carry out their plan, they were ambushed by the alert Indians. There followed a fight of several hours that saw the outnumbered troopers using their "repeating carbines" [sic] to hold off their attackers. After Chief Feathertail and forty-four warriors were killed, the rest of the Comanches fled for the hills. The soldiers suffered five killed and fifteen wounded. The wounded were treated by the fort's "two surgeons" [sic] who had accompanied the expedition. Arnold ordered his dead buried on the spot; the wounded were loaded up and carted back to Fort Worth.

Six months later, Chief Jim Ned led another war party against Fort Worth, this time getting as close as "the hillside southwest of the Fort" (near the point where Summit Avenue crosses the West Freeway today). Their planned attack was broken up, however, when the fort's six-pound howitzer was brought to bear, dropping a shell in their midst. That took the fight out of them and they fled, never to bother the fort again. Chief Jim Ned even reformed, secured an official amnesty, and led a peaceful life until death took him some years later.[39]

This story invites skepticism on several points: the names of the officers who led the expedition and the surgeons who accompanied it, the trooper casualties, and the type of arms carried by the troopers, none of which match the official records.[40] What helps keep this apocryphal tale alive is a historic marker—a simple concrete shaft erected in the flurry of public works projects during the heyday of the New Deal in the 1930s—that marks the spot of this supposed "Indian battle."

The official record shows that the garrison at Fort Worth never had to deal with a war party of Comanches or any other

Historic marker at the alledged site of an Indian attack on Fort Worth— more a monument to WPA activism in the 1930s than to historical accuracy.

hostile Native Americans. There are no reports apart from Howard Peak's of Comanche depredations in the vicinity of Dallas and Fort Worth until the 1860s.[41] All told, the Indian threat could not have been too serious if Major Merrill, the army's most experienced Indian fighter in Texas, could close his report to the superintendent of Indian affairs by saying, "Both policy and humanity would urge that these Indians be clothed and fed till otherwise provided for by donations of land and settlement."[42]

Of more serious concern to the army than imagined Indian raids was the widespread "illicit trade" with the Indians34 being carried on brazenly by some of the unscrupu-

lous men to be found around many frontier posts. This commerce in guns and liquor could stir up a war faster than almost anything, and for this reason it infuriated both the army and the Indian Bureau. The problem reached such proportions that it was made the subject of special orders sent out in May 1851 directing post commanders to do everything in their power to stamp it out. To promote better relations with the Indians and encourage legitimate trade, while economizing on the annual largesse handed out to the tribes, post commanders were instructed in July 1851 to issue their condemned provisions to the Indians.[43] Whether this practice won much goodwill is another question. As Arnold discovered at Fort Worth, it helped turn some of the Indians into shameless beggars.

In the summer of 1853, Fort Worth troopers got their first look at a large band of Native Americans—somewhere between fifty and 350 according to various observers—mostly Shawnee and Delaware.[44] It was not a war party; they came in peace, though not willingly. Forcibly driven north by the army to the Indian Territory across the Red River, the old and infirm, and the women and children outnumbered the men.

The Texas legislature had been looking for a way to expel the Indians from the state and passed a resolution to that effect in 1850, calling on United States troops for the job.[45] Congress obligingly appropriated $25,000 for the operation, and the docile Shawnees and Delawares were the first to be rounded up. This small-scale "Trail of Tears" began on the Llano River about the first of May, then moved north past Fort

Graham and arrived at Fort Worth early in June. The uprooted Indians—traveling in the white man's wagons—brought everything they owned, including pigs, goats and chickens. A few wayward Comanches, intent on getting to the Indian Territory, attached themselves to the procession, but they proved to be models of decorum while they were under close army scrutiny. The caravan sojourned at Fort Worth for a day or two, using the respite to deal in horseflesh and whiskey with the locals. No unfortunate incidents occurred. As soon as they moved on, they were forgotten—except in the records of the Bureau of Indian Affairs. Sadly for the cause of Indian-white relations, the Shawnees and Delawares were considered by those who knew them to be "honest people who never made a living other than by honest means." Major Merrill described them as "useful people" in recognition of their service as guides, scouts and diplomats. (When Major Merrill reported to Lieutenant Colonel Freeman in September 1853 that he had seen no Indians in nearly a year, he must have forgotten this caravan, or he discounted it because they were under close army supervision.)[46]

It had been an odd encounter, completely different from Howard Peak's fanciful reminiscences of Comanche raiding parties, and far more representative of the true state of Indian affairs on the North Texas frontier.

In 1854, the year after Fort Worth was abandoned, Secretary of War Jefferson Davis, in his annual report to Congress, took special note of the "bleak military situation" in Texas. With an estimated Indian frontier of nearly 2,000 miles, he said the citizens needed more protection and urged Congress to authorize additional mounted and foot regiments. He supported his request with telling figures, in particular 30,000 "nomadic and predatory Indians" being held back by only 2,886 officers and men.[47] The figure 30,000 was even more inflated than what Indian agent Robert Neighbors had turned in to the Indian Bureau some five years earlier. If anything, the numbers of Indians inside Texas borders had *decreased* in that time. There is a strong suspicion that the number of Indians was grossly exaggerated by Davis in order to get more troops. This suspicion is supported by the fact that even after virtually all the U.S. Army troops were pulled out of north Texas in 1853, not to mention similar pull-backs in other sectors of the frontier, there followed no onslaught against defenseless frontier communities. On the contrary, the area of the upper Trinity continued to fill with settlers who felt safe enough, even without an active garrison nearby, to stake out homesteads and bring in families.

The experience of Frances Caroline Terry, who came to Fort Worth with her husband Stephen in 1854, is illustrative. When they arrived at Dallas, the Terrys were warned of bloodthirsty Indians rampaging along the Trinity River. Mrs. Terry took the alarm lightly, telling fear-mongering Dallasites, "If wild Indians [were] only thirty miles away, you wouldn't be here."[48]

Captain Randolph B. Marcy of the Army Topographical Corps, another official visitor to North Texas in 1853, was impressed by the numbers of white settlers he saw moving into the area.[49] Like earlier army observers, he considered the Indians to be peaceful and the future to be bright. But that situation was destined to change. Eighteen years later when he returned as General Marcy, he saw many abandoned ranches and fewer white people than he had encountered on his first visit.[50] In the interim the need for soldiers during Civil War stripped the frontier of its protective garrisons, and the Indians, recognizing an opportunity, struck the vulnerable settlements and isolated ranches at will.

The 1860s and 1870s were truly the most dangerous days for frontier settlers. Much of the historical memory of Indian depredations dates from this later period and has no bearing on the time when Fort Worth stood guard on the north Texas frontier. Moreover, during the Civil War years—the darkest days of Indian depredations—Fort Worth remained relatively safe from raids. As one reporter for the *Fort Worth Daily Gazette* noted in 1889, after 1853 "little or nothing was subsequently seen of the Indians with the exception of a few from the friendly tribes."[51]

12
TATTOO

By mid-1853, Fort Worth was literally falling down. Poor construction skills and poor materials were the chief culprits from the very start, and the problem was exacerbated by the army's unwillingness to commit the necessary funds for repairs. Even minor repairs were scrutinized with Scrooge-like efficiency. Cosmetic mending in 1851, for example, totalled only $133. In 1853, an inspector reported that the buildings at Fort Worth *might* last another year before they collapsed, but by that time they would either require major repairs or complete abandonment. Under the impression that the post had originally been built for two companies, the inspector estimated the cost of completing additional quarters for a second company to be $5,027.50. The cost of repairs to standing buildings, estimated at $1,246.75, brought the total to $6,274.25.

By its fourth year, Fort Worth had become a stopover and base of supplies for more distant posts, principally Fort Belknap, but also Forts Griffin and Richardson and Camp Cooper, all northwest of Fort Worth a hundred or more miles. Detachments of raw recruits marched through going west; the bad actors of other commands were confined in the post guardhouse on the way back to regimental headquarters; and the sick from more distant posts rested in the hospital under Dr. Williams' care. All were going elsewhere when they reached Fort Worth.

In August 1852, Arnold was relieved once and for all by Brevet Major Hamilton Merrill. Merrill's tenure was brief. Almost exactly a year later, when the garrison received its regular mail delivery via "express" on September 29, among the official correspondence were orders which the Major had been expecting for some time. Orders No. 50, issued at Headquarters Eighth Military Department, Corpus Christi, Texas, on August 20, 1853, dealt with troop redeployments and "dispositions" within the department, but the part that caught Merrill's attention was Section III which said, "In continuance of the

Early Fort Worth *as described by Florence Peak, widow of Dr. C. M. Peak, to artist Christina McLain. This is the only known representation of the fort based on the recollections of someone who lived there. Copies of this sketch were given out as souvenirs by M. G. Turner at an "Early Settlers' Barbecue" in 1907. (Courtesy of William Collins, Fort Worth.)*

above dispositions, Forts Croghan, Graham, and Worth, will forthwith be abandoned, and the companies now occupying them will proceed to the [new] posts to which they are assigned."[1]

Company B was ordered to Fort Mason, located between San Saba and the Llano River, a long march to the southwest. Ironically, Fort Mason had been founded by Merrill and two companies of the Second Dragoons in July 1851. From that time on, it had been a much more important post than Fort Worth, much closer to the main trade and communication routes going west. Company B was assigned to replace elements of the 5th Infantry at Mason who had been ordered to march "without delay by the most direct practicable route" to the Rio Grande.

The cause of this rapid mobilization on the Rio Grande was another international crisis. Relations between the United States and Mexico were deteriorating and perennial dictator Santa Anna was back in power. Problems between the two countries included lingering boundary questions and Indian raids back and forth across the border. Embracing the philosophy of Manifest Destiny, many Americans looked upon the Mexican people as "ignorant cowards and profligate ruffians" unfit to rule any part of North America.[2] The U.S. Government was also in the process of negotiating the Gadsden Purchase in late 1853 to provide right-of-way for the projected southern transcontinental railroad. For all these reasons, the army wanted to make a strong showing on the Rio Grande, and that meant stripping troops from the frontier garrisons of Texas to reassign them to the border. In a domino effect, troops withdrawn from posts closer to the Rio Grande were replaced by troops from garrisons farther north. Forts Croghan, Graham, and Worth were closed entirely.

When Lieutenant Colonel Freeman arrived for his inspection at the beginning of September, Merrill was still waiting impatiently for the transportation to arrive that would "remove his Company to Fort Belknap." A contract was eventually signed with Elijah Farmer, Tom Johnson (son of M. T. Johnson) and Squire Thomas to take all the company's baggage by ox-drawn wagon to its next post.[3]

Local lore says that the dragoons were dispatched to Fort Belknap, but this is not true. After the border crisis passed, Merrill's Company B did end up at Belknap before the year was out, but only after a brief tenure at Fort Mason. Meanwhile, Arnold's Company F was at Fort Belknap in August 1853 when the orders to abandon Fort Worth were issued, but by the time those orders were received on September 29, Ripley Arnold was dead, murdered in a personal confrontation at Fort Graham. In a classic example of how official communications lag, the orders that arrived in Fort Worth at the end of September still referred to "Bvt. Major Arnold's company, F, Second Dragoons." Company F subsequently finished out the year at Fort McKavett, situated near the ruins of an old Spanish mission and presidio on the road from San Antonio to El Paso. Men of the former Fort Worth garrison appreciated the snug stone buildings of Fort McKavett compared to the drafty wooden quarters they had known for three years. Company F next went to Fort Chadbourne before being reunited with the rest of the Second Dragoons in August 1855 at Fort Belknap. Later they were shipped up to Fort Riley, Kansas, never to return to Texas.[4]

The only member of the garrison to go directly from Fort Worth to Fort Belknap in the fall of 1853 was Assistant Surgeon Thomas H. Williams, who had been posted at Worth virtually without a break since December 1849. His last major duty at Fort Worth was to handle one of the debilitating epidemics that periodically afflicted frontier posts short of medicines, doctors and proper hygiene. In August an unidentified illness left fifteen men in the hospital. Apparently all recovered. Dr. Williams' orders took him to Fort Belknap to join a battalion of the Fifth Infantry that was being moved to the Rio Grande.[5]

Why Orders No. 50 took more than five weeks to arrive is a mystery, but the delay did not permit Major Merrill to tarry in carrying them out. He had only a few weeks to shut Fort Worth down and present himself at his new post. All medical stores and quartermaster's stores, "as far as possible," had to be packed up to accompany or follow the command to Fort Mason. Whatever subsistence stores that could not be carried along were to be transferred to the regimental depot at San Antonio while surplus medical stores were to be turned over to the "medical purveyor" at Fort Mason. The only exception to these instructions was to allow more distant posts to draw on Fort Worth supplies to fill their requisitions. Merrill locked up and packed up everything he could, then hastened to Fort Mason with the first contingent of Company B. In accordance with military practice, he left behind a small crew to finish the closing process. His orders were also explicit on this point: "A small guard, under the command of an officer, will remain in charge of the public property, until it is removed." The selection of that officer was not difficult—Merrill had only one junior officer on hand at the time. Second Lieutenant Jonas P. Holliday got the job of transporting the remaining supplies and the rest of the men to Fort Mason as soon as possible.

Holliday had joined Company B the previous October, on Halloween Day, after a two-month delay due to illness. He came with orders and a new promotion fresh in his pocket and was immediately handed the duties of assistant acting quartermaster, assistant acting commissary supplier, and post adjutant, by Major Merrill, who had filled all three positions since his arrival in August of 1852.

While the majority of the garrison, with their personal belongings and subsistence stores, headed off to Fort Mason, Holliday assumed the role of the commander. Staying behind with Lieutenant Holliday, with orders to take charge of "Public Property," were Sergeant Marshall Thomas, Corporal Frederick Williams, and Privates John Gross, John Laird, Levi Patterson, George Wayne and Charles Raynor. Two other members of Company B also remained behind, but their days of official

duty were over. Privates Louis Batty and John Kinsley were mustered out "by expiration of service." Though both men had started their service in eastern cities, they decided their fortune was to be made in north Texas.

In October, Sergeant Patrick Murphy of Company B returned with an ox train to take away everything Holliday's men had collected. Other men of Company B returned on special assignment at different times during the next two months, including Private Henry Brier as "post baker" and Private James Ennis as "mail rider." While the post was officially closed, it was not yet dead. Holliday finally rejoined the company from "detached service at Fort Worth" on December 9, the last soldier to leave the post on the Trinity. Ironically, he was sick at the time.[6]

The combined command at Fort Worth in August 1853 had consisted of only sixty-three men, including the post surgeon and the express courier who brought the last mail delivery and was present on the official count day. When Holliday pulled out in October, he probably had no more than a half dozen men with him. One of his last acts was to give Dr. Carroll M. Peak's wife a small, handmade rocking chair. That rocker remained a part of the small civilian community for years, much used by women who wanted to rock their babies to sleep.[7]

One of Major Hamilton Merrill's last official acts was to submit a budget request to the Quartermaster Department for the fiscal year 1853-1854. On August 15, practically as he was going out the gate, Merrill itemized a budget that included such things as "fuel for use of blacksmith shop" ($60), "postage" ($36) and "100 bushels of corn for passing trains" ($45). He estimated total expenses for the coming year at $6,861.[8] This last piece of regulation correspondence reached the Quartermaster Department in Washington and was promptly forgotten.

Merrill also left behind some unfinished business that was not so easily forgotten by his superiors. In the final months, the major had signed a contract with local farmer George Wilson to deliver 200 tons of hay to Fort Worth. Merrill then sent a routine copy of the agreement to the Quartermaster Department with his "bond." The response from Washington: "A copy cannot be substituted in the files for the contract." The paperwork was returned and he was instructed to forward the original contract and the bond immediately. The bureaucracy took longer than the dragoons to close the book on Fort Worth, for the matter was not cleared up until January 23, 1854.[9]

Local lore does not record any send-off for the garrison. During the life of the post the civilian community had grown from a clutch of five families numbering some twenty to thirty people to about a hundred. Those first families of Fort Worth included the Press Farmers, the Arch Robinsons, the Littles, and the S. P. Lovings. In the next eight years the number would grow to some 350 solid citizens.[10] Despite the natural attractions of the area, the village that kept the name of Fort Worth did not prosper. It consisted of the abandoned military quarters and a few rude houses, described by one source as "little better than huts."[11] A handful of unpaid county officials, led by County Clerk Benjamin P. Ayres and Sheriff John B. York, presided over virtually nothing — they had no courthouse, no school nor church.

When the dragoons rode out for the last time, buildings that had been home to more than a hundred men at times during the last four years were abandoned and free to anyone who wanted them. The locals did not waste any time moving in and taking up occupancy, a pattern of re-use not seen at many other Texas posts. The abandoned buildings at Fort Worth took on a different character when the site passed into new ownership. Captain Ephraim Daggett, brother of Henry Daggett the post trader, bought out the dry-goods store of one Lewis Kane, a settler whose place was located on the future Samuels Avenue near "the old cemetery," and then moved it into the former commissary building. He formed a partnership with Charles Turner, one of the men who first guided Arnold's dragoons to the Trinity site. The enterprising Daggett also played a part in opening the town's first commercial lodgings in another of the fort's abandoned buildings. According to Howard Peak, Daggett "bought the cavalry stable on the bluff and converted it into a hostelry which, while it had a dirt floor, served its purpose very well." The cavalry stable to which Peak refers could only have been the uncompleted quartermaster's stable since the 1849 structure was falling down and unfit for human habitation.

Legend has it that Daggett converted the dirt-floor and log-wall structure into a two-room hotel.[12]

The adaption of the fort's buildings did not stop there. John Peter Smith, another pioneer from Kentucky, took over the hospital and turned it into the community's first schoolhouse. Another enterprising settler was Julian Feild, who arrived in 1853 and moved into a cabin on the west end of officers' row. Feild bought the sutler's store and reopened it to serve the growing civilian population. The town's first civilian doctor, Carroll M. Peak, came from Dallas with his new wife and set up his practice in the cabin at the east end of officers' row that had housed Lieutenant Holliday earlier.[13] Most of the other buildings were in such a state of disrepair that they either fell down in the next few years or had to be substantially rebuilt. But the buildings of the fort formed the core of the subsequent Fort Worth business district. The ruins did not go to waste, however. Some of the salvaged logs were used in later years for construction of new houses. In 1870, John C. Gambrell moved into town from Marine Creek and built a snug cabin on Belknap Street using logs from the fort. The Gambrell cabin was still standing fifty-three years later, suggesting that Gambrell was a far better carpenter than any dragoon of 1849.[14]

Abandoning a military post to the benefit of the civilians did not please all the bureaucrats in Washington, D.C., however. Two years after Fort Worth closed (1855), U.S. Army Quartermaster Thomas Jesup recommended that all govern-ment structures "be removed" when posts were abandoned.[15] Moving rude log cabins was not always practical, however, and in many cases on the rapidly expanding frontier, buildings were simply abandoned or destroyed.

Daggett and Feild came as settlers after the fort was built and stayed on to become founding fathers of Fort Worth. Some others got their first introduction to Fort Worth as members of the U.S. military and chose to stay after their time was up. Of the five civilians who guided Arnold to the bluffs overlooking the Trinity in 1849, all except Dr. Echols stayed on, becoming traders, farmers, and ranchers.[16]

Abe Harris was a relative latecomer, probably arriving with the Eighth Regiment in the fall of 1849 as part of the infantry support for the Second Dragoons. He had been a member of Company F of the Eighth since the Mexican War. There was still plenty of construction work at that time and he helped build the double log cabin that Major Arnold used as quarters for his family. Harris was discharged in 1852, but when the Civil War began, he joined the Confederate army, rising to the rank of colonel by the time the war was over. Between his U.S. and Confederate service, he settled down in Tarrant County, marrying a local girl, Margaret Conner, who died right before the Civil War. He retired to Fort Worth, living there until his death in 1915. During the latter years of his life he became a colorful local character, celebrated as the oldest surviving member of the original party who founded Fort Worth.[17] Harris played up this connection, giving speeches and newspaper interviews wherein he told some remarkable stories. He particularly liked to tell the story of the "Battle of Fort Worth," fought against the Comanches when the fort was still active.

Alphonso Freeman, credited with cutting down the trees used to make the fort's first flagpole, liked the area so much he also settled to rear a family after his soldiering was done. By the time he died in 1905 at the age of ninety-two, he could count seventeen grandchildren, seventy-one great grandchildren, forty-one great-great grandchildren, and two great-great-great grandchildren.

Others who stayed on to become leading citizens included Francis Knarr, the dragoon blacksmith, and Louis Wetmore, who helped build the first county roads. Wetmore received a small piece of land several miles south of town and established title to it in 1858. Unlike most of his fellows, he put down deep roots locally, marrying into the prominent James F. Ellis family and enlisting in Confederate service with a local company when the Civil War came. He died during the war.

Among the direct beneficiaries of Fort Worth's founding, none had more to be thankful for than Tate Johnson. He owned more than a thousand acres on the upper Trinity, but it was useless as long as the Indians controlled the area. As soon as the army arrived to pacify the upper Trinity region, however, he put down roots. It was said he possessed "that intuition which enabled him to foresee the possibilities of this immediate section of the State."[18] Johnson took up land speculation, financing his dealings with profits from his cot-ton plantation on Marrow LeBone Creek. He sometimes paid squatters to move off their land and turn the rights over to him, thus allowing him to amass quite a collection of head-rights without filing any claims.[19] Soon his name was all over survey maps of Tarrant County. Starting in 1854 and continuing to the end of the decade he patented valuable pieces of land along the river where Samuels Avenue now runs, the same area where he had first led Arnold's dragoons to camp in May 1849. He may have even been thinking of future land deals as he led them from Live Oak Point up the trail to the top of the bluffs. He re-established his home at Johnson's Station, where he achieved a genuine reputation for hospitality, but he focused his land deals on the Trinity bluffs. He claimed property without legal title, using the questionable device of "certificates" to sell real estate to unsuspecting settlers who had to fight to establish legitimate claim in court. The first city directory called him a "liberal proprietor," which was a generous assessment of his dealings. In the mid-1850s, he was also one of the organizers of the Southern Pacific Railway Company, bringing the proposed transcontinental railroad through Fort Worth; he also pursued grandiose political ambitions which included several races for governor. But for his premature death from a stroke in 1866 while returning from business in Austin, Johnson might have become the most powerful man in Texas. Instead, he is remembered for putting Fort Worth on the map, both literally and figuratively. As one of his many admirers said, "Fort Worth is indebted to him for existence probably more than to any other man."[20]

Long after civilians had taken over the fort, the story grew that the land on which it was constructed legally belonged to Middleton Tate Johnson and Archie Robinson. But the nature of their claim is open to question. According to local lore, Johnson and Robinson "granted" the site to the government "during the time of [its] occupancy as a military post."[21] Such a statement begs questions. The pioneer developers' motives are unknown, for instance. Did they grant the land out of generosity or shrewdness? Were Johnson and Robinson's supposed rights legal, or were they squatter's rights? The historical record does not bear the legend out, but Johnson's demonstrated talents as a promoter and self-made land baron ensured that his name would be connected to Fort Worth long after the events of 1849. No matter. The story has been passed down that Johnson and Robinson owned the original surveys, that they donated the property to the army and that it reverted back to them when the army left. As one authority stated, the two men "[re]took possession of the premises."[22]

Archibald Robinson is not as well recognized in public memory as is Tate Johnson. He was a native of Kentucky who came to Texas in 1843 with his wife and children. In July of 1849 he claimed a headright "embracing what is now that beautiful portion of the city west of Throckmorton Street and north of Johnson Avenue." The genial "Uncle Archie" as he was known locally, maintained a cabin on this land until he

was "induced to dispose of his interests here," after which he retired to a farm on the northern Tarrant County line where he lived for many years.[23]

In fact, neither Johnson nor Robinson owned the land on the bluff in 1849. Until 1856, Robinson resided on his headright, but his legal status was that of a squatter. Until 1848 almost the entire area of Tarrant County was part of the Peters Colony land grant; in that year the grant, originally chartered by the Republic of Texas, expired. The records of the colony were in litigation for years while rival claims and shady transactions were sorted out. However, the most authoritative list of landholders to come out of those years of legal wrangling did not include the names of either M. T. Johnson or Archibald Robinson. Assigning property rights to M. T. Johnson and others during the years before 1854 is simply one more legend added to the folklore about Fort Worth.[24]

The oldest survey maps of Tarrant County show two pieces of property (or "surveys") in the area of the bluff that could have included the site of the fort. One did bear Robinson's name and stretched from the present downtown all the way to the Clear Fork. The other one, belonging to Mitchell Baugh, lay just to the east of the Robinson survey and stretched northward taking in Samuels Avenue and both sides of the river. By Texas law, a certificate entitled the owner to claim so many acres of land, but the claim had to be patented to become legal. A certificate holder would have his acreage surveyed then build a shack to establish squatter's rights. While particular surveys which show up on the maps were named for the certificate holders, the actual title belonged to whomever later patented it. The name attached to the survey was simply a convenient designation firmly entrenched in custom.[25]

Archibald Robinson patented his 160-acre survey in 1856. The 320-acre Baugh Survey was patented by Middleton Tate Johnson but not until August 15, 1854.[26] However, no titles were established until *after* the fort was abandoned. No one had clear claim to the land atop the bluffs in 1849 or during any time in the next four years, except the U.S. Army, and that was by right of possession. The statement that, "Upon the evacuation of the Post by the troops, immediate possession was entered upon by Col. M. T. Johnson and Archie Robinson, the landed proprietors of the surveys upon which the Post was located," is simply unsupportable.[27]

Recycling of the old post did not stop with the handful of buildings that were reoccupied. The former parade ground became the public square of a budding new town. For several years it was not much of a public square but more of a convenient campground where "transient immigrants pitched their tents for the night" and across which cattlemen drove their herds heading for one of the Trinity River crossings.[28]

With the Indian threat receding and the permanent population growing, the first settlers were glad to see their property values go up. Some of those early citizens eventually did quite well by their original investments. Just a mile due south of the bluff the Daggett farm stood alone for years, Daggett waiting for the town to grow out to them. While running a quiet little dry-goods store, Captain Ephraim Daggett was actually staking his future on the expectation that his land was destined for greater things than farming. His faith was borne out as the Daggett Addition and part of the Railroad Reservation were carved out of his holdings in the 1870s, just in time for the town's first great boom after the Texas & Pacific came.

13
TAPS

Most of the principal actors in the drama on the Trinity went on to better things—except for Ripley Arnold. The major left Fort Worth on August 17, 1852, leading Company F of the Second Dragoons to their new assignment at Fort Graham. He had officially turned over the post the day before to Major Hamilton Merrill, who had arrived with Company B, Second Dragoons, on August 13.[1] Arnold had been preparing his command for the move since the middle of July after receiving transfer orders from departmental headquarters in Corpus Christi. He left behind his two younger children, Sophia and Willis, who had died of natural causes and were buried in the little community's only cemetery.[2]

Fort Graham, the first post founded by Arnold, was also his last assignment. On September 6, 1853, the thirty-six-year-old major was shot to death by the post surgeon. Whether because of fond memories from her husband's longest assignment, or a desire to keep the family together even in death, Mrs. Arnold decided his final resting place should be in Fort Worth beside Sophia and Willis. A year and a half after his original burial, Tate Johnson, Alphonso Freeman, and Adolphus Gouhenaught made the trip to Fort Graham to bring the body back, and Arnold was re-interred with proper Masonic ritual in the little cemetery near Live Oak Point. Family history has it that his personal black servant was also buried in the same plot.[3] The major's murderer, Dr. Josephus Steiner, was never brought to justice by either civil or military authorities. Mrs. Arnold, only thirty-two years old when her husband was killed, continued to reside in Texas with her two remaining children, Katherine and Florida, cherishing her husband's sword, dress uniform, and personal papers to the day she died.

As for the other officers who played prominent roles in the history of Fort Worth, the man who probably issued the orders that sent Arnold to the Trinity, William S. Harney, had the most flamboyant and controversial career. He was transferred to the Department of Oregon in the middle of the decade, where he tried to provoke a war with the British over a boundary dispute. A disgusted settler living on the Washington coast wrote a dispatch to the *New York Times*, mincing no words in his opinion of Harney: "General Harney, who is here called 'Goliath'—for two reasons, first, that he is a very large man; and second, that he is all matter and no mind—ought, I think, to be court-martialled, and dismissed from the service."[4] More than one of his superiors in Washington, D.C., agreed with that assessment. Harney's career survived, but he was relieved of his duties in the Northwest and transferred to a less sensitive area. He was commanding U.S. forces in Missouri when the Civil War started. On the way back to Washington, D.C., to confer with Lincoln administration officials, he was detained at Harper's Ferry, Virginia, by the Confederates, thus becoming the first general officer captured during the Civil War. Released and back in Missouri, his loyalties came under suspicion, and he was once again removed from duty, this time forcibly retired. In belated recognition of his forty-seven years of service to the government, he received a long-awaited promotion to major general at the end of the Civil War. Discredited but still defiant, Harney died in 1889, but not before he saw to it that his authorized biography was completed by a hand-picked writer.[5]

Major Hamilton Wilcox Merrill, after leaving Fort Worth, spent three more years on the Indian frontier, first at Fort Belknap then at Fort Riley, Kansas. Never in good health, he spent much of his service on sick leave, but always performed creditably when he was able to carry out his duties. He enjoyed a distinction few other living officers could claim: Fort Merrill (Texas) was named after him in 1850 in recognition of his outstanding frontier service pacifying the state's Indian population. The fort guarded the road between San Antonio and Corpus Christi until it was abandoned in December 1855. By then Merrill was off chasing Indians in Kansas. In February 1857, he resigned his commission and returned to private life as a highly respected expert on Indian affairs. He spent his last years researching and writing on some of the more esoteric aspects of arms and ammunition, dying in 1892 at the age of seventy-eight.[6]

Captain Robert Plunket Maclay, who commanded the infantry troops at Fort Worth, spent the rest of the 1850s on similar frontier assignments. With the Civil War rapidly approaching, however, he resigned his commission on December 31, 1860, and returned to his Louisiana plantation. He was there when the Confederacy called, and he accepted a major's commission in the Confederate army. In 1864 he was appointed a brevet brigadier general over a brigade of Texans by the commander of the Trans-Mississippi Department, Edmund Kirby Smith, acting without the approval of either the Confederate congress or president. Maclay's highly unconventional appointment also antagonized Governor Pendleton Murrah of Texas, and Maclay never assumed full command of the brigade. When the war ended he was still awaiting confirmation of his appointment by Richmond. Thus ended his military career. He died in 1903.[7]

Perhaps the most distinguished alumni of Fort Worth was Assistant Surgeon Thomas H. Williams. He was thirty-one when he said farewell to Fort Worth. After nearly four years of service at the Trinity outpost, he took an extended leave of absence in 1854, then was reassigned to the frontier, this time at Fort Washita in the Indian Territory. He accompanied the Utah Expedition in 1858-1859, then resigned his U.S. Army commission in 1861. He assumed the duties of medical director for the main Confederate army in northern Virginia, a post he kept until Robert E. Lee assumed command of that army in June 1862. Williams then held a succession of high medical posts in Confederate service which allowed him to organize the medical corps and to set up most of the large hospitals operated by the Rebels. After the war he continued to practice medicine in Virginia and Maryland. He died in 1904.[8]

Lieutenant Samuel Starr had a distinguished, if somewhat checkered, career after he left the Trinity. He was next stationed at Fort Mason, Texas, where in July 1853 he was placed under arrest for striking an enlisted man and being disrespectful toward his commanding officer. He was suspended from rank and pay for nine months and given an official reprimand, which had the desired effect. After the Second U.S. Cavalry was created in 1855, later incorporating the Second Dragoons, he became a member of that crack Indian-fighting unit. Starr got his captain's bars in 1858, and when the Civil War began he remained with the Union. Early in the war, he enlisted in the Volunteers from his home state of New Jersey, serving in the eastern theater as the colonel of the Fifth New Jersey Infantry. At Gettysburg in July 1863, he fought with the Sixth U.S. Cavalry (Regulars), losing an arm in the battle, but winning plaudits from his superiors. Those plaudits included a battlefield promotion to colonel on July 2 for "gallant and meritous service." When he retired in 1870 he could point to the distinction of being that rare example of a soldier who rose up through the ranks from ordinary private to receive a field officer's commission. No more than a handful of officers have ever accomplished that feat in the history of American arms. He died November 23, 1891, and is buried in Arlington National Cemetery.[9]

Lieutenant Colonel William G. Freeman, the army inspector whose perceptive observations of the state's frontier posts in 1853 provided the most complete description of Fort Worth, never rose higher in rank or responsibility. His exhausting inspection of the Eighth Military Department capped his military career. He resigned from the service less than three years later and died in 1866. Too old and tired to fight in another conflict, Freeman did not serve in the Civil War. He had made his greatest contribution to his country (and to historians) through his detailed inspection reports of the western posts.[10]

W. H. C. Whiting, the indefatigable army engineer and explorer who left behind so much information on Fort Worth from his visit in 1849, never lived up to the promise of his early career. When he graduated from West Point at the head of his class in 1845, he set the standard for the highest grades ever made by a cadet up to that time and his record as an engineer in the years that followed upheld that promise. During his travels through Texas, he met Teresa Griffin Viele, wife of Lieutenant Egbert L. Viele of the Second Dragoons, and much impressed her with his Mississippi-bred manners. She praised him as "a polished gentleman of the old school, bland, courteous, and possessed of an affability that made him extremely popular." She also commented on his demeanor which "would meet the most startling emergency calmly yet with undaunted courage."[11]

Then came the Civil War. He joined the Confederacy and was almost immediately appointed chief engineer of the Provisional Army. But he never distinguished himself on the battlefield. Apparently an alcoholic with a "too-long-indulged habit of inebriety," and at odds with President Jefferson Davis, Whiting was passed over for choice assignments and saw his talents wasted.[12] In January 1865, he was mortally wounded while helping to defend Fort Fisher, North Carolina, and died a lonely, lingering death in a federal prison camp. Much of the knowledge of the terrain and topography for the region where the U.S. Army built its first line of frontier forts in Texas came from Lieutenant Whiting. Ironically, he was never impressed with the site of Fort Worth, and recommended downgrading the post further by splitting up its garrison in 1849.[13]

§

When the garrison scattered and went on to other duties, Fort Worth's military significance quickly faded. In the summer of 1854, General Persifor Smith, commanding the Department of Texas, called on Governor Elisha M. Pease for six companies of rangers to take the field against a resurgent Indian population. The state legislature authorized the call-up and the troops were mustered into federal service on November 1 for a twelve-month term. In North Texas the designated rendezvous point was McKinney in Dallas County, and it was originally planned to station two companies at Fort Worth, but they were subsequently sent farther west to Fort Chadbourne on the Colorado River where the threat was much greater. Fort Worth never saw any of the rangers, and by the spring of 1855, most of the six companies had been sent home. While everyone wanted more troops in the field, neither Texas nor the United States could afford the expense of continuous campaigning.

As early as April 1851, when General Smith took over the Eighth Military Department, he was warned by the secretary of war, "Serious doubts are entertained whether the posts now occupied by the troops [in Texas] are the most eligible." He was further advised to "make such changes as you may deem proper," consistent with protecting the inhabitants of the state and preserving a strict economy.[14] All remaining active federal posts in Texas after 1853 were in a strictly defensive posture. Only four companies of infantry and two companies of dragoons were left on the Texas frontier, the closest to Fort Worth being posted at Fort Belknap.[15]

Circumstances combined to draw federal attention away from Texas. First, the creation of two state-controlled Indian "reserves" on the upper Brazos in 1854 seemed to hold out hope for better relations with the native population and therefore less need for army watchdogs. "No Indians were to be located more than twenty miles south or east of the most northern line of military posts extending from [the] Red River to the Pecos River."[16] Coincidentally, "Bleeding Kansas," so named because of the violent sectional conflict raging for control of that territory, demanded every soldier the U.S. Government could spare. Texas was stripped of troops to meet the crisis in Kansas in the summer of 1855. The next year the situation was somewhat restored with the arrival of the brand-new Second U.S. Cavalry in Texas to challenge the Plains Indians. But the elite Second Cavalry fought a mobile style of warfare. Gone forever were the old days of a dozen or more forts and their garrisons standing guard over the frontier.

The U.S. Army, too, changed during these years. The Second Dragoons, who had played the leading role in founding Fort Worth and garrisoning it for four years, became victims of modernization. By act of Congress on August 3, 1861, dragoons ceased to be part of the U.S. force. Their place was taken by new cavalry regiments while the term "dragoon," along with the two regiments that had proudly worn it since the 1830s, was retired from the service. The Second Regiment of Dragoons had served in Texas for all but one year between 1848 and 1861.[17]

Nothing short of a miracle could have resurrected Fort Worth as a front-line military post after 1853, and for good reason: the fort had never justified its existence. From the beginning, its location was based on considerations of geography and popular alarm rather than far-sighted military planning. The site Major Arnold chose was only vaguely connected to a master plan for the Texas frontier that existed mostly in General William Jenkins Worth's mind. The site was selected with no thought given to its place in the bigger picture of western expansion, transportation, communication, or security.

Toward the end, there was talk of turning Fort Worth into a supply and remount depot for posts farther west (much like the "base realignments" of the 1990s). The fort's "size and favorable location" might merit a conversion.[18] The building of the second (or quartermaster's) stables showed that such a mission change was probably imminent, as did the construction of barracks beyond the needs of the small, regular garrison. Further evidence is found in the post returns which show that in 1853 the size of the garrison actually increased on several occasions as troops stopped over on the way to or from Fort Belknap or one of the other posts guarding the new frontier line. If Fort Worth had been turned into a supply and remount center, huge quantities of munitions and supplies would have had to be hauled in from Shreveport, Houston, or San Antonio, by oxen and mule teams over bad roads, and stored on site. The idea was never fully articulated—obstacles were too many and the benefits too few to justify it. Yet early local historians continued to record that Worth had been intended, perhaps from the beginning, as "a base of supply to more distant posts."[19]

The paradox of Fort Worth was that although it was established to guard the northern frontier, its location worked against it. At no time was Fort Worth ever located on a military road, like Fort Bliss and Fort Lancaster, so its role was severely limited from the beginning. Much of the exploration of 1849 and 1850 was to survey routes across west Texas with the aim of linking isolated settlements and laying out a secure route to California where the gold rush was in full sway. Most of the attention of the U.S. Army was in this direction, across southwest Texas—focused on tying New Mexico and California to the rest of the Union, plus protecting emigrants and military movements. Because Fort Worth was far off the main trails going west, its garrison was never called upon to perform escort duty, which removed a principal reason for keeping it open.

As a sentinel on the frontier, its garrison was too small and too weak to guard much more than its own parade ground. The chain of scattered army posts on the frontier was never capable of preventing Indian incursions across the white man's boundary line and most senior officers recognized this. Troops at Fort Worth, keeping an eye on Anadarkos, Wacos, and Wichitas, were an unnecessary expense.

Nor was Fort Worth located on the proposed southern transcontinental railroad route which Secretary of War Jefferson Davis ordered surveyed in 1853. Ripley Arnold's command lay north of the recommended line going from the Red River to the Rio Grande. When the southern transcontinental line was eventually built, it did indeed run through Fort Worth, but no one could have anticipated Fort Worth being a rail center in 1849. Fort Worth was not on any stage lines or important mail routes during its brief existence as a military post. Before 1852, commercial, long-distance coach service in Texas ran only as far north as Austin, and there was not enough demand for regular service to the far reaches of the state. Any intrepid traveler desiring to reach Fort Worth could pay $20 and make the three-day trip to Austin, but then had to hire a horse for the second leg of the journey, or hook up with one of the freighters going north to the Trinity.[20] All together, it was a dusty, bone-jarring six-day journey over unimproved roads with no public accommodations along the way. In 1852, commercial service was extended into the western region of the state, following the emigrants' trail, thanks to the efforts of Henry Skillman. Skillman began running coaches carrying mail and passengers between San Antonio and El Paso, making a name for himself as one of the "pioneer [courier service] operators in the West" before the Civil War.[21] But no entrepreneur was rich enough or foolish enough to try to make money running stagecoaches up to the Trinity at a time when the area was still considered Indian country by most Texans.

The bigger and better financed Southern Overland Mail

Route, which, after several false starts, began operating in 1858, came nowhere near Fort Worth. It connected isolated communities in West Texas until permanent railroad, highway and telegraph systems were established and stretched from Fort Belknap to Clear Fork Station to Fort Phantom Hill to Fort Chadbourne.

Fort Worth was never more than temporary, beginning life as a humble "outpost." One sign of its low standing was that no court-martials, as far as the record shows, were ever convened at the place, despite the fact that every military post experiences problems that require formal adjudication. When Brevet Lieutenant Colonel James Bomford requested authorization to convene such a court in 1851, his request was denied. Headquarters sympathized but maintained that there were not enough commissioned officers on the post to constitute a proper court. This problem arose more than once during the lifetime of Fort Worth. Whenever serious matters arose that demanded a full-scale court-martial, the proceedings had to be convened at Fort Graham or Austin. Headquarters advised Bomford in 1851 that court-martials "will be ordered from time to time on application, as the necessities of the service may require."[22]

And it would not be until the World War I years that federal troops would make an appearance when Camp Bowie was established on the western edge of town in 1917. By that time the army had learned one lesson: land for Camp Bowie was

Artist's view of Fort Worth on the horizon as it probably appeared in 1872 when easterner John Forney came through. The country looked much the same to members of the Second Dragoons twenty years earlier. (From What I Saw in Texas.)

leased from the city for a token of $1 per year.[24] There would be no disputes this time over ownership and usage payments.

The name Fort Worth stuck to the city that grew up on the site. What made Fort Worth different from places like Fort Belknap and Fort Phantom Hill was the people left behind. They were men of ambition and vision. Former ranger Simon Farrar stayed and watched the city grow, expressing the wish in later years that Fort Worth might someday become the "capital city of the grand northwest of Texas." He said, "I have at all times entertained great confidence in the people of Fort Worth," whom he had known as dragoons, pioneers, and citizens.[25] Always, they displayed an enduring spirit that worked to bring the railroad to town in 1876, to build the Texas Spring Palace in 1889, to attract Camp Bowie in 1917, and to perform countless other tasks when the city needed them. Without those men, Fort Worth today would probably be little more than the site of a minor historic state park on the bluffs over the Trinity, or perhaps a small, sleepy town living in the shadow of its giant neighbor to the east.

APPENDIX

Roll of Captain and Bvt. Maj. R. A. Arnold's Company (F) Second Regiment of Dragoons, stationed at Fort Worth, West Fork of Trinity River, Texas, June 19, 1849.*

RANK	NAME	COUNTRY/STATE OF ORIGIN	RANK	NAME	COUNTRY/STATE OF ORIGIN
Sgt.	Dearing, Jacob	Unknown	Pvt.	Hughes, Johnston	Ireland
Sgt.	Slade, William	Unknown	Pvt.	Helmering, Augustus	Germany
			Pvt.	Hanna, James	Ireland
Cpl	Kepner, James	Unknown	Pvt.	Hannibal, John	Unknown
Cpl.	McCauly, Daniel	England	Pvt.	Kaas, Otto	Denmark
Cpl.	Schaffer, Joseph	Unknown	Pvt.	Knaar, Francis	Germany
Cpl.	Zorkowsky, Nathan	Poland	Pvt.	Keough, Peter	Ireland
			Pvt.	Law, John	England
Musician	Noland, Thomas	Unknown	Pvt.	McCullough, Moses	Unknown
Farrier	Kemp, Anthony	Germany	Pvt.	Mendez, Anthony L.	Louisiana
			Pvt.	Miller, Blassis	Virginia
Pvt.	Anderson, Phillip	Scotland	Pvt.	Patterson, Matthew R.	Unknown
Pvt.	Beyer, Nicholas	Unknown	Pvt.	Poggenfruhl, August	Germany
Pvt.	Burlage, Frederick W.	Germany	Pvt.	Porthouse, Thomas	England
Pvt.	Bohrman, Christian	Germany	Pvt.	Schultz, Ferdinand	Unknown
Pvt.	Dilcher, William	Germany	Pvt.	Senn, John	Switzerland
Pvt.	Dixon, William H.	Massachusetts	Pvt.	Wagner, John	Unknown
Pvt.	Durfee, George	New York	Pvt.	Weaver, Samuel	Unknown
Pvt.	Doyle, Hugh	Ireland	Pvt.	Wetmore, Louis	Germany
Pvt.	Donelly, Thomas	Ireland	Pvt.	Yolbel, William	Unknown
Pvt.	Freeman, Alphonso	Unknown	Pvt.	Zeckler, William	Unknown
Pvt.	Gerstring, Simon	Germany			
Pvt.	Gross, Joseph	Germany			
Pvt.	Gwynne, William A.	Ireland			
Pvt.	Harrison, Andrew I.	Maryland			

Muster Rolls, Second Dragoons, Company F, Report of June 30, 1849, RG 94, NA. Ruby Schmidt provided data for "Country/State of Origin."

NOTES

1-BOOTS AND SADDLES

1. The well-known eccentricities and non-regulation attire of the dragoons was well documented by long-time member of Company B, Second Dragoons. Although Percival Lowe never served in Texas or was personally acquainted with members of Ripley Arnold's command, he is the best primary source on life in the dragoons. See Lowe, *Five Years a Dragoon, '49-'54* (Kansas City, Missouri: Franklin Hudson, 1906, reprinted by University of Oklahoma Press, 1965). The descriptions used here are based on Lowe's accounts plus the reminiscences of another contemporary observer of the cavalryman's life in the field, Washington Irving, who was a guest of the dragoons in the 1830s. See Irving, *A Tour on the Prairie*, John Francis McDermott, ed. (Norman: University of Oklahoma Press, 1956). The lashing of carbine to saddles, for instance, was a popular but strictly non-regulation way of carrying the weapon on long journeys.

2. This spring was later called Terry Spring, after Nathaniel Terry, a pioneer who arrived in October, 1853, purchased the surrounding land from Middleton Tate Johnson. Later the land was divided and re-sold, but Terry's name remained on the cold spring among old-timers. (Ruby Schmidt to Richard F. Selcer, February 8, 1995 [hereafter cited as Schmidt to Selcer].)

3. See example of Frank R. Murray, a member of the Eighth Infantry posted briefly to Fort Worth, who "intended to homestead a piece of land" in Texas just as soon as his "term" was up. Cited in Jerry Flemmons, "Texas Siftings," *Fort Worth Star-Telegram*, May 22, 1994, p. 5 D.

4. Bird's Fort, located in eastern Tarrant County near the Trinity River, was founded by a company of state militia ("rangers") led by Captain Jonathan Bird in the winter of 1841-42. They put up cabins and constructed a stockade for protection, all aimed at opening the area for white settlers. But when a series of misfortunes struck and the militiamen's terms of enlistment expired that spring, they disbanded and returned to their homes, leaving the site unoccupied until the end of the decade.

5. "History of the City of Fort Worth," introductory essay by Charles Swasey and W.M. Melton in *Fort Worth City Directory, 1877*, p. 4, microfiche, Local History and Genealogy Department, Fort Worth Public Library, Central Branch (hereafter cited as Swasey and Melton, "History," FWPL).

6. Descriptions of the country the dragoons passed through, including distances, fauna and flora, etc., come from several sources, including: "Copy of Report of Col. Samuel Cooper, Assistant Adjutant General of the United States of an Inspection Trip from Fort Graham to the Indian Villages on the Upper Brazos Made in June, 1851," E.B. Ritchie, ed., *Southwestern Historical Quarterly* (hereafter cited as *SWHQ*), Vol. 42, April, 1939, pp. 328-331, ff;

"Report of Inspection of Eighth Military Department Made by Bvt. Lt. Col. W.G. Freeman, Assistant Adjutant General, Pursuant to Instruction from Headquarters of Army, dated April 22, 1853," Records of the Adjutant General's Office, 1780s-1917, Entry 287, Box 17, Miscellaneous Files, pp. 95-98, Record Group (hereafter cited as RG) 94, National Archives (hereafter cited as NA), Washington, D.C. (hereafter cited as Freeman, "Report of Inspection," RG 94, NA); Assistant Surgeon Thomas H. Williams, "Medical Topography and Diseases of Fort Worth," Statistical Report on Sickness and Mortality in the Army of the United States, Records of Surgeon General's Office, January, 1839-January, 1855, 34th Congress, 1st Session, Senate Executive Document No. 96, p. 373 (hereafter cited as Williams, "Medical Topography," Senate Executive Document No. 96); Report of A.W. Speight, Commissioner of Statistics, "Resources, Soil, Climate of Texas, Tarrant County," 1882, in "WPA Fort Worth—City Guide and History," Box 4J78, File 2, Center for American History, University of Texas, Austin (hereafter cited as CAH, UT, Austin); "Report on Texas Forts by Surgeon General Conley, U.S. Army," in M.L. Crimmins Papers, Box 2, D16, CAH, UT, Austin; "The Report of Lt. W.H.C. Whiting's Reconnaissance of the Western Frontier of Texas," 1850, in Report of the Secretary of War, Senate Executive Document No. 64, 31st Congress, 1st Session (hereafter cited as "Report of Whiting's Reconnaissance," Senate Executive Document No. 64); A.B. Bender, "Opening Routes Across West Texas, 1848-1850," *SWHQ*, Vol. 37, October, 1933, pp. 116-135; and Edward J. Smith, *The Capitalist; or The City of Fort Worth, A Parody of "The Mikado"* (Fort Worth: n.p., 1888), pp. 20-25. The actions of the men who accompanied Arnold, and their response to what they saw, come from Simon B. Farrar to C.C. Cummings, "Palmer, Ellis County, Texas," September 23, 1893 (hereafter cited as Farrar to Cummings, September 23, 1893). Copy of original hand-written letter in pos-

session of Ruby Schmidt. Typescript in vertical files of Tarrant County Historical Commission (hereafter cited as TCHC). C.C. Cummings was a Civil War veteran who rose to the rank of Captain, lost an arm at Gettysburg, then settled in Fort Worth after the war. In addition to becoming a prominent local judge, he was the long-time historian of the United Confederate Veterans' R. E. Lee Camp in Fort Worth.

7. For physical description of and background on Middleton Tate Johnson, see John Henry Brown, *Indian Wars and Pioneers of Texas* (Austin: L.E. Daniell, n.d.); and Michael Walter Farrington, "Middleton Tate Johnson: Texas' Would-Be Governor, General, and Railroad Entrepreneur," M.A. Thesis, University of Texas at Arlington, 1980.

8. During its first three years of statehood, Texas had to rely on these state troops to patrol its borders and protect against Indians. They have been described variously as "mounted militia," "frontier guards" (by Simon B. Farrar), or "frontier rangers" to distinguish them from the Texas Rangers. W.H. King, an early historian of the law enforcement Rangers, defines the other rangers as "Volunteer companies of citizens raised frequently to repel Indian attacks and to suppress domestic commotion." See Dudley Goodall Wooten, ed., *A Comprehensive History of Texas. 1685-1897* (Dallas: G. Scarf, 1898), Vol. 2, p. 329. M.T. Johnson (for whom Johnson's Station was named, and a native of South Carolina who came to Texas in 1840) was elected to the legislature, and served with the U.S. Army under the legendary "Coffee Jack" Hays in the Mexican War. Afterwards, he served in the rangers until February, 1849. "Tate" Johnson was acknowledged as Tarrant County's most influential citizen before the Civil War. See Seymour V. Connor, *Texas: A History* (Arlington Heights, Illinois: AHM Publishing, 1971), p. 167; and Swasey and Melton, "History," FWPL, p. 5.

9. Farrar to Cummings, September 23, 1893, TCHC. Ranger Farrar is

the only one of the original party to leave a written account of the founding of Fort Worth, although he did so only upon the request of Judge Cummings many years later. Farrar claimed to be the last survivor of the original locating party.

10. Local lore is insistent that Tate Johnson and his friends were Rangers at the time of the expedition. This is not correct. Johnson was discharged from state service on February 3, 1849, according to an affidavit dated January 28, 1851, in the State Archives.

11. Simon B. Farrar and Mrs. Henry C. Daggett are the primary sources for the names and backgrounds of the men who accompanied M.T. Johnson. Mrs. Daggett was the widow of Henry Daggett who is recognized as one of the earliest pioneers of Fort Worth. However, her recollections and Simon Farrar's differ on the identities of the four men with Johnson. In Farrar's letter to Cummings, Echols, Turner, Parker, and Farrar are named. Judge Cummings in an article he wrote for *The Bohemian*, citing Mrs. Daggett as his source, identifies the civilians as Farrar, Daggett, Turner and Echols. Thus it seems Cummings either changed his mind or else did not recognize the contradiction in his sources. Some later newspaper accounts, giving no source, cite three "Rangers" instead of four, leaving out Henry Daggett and William Echols. When Mrs. Daggett wrote about it many years later, she said that the five Rangers visited the future fort site some time *ahead* of the dragoons. Since Farrar was very specific about the sense of wonder he felt upon first seeing the site with the Arnold expedition, his recollection carries more weight than Mrs. Daggett's, who was repeating the stories of her husband, who may or may not have been there. See Farrar to Cummings, September 23, 1893, TCHC; and C.C. Cummings, "First Days in Fort Worth," *The Bohemian*, Souvenir Edition, 1904, p. 210, Genealogy and History, FWPL.

12. Farrar to Cummings, September 23, 1893, TCHC.

13. According to Lt. Whiting, "These belts [the Cross Timbers] are important as being a favorite range for many of the Texas Indians, and their usual home in the winter." See "Report of Whiting's Reconnaissance," Senate Executive Document No. 64, p. 238. Description of Comanche Peak comes from Elijah Hicks, a member of the Indian Commission who negotiated the Texas Comanche Treaty of 1846, and whose diary was published as "The Journal of Elijah Hicks," Grant Foreman, ed., *Chronicles of Oklahoma*, Vol. 13, March, 1935, p. 79.

14. The Cross Timbers consist of two great belts of post-oak forests, extending from the Brazos River to the Red River, separated by prairie. The site of Fort Worth lay on the southern edge of this prairie. The trees of the Cross Timbers were perfect hiding places for wild creatures, Indians, and later, outlaws on the run. Lt. W.H.C. Whiting, who came through Fort Worth on an extended reconnaissance of the western frontier of Texas in 1850, reported seeing "a coarse-grained marble. . . in the neighborhood" of Fort Worth. See "Report of Whiting's Reconnaissance," Senate Executive Document No. 64, p. 241. Dr. Thomas Williams, post surgeon at Fort Worth in 1852, also reported what he believed to be "a species of marble of the lumachella variety . . . scattered upon the surface of the prairie." Also, Surg. Gen. Conley's report to Col. M. L. Crimmins (no date), cited in *The Federal Writers' Project*, Vol. 4, p. 1226, mentions "a specie of marble . . . scattered upon the surface of the prairie" and "a great variety of marble deposits along the ravines and in the beds of the small streams." (This is probably the same report as Williams'.) However, none of these reported sightings have any scientific basis since there are no marble deposits in Texas. What they probably mistook for marble was limestone. Williams did report accurately that "the buffalo have entirely disappeared" from the vicinity of Fort Worth. For both observations, see Williams, "Medical Topography," Senate Executive Document No. 96.

15. Farrar to Cummings, September 23, 1893, TCHC. Farrar writes: "It is not a fact that I belonged to Col. Johnson's command at that time, though I had been a member of Captain Johnson's company in the first year of the war between the United States and Mexico."

16. Fort Graham's Post Returns for May, 1849, show Maj. Ripley Arnold to have been "sick" at the end of the month. The physician of record at Fort Graham was Josephus Steiner, the same man who shot and killed Arnold in 1853. Post Returns for Fort Graham, May, 1849, Returns from U.S. Military Posts, 1800-1916, Records of the Adjutant General's Office, M-617 (Microfilm), RG 94, NA.

17. Simon B. Farrar's recollections, on which this section is largely based, are taken from his 1893 letter to Judge C.C. Cummings, cited above. The exact credit for picking this particular site has never been established. Compare family history among the Farmer clan claims that John "Uncle Press" Farmer "chose the camp site on the courthouse bluff. . . at the request of Maj. Ripley Arnold." (From Farmer family history in *Baptist Standard*, n.d., typescript in Tarrant County Scrapbook No. 1, filed with "Excerpts from Scrapbook of Mrs. Grover Leigh," CAH, UT, Austin). This story is supported in an early city publication, *Charter and Revised Civil and Criminal Ordinances of the City of Fort Worth*, "By Authority" (Fort Worth: Texas Printing and Lithographing, 1889), p. iv. Copy at Fort Worth Public Library, Local History and Genealogy Department, Central Branch (hereafter cited as *Charter and Revised Civil and Criminal Ordinances*, FWPL). That source says that Farmer, a local settler at the time, visited the soldiers' camp in June when it was at Terry's Spring and recommended they move to the high bluff, which they did. Thus the unsolicited suggestion of a local homesteader becomes the basis for the placement of the fort, an unlikely scenario. The official records do not show John Press Farmer connected in any way with the military expedition that founded Fort Worth, so the family legend must be discounted. Not everyone agrees that the fort was named for Gen. Worth. One early pioneer signed an affidavit in 1924 stating that "Fort Worth was not named for Gen. Worth" but for "Old Man Worth," a squatter who was persuaded to vacate his land by M.T. Johnson in favor of the army. See George L. Harris, "Remarks on Early History of Fort Worth," typescript affidavit, pp. 1-2, in vertical files of FWPL. The overwhelming historical evidence is that Fort Worth was named for Mexican War hero and recently deceased Department commander William Jenkins Worth. (See, for instance, *Charter and Revised Civil and Criminal Ordinances*, FWPL.) The copse of trees was a well-known spot in the city for many years which old-timers swore was where Maj. Arnold had first tethered his horse on his initial visit to the site of the future fort. There was some discussion at the time of the Texas Centennial about marking it as a historic site. See "Imprints of Frontier Adventure" in *Fort Worth Star-Telegram*, June 6, 1948.

2-TO ARMS

1. "Register of the Officers and Cadets of the U. S. Military Academy, June, 1839," USMA Library, West Point, New York.

2. Paul I. Kliger, "The Confederate Invasion of New Mexico," *Blue & Gray Magazine*, Vol. 11, June, 1994, p. 12.

3. George W. Cullum, *Biographical Register of the Officers and Graduates of the U.S. Military Academy*, Vol. 1 (New York: Houghton, Mifflin and Company, 1891), pp. 722-723.

4. See various entries under Bvt. Maj. Ripley A. Arnold in Registers of Letters Received, Adjutant General's Office, 1822-1860, and Letters Received, Adjutant General's Office, Main Series, 1822-1860, for the years 1849-1853, M-711 (Register), M-567 (Letters), RG 94, NA.

5. "Doughboys" is usually associated with World War I as a term for American soldiers. It originated, however, in the Mexican War

from the infantry's practice of applying clay whitener to their white criss-crossing belts. See Samuel E. Chamberlain, *My Confession, The Recollections of a Rogue*, Roger Butterfield, ed. (Omaha: University of Nebraska Press, 1987, reprint); and William H. Goetzmann, *Sam Chamberlain's Mexican* War (Austin: Texas State Historical Association, 1993), pp. 11, 32 (note 25).

6. Bvt. Maj. Ripley Arnold to Maj. Gen. Roger Jones, Adjutant General, U.S. Army, June 15, 1849, Letters Received, Adjutant General's Office, 1822-1860, M-567, RG 94, NA.

7. Quoted in Sam Kinch,"Slayer of Fort Worth Founder . . ." *Fort Worth Star-Telegram*, October 30, 1949, p. 4.

8. Captain R.A. Arnold to Maj. Gen. Roger Jones, June 2, 1849, Letters Received, Adjutant General's Office, 1822-1860, RG 94, NA. Arnold always signed himself, "R.A. Arnold, Bvt. Maj. Gen., 2nd Dragoons," but in filing the correspondence, the army always listed him by his official rank, "Captain."

9. The chronology of these events is confusing. There is no extant report by Arnold giving the date when he arrived back at the Twin Forks. In a Quartermaster's Report the following year, Lt. Samuel Starr gives June 6 as the date when Fort Worth was officially established. This is the first time that date is mentioned in any official records. Therefore, Starr is the original source for the often cited June 6 founding date. The chronology is further complicated by the fact that Arnold was at the Twin Forks at the end of May 1849 with Col. Johnson, returned to Fort Graham, then came back with his men at the beginning of June. These two trips, so close together, are often combined in later, popular accounts of the founding of Fort Worth.

10. Robert M. Utley, *Frontiersmen in Blue: The United States Army and the Indian, 1848-1865* (Lincoln: University of Nebraska Press, 1981, reprint of 1967 ed.), assigns credit differently: "To Bvt. Maj. Gen. George Mercer Brooke, who assumed command in 1849, fell the task of laying the groundwork of the Texas defense sys-

tem" (p. 71). By the time Brooke took over in the summer of 1849, that "groundwork" had already been largely laid.

11. Elements of the 1st Infantry and 3rd Infantry were also stationed in Texas in the early months of 1849.

12. Both swords were captured by Federal forces when New Orleans fell in April, 1862. Union General Benjamin F. Butler who commanded the occupation forces, "sequestered" Twiggs' home and personal property in the name of the U.S. Government, sending the two swords to Washington for appropriate disposition by President Lincoln. According to legend, the man the South dubbed "Spoons" Butler kept Twiggs' silverware for his own use. See Robert Werlich, *"Beast" Butler* (Washington, D.C.: Quaker Press, 1962), pp. 42-45; and Robert S. Holzman, *Stormy General Butler* (New York: Macmillan, 1954), pp. 101-102.

13. For brief biographical sketches of David Emanuel Twiggs, see Roger J. Spiller, ed., *Dictionary of American Military Biography* (Westport, Connecticut: Greenwood Press, 1984), Vol. 3, pp. 1119-1122; and William C. Davis, ed., *The Confederate General* (Harrisburg, Pennsylvania: National Historical Society, 1991), Vol. 6, pp 64-65; for Twiggs' orders, see Col. M.L. Crimmins, "The Second Dragoon Indian Campaign in Texas," *West Texas Historical Association Year Book*, Vol. 21, October, 1946, p. 50 (hereafter cited as *WTHAYB*).

14. Samuel G. French, *Two Wars: An Autobiography of General Samuel G. French* (Nashville: Confederate Veteran, 1901), p. 102.

15. M.L. Crimmins, "An Episode in the Texas Career of General David E. Twiggs," *SWHQ*, Vol. 41, October, 1937, pp. 167-168.

16. All quotations by David Twiggs to Secretary of War William Marcy, from Galveston, Texas, November 4 and 6, 1848, Letters Sent, Eighth Military Department, November-December, 1848, Pt. 1, Entry 69, RG 393, NA.

17. *Ibid.*, Order No. 2 from Headquarters Eighth Military Department, Galveston, November 7, 1848.

18. *Corpus Christi Star*, December 16, 1848. Cited in William C. Holden, "Frontier Defense, 1846-1860," *WTHAYB*, Vol. 6, 1930, p. 41.

19. David Twiggs was back in the Lone Star State in March, 1857, commanding the Department of Texas, but his second tour of duty continued to be marked by what one historian has called highly publicized "episodes." William C. Davis, ed., *The Confederate General*, Vol. 6, pp. 64-65. For additional information on Twiggs, see Crimmins, "An Episode in the Texas Career of General David E. Twiggs," *SWHQ*, pp. 167-173; and Post Returns for Fort Graham, Returns from U.S. Military Posts, 1800-1916, Records of the Adjutant General's Office, 1780s-1917, M-617, RG 94, NA (hereafter cited as Post Returns . . .[with date], RG 94, NA).

20. For a brief survey of Worth's background and career, see Edward S. Wallace, "General William Jenkins Worth and Texas," *SWHQ*, Vol. 54, October, 1950, pp. 159-168.

21. *Ibid.*, pp. 166-167. Worth saw it this way, but that does not mean that the government's intention was to send him into exile in Texas. See Worth to James Duncan, San Antonio, February 26, 1849, Worth Letters, United States Military Academy Library.

22. Worth to Brig. Gen. Roger Jones, Adjutant General's Office, February 1, 1849, in Letters Received, Adjutant General's Office, 1822-1849, M-567, RG 94, NA.

23. William L. Marcy to Worth, December 10, 1848, Letter Books, Secretary of War, Old Records Section, Adjutant General's Office, RG 94, NA. Cited in A.B. Bender, "Opening Routes Across West Texas, 1848-1850," *SWHQ*, Vol. 37, October, 1933, p. 119.

24. Bender, "Opening Routes Across West Texas," *SWHQ*, p. 126. There were forty-six U.S. Army posts in the Southwest in 1851, compared to sixty-three for the rest of the country. R.C. Crane, "Some Aspects of the History of West and Northwest Texas Since 1845," *SWHQ*, Vol. 26, July, 1922, p. 32. The total number of U.S. Army troops in Texas reached a maximum of 3,265 in 1853. See 33rd Congress, 1st Session, Senate Executive Document No. 1, Pt. 2, pp. 118-119. In 1861, Texas troops still represented one-fifth of the entire U.S. Army. See Sam Houston's message to the Texas legislature, January 21, 1861, Texas State Archives. Cited in Holden, "Frontier Defense, 1846-1860," *WTHAYB*, p. 63.

25. For Whiting's and Smith's orders, see Maj. George Deas, Adjutant General, Eighth Military Department, to W.H.C. Whiting, February 9, 1849, Records of the Office of the Chief of Engineers, Letters Received by the Topographical Bureau of the War Department, 1824-1865, M-506, RG 77, NA.

26. W.H.C. Whiting to Gen. Joseph G. Totten, Office of the Chief of Engineers, July 24, 1849, Registers of Letters Received, Engineers Department, January 1, 1849-December 31, 1851, Entry 17, RG 77, NA (hereafter cited as Whiting to Office of the Chief of Engineers, Registers of Letters Received, RG 77, NA).

27. Whiting's second expedition was ordered by Bvt. Maj. Gen. George Brooke, as successor to Gen. Worth at the head of the Eighth Military Department. Whiting's report of his second expedition, submitted in two parts, January 21 and March 14, 1850, and subsequently incorporated into the *Congressional Record*, is one of the most valuable sources for understanding the "General character of the country, condition of the roads, building material, fuel, water, subsistence, forage, population, and climate" in central Texas. Whiting also visited eight military posts en route—including Forts Graham and Worth—which he described in detail. For the best summary account of Whiting's and others' expeditions of this period, see Bender, "Opening Routes Across West Texas," *SWHQ*, pp. 126-127.

28. There is considerable confusion in this matter. In his standard *History of Texas: Fort Worth and the Texas Northwest Edition*, B.B. Paddock claims, "The post was first called Camp Worth in honor of Brigadier-General William Jennings *[sic]* Worth" (Vol. 2, p. 599). Unfortunately, Paddock makes two mistakes in that simple statement: 1) it was never Camp Worth, and 2) its namesake was

William Jenkins Worth. Since most subsequent histories of Fort Worth have relied on Paddock as a primary source, the error has been frequently repeated. It is also compounded by a history of the Second Dragoons entitled *The Dragoons' Story*, Wolf W. Schmoekel (Washington, D.C.: Randall Printing, 1958), which says, "Among the various posts established by the regt. during its service in west Texas as Camp Worth, on the site of the present Fort Worth, Texas" (p. 34). *The Dragoons' Story* is an obscure and long-out-of-print source, but a recent source, Ray Miller, *Ray Miller's Texas Forts* (Houston: Gulf Publishing, 1985), repeats the same error (p. 44). The most conclusive evidence against the "Camp Worth" name comes from a letter written by a man who was with Ripley when they chose the location. Simon B. Farrar, writing to C.C. Cummings years later, states unequivocally that "in honor of that grand old hero [we] named the point *[sic]* Fort Worth." Farrar to Cummings, September 23, 1893, TCHC. The confusion probably arises from the dateline on official correspondence between Fort Worth and Eighth Infantry Headquarters in San Antonio, which was designated "Camp Worth" in 1849.

29. Col. M.L. Crimmins, U.S. Army veteran, Tarrant County judge, and long-time authority on Fort Worth history, says, "It is not improbable that this regiment was organized in anticipation of events which would result from the possible acquisition of Texas to our Union." Crimmins, "Fort Worth Was an Early Army Post," *Frontier Times*, Vol. 16, January, 1939, p. 139. Henry Puntey Beers, *The Western Military Frontier, 1815-1846* (Philadelphia: Porcupine Press, 1975), p. 120, writes, "The war with the Seminoles in Florida was under way, and to it more than to events on the western frontier was due an act of May 23 for the creation of the Second Dragoons." Other authorities, such as T.F. Rodenbough, *From Everglades to Cañon with the Second Dragoons* (New York: D. Van Nostrand, 1875), p. 15, agree with Beers.

30. Russell F. Weigley, *History of the United States Army* (New York: Macmillan, 1967), p. 159.

31. Gregory J.W. Urwin, *The U.S. Infantry: An Illustrated History* (New York: Sterling Publishing, 1991), pp. 76, 78.

32. Philip Katcher, *The Mexican-American War, 1846-1848*, Vol. 56, in the "Men-at-Arms Series," Martin Windrow, ed. (London: Osprey Publishing Ltd., 1976), pp. 3-4.

33. Wallace, "General William Jenkins Worth and Texas," *SWHQ*, p. 162.

34. Report of the Committee on Indian Affairs, April 24, 1850, House Reports, 31st Congress, 1st Session, Report No. 280, p. 3.

35. Quotation from anonymous manuscript, "Fort Worth," vertical files, TCHC.

36. According to 1841 U.S. Army Regulations (Paragraph 1292), only dragoons were allowed to wear mustaches. Otherwise, the hair was to be "short, or what is generally termed cropped; the whiskers not to extend below the lower tip of the ear, and a line thence with the curve of the mouth." Cited in Randy Steffen, *The Horse Soldier, 1776-1943*, Vol. 1, *The Revolution, The War of 1812, The Early Frontier, 1776-1850* (Norman: University of Oklahoma Press, 1977), p. 119.

37. Katcher, *The Mexican-American War*, p. 4.

38. Unnamed newspaper of 1858, as reported in *The Old Tarrant County & Fort Worth Chronicle*, Vol. 2, No. 9, 1994, p. 55.

39. Richard H. Wilson, "The Eighth Regiment of Infantry," *The Army of the United States*, Theodore F. Rodenbough and William L. Haskin, eds. (New York: Maynard, Merrill, & Co., 1896), pp. 511-513.

40. *Ibid.*, pp. 513-518.

41. *Ibid.*, pp. 518-520. While the Eighth Regiment benefitted from its long association with William Jenkins Worth, it suffered under Department Commander David Twiggs, who surrendered both his regiment and his department to Rebel forces without a fight

after Texas seceded from the Union in 1861. Most of the troops were marched into captivity, and the regiment did not recover as a fighting force until late 1863.

42. Ultimately, a chain of eight forts marked the first line of frontier defense set up by the U.S. Army in Texas after the Mexican War. These included, from north to south: Worth, Graham, Gates, Croghan, Martin Scott, Lincoln, Inge, Merrill. All were established in the fifteen months between December, 1848 (Martin Scott) and March, 1850 (Merrill), and all were abandoned by the U. S. Army by the mid-1850s.

43. Charles J. Peterson, *The Military Heroes of the War With Mexico: With a Narrative of the War* (Philadelphia: William A. Leary, 1848), pp. 275, 278.

44. *Ibid.*, p. 278; and L.U. Reavis, *The Life and Military Services of General Willaim Selby Harney* (St. Louis: Bryan, Brand & Co, 1878), pp. 308, 465.

45. Bvt. Maj. Gen. G.M. Brooke to Bvt. Brig. Gen. Harney, August 5, 1849, Record of the Army Headquarters, Registers of Letters Received, Entry 21, RG 108, NA.

46. General Orders No. 13, February 14, 1849, Headquarters Eighth Military Department, San Antonio, "By order of [Maj.] Gen. William Worth," Adjutant General's Office, 1780-1917, RG 94, NA.

47. See Post Returns, Fort Graham, May, 1849, Orders Received, RG 94, NA. "Orders No. 16" has a specific connotation in military parlance used by the U.S. Army. The designation "Orders" (as opposed to "General" or "Special Orders") usually means that they were issued by regimental headquarters dealing with routine matters.

48. Geoffrey Perret, *A Country Made by War* (New York: Random House, Vintage Books, 1990), p. 172.

49. Francis B. Heitman, *Historical Register and Dictionary of the United States Army* (Washington, D.C.: Government Printing Office, 1903), Vol. 1, p. 248.

50. J.U. Salvant and Robert M. Utley, *If These Walls Could Speak: Historic Forts of Texas* (Austin: University of Texas Press, 1985), p. 12.

51. For Smith's military career, see *Webster's American Military Biographies* (Springfield, Massachusetts: G.C. Merriam, 1978), p. 400. Smith died in harness, organizing his forces for the Mormon Expedition in May, 1858. At that time he commanded the Department of Utah. For Arnold's official correspondence, see Registers of Letters Received, Adjutant General's Office, M-711, and Letters Received, Adjutant General's Office, 1822-1860, M-567, RG 94, NA.

52. In the summer of 1849, Bryan and Michler separately conducted wide-ranging explorations of West Texas. Both men were looking for practicable routes to El Paso. In the fall of 1849, Michler was ordered to the northern reaches of the state to conduct further explorations. Both men reported the emptiness of the land but also its great potential for development and settlement. See Bender, "Opening Routes Across West Texas," *SWHQ*, pp. 125, 130-132.

53. To cover the Rio Grande border, another line of forts was constructed between 1846 and 1852. These included Brown (1846), Ringgold (1848), Bliss (1848), McIntosh (1849), Duncan (1849), and Clark (1852). Most of these posts were not established on Worth's watch, but his Orders No. 13 (February 14, 1849) sketched out the first strategic plan for the "Rio Grande Department, Eighth Department."

54. Leonora Barrett, "Transportation, Supplies, and Quarters for the West Texas Frontier Under the Federal Military System 1848-1861," *WTHAYB*, Vol. 5, June, 1929, p. 97.

55. Other examples of Texas posts named after Mexican War heroes include McKavett, Chadbourne, Terrett, Martin Scott, and Mason. Miller, *Ray Miller's Texas Forts*, pp. 37, 42, 58, 68, 71, and 81.

56. D. Port Smythe, "A Journal of the Travels of D. Port Smythe,

M.D., of Centerville, Texas, From That Place to the Mouth of the Palo Pinto, on the Upper Brazos," *The Texas Geographic Magazine*, Vol. 6, Fall, 1942, p. 14 (cited in James Reese, "The Murder of Maj. Ripley A. Arnold," *WTHAYB*, Vol. 41, October, 1965, p. 144).

57. J. Evetts Haley, *Fort Concho and the Texas Frontier* (San Angelo: *San Angelo Standard*, 1952), pp. 53, 156; Ray Miller, *Texas Forts, A History and Guide* (Houston: Gulf Publishing, 1985), pp. 66, 104.

58. Whiting to Office of the Chief of Engineers, September 8, 1849 and July 4, 1849, Registers of Letters Received, M-505, RG 77, NA.

3-REVEILLE AND FATIGUE

1. Randy Steffen, *The Horse Soldier 1776-1943*, Vol. 1, *The Revolution, the War of 1812, the Early Frontier, 1776-1850* (Norman: University of Oklahoma Press, 1977), p. 174. A "Memorandum of Public Property" from Lt. John Bold, Acting Assistant Quartermaster at Fort Worth, dated August 3, 1851, states that there were four wagons on the post. He described them at that time as "old, worn out." See Lt. John Bold, "Report of the Condition and of the Public Property at Fort Worth, Texas," October 5, 1851, Office of the Quartermaster General, Consolidated Correspondence File, 1794-1915, Box 1262, Entry 225, RG 92, NA (hereafter cited as "Report of John Bold on the Condition," RG 92, NA).

2. For movements, see Muster Rolls, Second Dragoons, Company F, Reports of December 31, 1848, February 28 and April 30, 1849. For Arnold being sick, see Post Returns, Fort Graham, May, 1849, RG 94, NA.

3. Adj. Gen. Roger Jones to Bvt. Maj. Gen. G.M. Brooke, July 7, 1849; and Bvt. Maj. Gen. G.M. Brooke to War Department, July 3, 1849, Record of the Army Headquarters, Registers of Letters Received, 1849-1854, Vol. 66, Entry 21, RG 108, NA.

4. From Arnold to Maj. Gen. George Brooke, Headquarters Eighth Military Department, reprinted in *Fort Worth Star-Telegram*, June 22, 1949. The twelve-pound howitzer could throw an 8.9 pound shell 900 yards at standard elevation, and gun crews required little training in its use. Robert M. Utley, *Frontiersmen in Blue* (Lincoln: University of Nebraska Press, 1981), p. 28.

5. Author and local historian Howard W. Peak tells a story about how the howitzer was fired just once, sometime in 1850-1851, to break up a Comanche attack forming on the "bluffs" west of Fort Worth. A shell from the gun dispersed the Indians and they never came back. See Peak, *A Ranger of Commerce or 52 Years on the Road* (San Antonio: Naylor Printing, 1929), p. 169.

6. Farrar to Cummings, September 23, 1893, TCHC.

7. For the "spring," see *Charter and Revised Civil and Criminal Ordinances*, FWPL. For "Trinity," see Howard W. Peak, "The Story of Old Fort Worth," p. 2, Genealogy and History, FWPL. Samuels Avenue is named for Baldwin L. Samuel (1803-1879), who bought a house on Live Oak Point from Nathaniel Terry to be near his farmland in the West Fork bottom. The location was subsequently referred to as "Samuel's Point" or Live Oak Point. The trail passing in front of his house, connecting the cold spring to the fort on the bluff was also named for old man Samuel. In later years Samuels Ave. became Fort Worth's first "silk stocking row" when the wealthy built their homes there. Samuel is buried in Pioneer's Rest Cemetery near the avenue named for him.

8. Swasey and Melton, "History," FWPL; "Report of Lt. Samuel Starr, Acting Assistant Quartermaster, on the Condition of Facilities of the Post," May, 1851, in Records of the Office of the Quartermaster General, Consolidated Correspondence File, 1794-1915, Box 1262, Entry 225, RG 92, NA (hereafter cited as "Report of Samuel Starr on the Condition," RG 92, NA). For Whiting's evaluation, see "Report of Whiting's Reconnaissance," Senate Executive Document No. 64.

9. The idea was firmly entrenched by 1889 when the authors of the

Charter and Revised Civil and Criminal Ordinances, FWPL, stated that Arnold first established the post "in a valley" (p. iv). However, the same source also pinpoints the site as being very near the "old cemetery" (Pioneer Rest), which suggests that the so-called "valley" might actually be a hollow or depression formed by water erosion around the cold spring.

10. Quotation in *ibid.* Whether Ripley Arnold or some other individual deserves credit for picking the bluff site has never been firmly established. Family history among the Farmer clan claims that John "Uncle Press" Farmer "chose the camp site on the courthouse bluff . . . at the request of Maj. Ripley Arnold." (From Farmer family history in *Baptist Standard,* n.d., typescript in Tarrant County Scrapbook No. 1, filed with "Excerpts from Scrapbook of Mrs. Grover Leigh," CAH, UT, Austin). Farmer family history, supported by the unknown authors of the "Introduction" to the *Charter and Revised Civil and Criminal Ordinances,* FWPL, make a strong case for Uncle Press. Nevertheless, it strains credulity that the offhanded suggestion of a local homesteader should be the deciding factor in the placement of the fort.

11. "How Fort Worth Became 'Gateway to the West,'" undated newspaper clipping in vertical files, "Fort Worth," FWPL.

12. Orders No. 13, February 14, 1849, "By order of Genl. Wm Worth, General and Special Orders, Eighth Military Department, Department of Texas, and District of Texas, 1849-1870," RG 94, NA.

13. *Charter and Revised Civil and Criminal Ordinances,* FWPL.

14. Leonora Barrett, "Transportation, Supplies, and Quarters for the West Texas Frontier Under the Federal Military System 1848-1861," *WTHAYB,* Vol. 5, June, 1929, p. 97.

15. J. Evetts Haley, *Fort Concho and the Texas Frontier* (San Angelo: *San Angelo Standard,* 1952), p. 134.

16. Ray Miller, *Ray Miller's Texas Forts: A History and Guide* (Houston: Gulf Publishing, 1985), p. 13.

17. Report of Secretary of War, 34th Congress, 1st Session, Senate Executive Document No. 1, p. 22.

18. "The Purchase of Military Sites in Texas," Report of Secretary of War, 34th Congress, 1st Session, House Executive Document No. 282, pp. 22-23.

19. "Report of Lt. Samuel Starr on the Condition," RG 92, NA.

20. "Report of Whiting's Reconnaissance," Senate Executive Document No. 64, p. 241.

21. This situation occurred at both Fort Chadbourne and Camp Cooper according to Col. J.F.K. Mansfield, who recorded, "In two instances I was witness to [this] description of coffins." M.L. Crimmins, ed., "Col. J.F.K. Mansfield's Report of the Inspection of the Department of Texas in 1856," *SWHQ,* Vol. 42, April, 1939, p. 378. Similar observations are attributed to Lydia Spencer Lane, author of *I Married a Soldier or Old Days in the Old Army* (1893) by Jerry Flemmons, "Texas Siftings," *Fort Worth Star-Telegram,* March 6, 1994, p. 5 C.

22. The next nearest saw mill for the dragoons in 1849 was that of Gen. Edward Tarrant at Tarrant Springs on the headwaters of Chambers Creek in Ellis County. According to one unverified source, Johnson also ran a gristmill at the same site and offered to let the garrison use it in turning their locally purchased wheat into flour. His operation at Johnson's Station was truly a godsend for the struggling troopers in the early months. For "horse-powered saw mill," see Peak, "The Story of Old Fort Worth," p. 3, FWPL. Gristmill information is from *Fort Worth Star-Telegram,* n.d., "Fort Worth," vertical files, TCHC. For Fort Belknap's daunting lumber problems, see Earl Burk Braley, "Fort Belknap of the Texas Frontier," *WTHAYB,* Vol. 30, October, 1954, p. 97.

23. Records of the Office of the Judge Advocate General (Army), "Court Martial Case Files, 1809-1894," File HH-93, RG 153, NA.

24. First Sergeant Jacob Dearing and Corporal Daniel McCauly. Corporal McCauly was a model non-com. He was promoted to

sergeant while the company was at Fort Worth. See Company F Roll in Appendix.

25. Report of the Secretary of War, 1851, 32nd Congress, 1st Session, Senate Executive Document No. 1-C, p. 271.

26. Private Frederick Kleinsmith died June 11 and Private William Whitburn died May 28, both at Fort Graham. Sergeant William Slade was sick the first month the company was at Fort Worth. Muster Rolls, Second Dragoons, Company F, Post Returns, June 30, 1849, RG 94, NA.

27. Swasey and Melton, "History," FWPL, p. 3.

28. Sam H. Starr to Mrs. Starr, January 18, 1850, Starr Papers, CAH, UT, Austin.

29. For instance, see example of Fort Belknap in Braley, "Fort Belknap of the Texas Frontier," WTHAYB, p. 96.

30. Though the exact cause of malaria was unknown in 1849, it was well known to be closely associated with low, swampy areas. Joseph Schmitz, ed., "Impressions of Texas in 1860," SWHQ, Vol. 42, April, 1939, p. 344.

31. In 1877, the bluffs above the river were reported as being 100 feet high (see Swasey and Melton, "History," FWPL, p. 1). In 1995, the city engineer's office said the top of the bluffs are 130 feet above the river at the highest point, testifying to the best efforts of nature and the civil engineers.

32. For "stagnant water," see Peak, "The Story of Old Fort Worth," p. 3, FWPL. Other primary sources are "Report of A.W. Speight, Commissioner of Statistics, Resources, Soil, and Climate of Texas, Tarrant County, 1882," in WPA, Fort Worth-City Guide and History, Box 4J78, File 2, CAH, UT, Austin; and I.C. Terry, "Reminiscences of the Fort Worth of Fifty Years Ago," unpublished manuscript, p. 5, Genealogy and History, FWPL.

33. Fort Belknap was closed by order of Gen. David Twiggs in February, 1859, because of insufficient water supplies: a seasonal well and a stream six miles away. The fort was reoccupied by U.S. troops after the Civil War but abandoned for good in September, 1867, due to the water situation. See Robert W. Frazer, *Forts of the West* (Norman: University of Oklahoma Press, 1988), p. 142; and Carl C. Rister, "Fort Griffin," WTHAYB, Vol. 1, June, 1925, p. 17.

34. Quoted in *Fort Worth Star-Telegram*, June 22, 1949. Arnold's use of the word "discovered" suggests that he was referring to the new well on the site, not to the spring at Live Oak Point, which was already a familiar landmark.

35. "Report of Samuel Starr on the Condition," RG 92, NA. When the town began growing up around the fort, additional wells were sunk all over the area, with an almost unbroken record of success in striking water on the first try.

36. "Report of John Bold on the Condition," RG 92, NA.

37. By contrast, Fort McKavett, built in 1852 "atop a stony plateau overlooking the head streams of the San Saba River," was constructed of limestone blocks cut and assembled by soldiers of the Eighth Infantry. The result was one of the most popular posts on the Texas frontier. See J.U. Salvant and Robert M. Utley, *If These Walls Could Speak: Historic Forts of Texas* (Austin: University of Texas Press, 1985), p. 27.

38. Orders No. 13, February 14, 1849. "General and Special Orders, Eighth Military Department, Department of Texas, and District of Texas, 1849-1870," RG 94, NA.

39. "Report of John Bold on the Condition," RG 92, NA. For Merrill's quotation, see Merrill to Thomas S. Jesup, Quartermaster General, Washington, D.C., August 20, 1853, RG 94, NA. The same words are used in the 1853 Report of the Secretary of War, 32nd Congress, 1st Session, House Executive Document No. 2, Pt. 1, p. 270.

4-CALL TO QUARTERS

1. Freeman, "Report of Inspection," RG 94, NA, "Figure Q—Rough Plan of Fort Worth, Texas," p. 96. This report has been repro-

duced in several places, including 34th Congress, 1st Session, Senate Executive Document No. 96, pp. 375-378; and *SWHQ*, in nine Parts: Vol. 51, Nos. 1 and 4, Vol. 52, Nos. 4 and 5, Vol. 53, Nos. 1-4, and Vol. 54, No. 2. Freeman's rough sketch is the starting point for all attempts to orient the fort with the local geography and relate it to the modern city.

2. The earliest description is contained in "Report of Samuel Starr on the Condition," May 22, 1851, RG 92, NA. Starr was the acting assistant quartermaster at the time. He made the report to Maj. E.B. Babbitt, Chief Assistant Quartermaster, Eighth Department, San Antonio. The second description is contained in "Report of John Bold on the Condition," RG 92, NA. Lt. Bold, Eighth Infantry, was acting assistant quartermaster at this time, and his report was addressed to Maj. Gen. Thomas S. Jesup, Quartermaster General, "Washington City." The third description is contained in Freeman, "Report of Inspection," October 1, 1853, pp. 95-98, RG 94, NA. Lt. Starr's report also served as the basis for the regular 1853 War Department report to Congress, in House Executive Documents, 32nd Congress, 1st Session, Document No. 2, Pt. 1, pp. 270-271. These are the only known descriptions of Fort Worth during the time it was an active military post.

3. "Report of Whiting's Reconnaissance," Senate Executive Document No. 64.

4. For Whiting, see "Report of Whiting's Reconnaissance," Senate Executive Document No. 64, p. 241. Most of the remaining description in this paragraph comes from Swasey and Melton, "History," FWPL. Information on "Belknap St." and location of flag pole come from "Fort Worth as Seen in 1853," notes by M.G. Turner and Mrs. M.A. Holloway in "Excerpts from Scrapbook of Mrs. Grover Leigh," Tarrant County Scrapbook No. 1, CAH, UT, Austin. Most descriptions place soldiers' quarters on the north side of the parade gound. Location of the sutler's store is based

5. From unidentified sources quoted in *Fort Worth Daily Gazette*, September 5, 1889, p. 8.

6. These locations have been estimated by comparing the descriptions in the *Fort Worth Daily Gazette* of September 5, 1889, with an 1885 Sanborn Fire Map of the City. The vaguely worded location of the stables would place them on the southwest side of the present courthouse block. According to the recollections (circa 1947) of one of Maj. Arnold's descendants, Mrs. W.H. Thompson, the first barracks were built on the site of the later Criminal Courts Building. See "Frontier Outpost . . ." *Fort Worth Press*, June 6, 1947, p. 1.

7. The reference to G.W. Newman's residence was used by Mrs. M.A. Holloway to pinpoint the location of the old sutler's store. See Recollections of Mrs. M.A. Holloway, Tarrant County Scrapbook No. 1, CAH, UT, Austin. Research by Frances M. Allen in recent years has located the Newman residence at the "northwest corner of the intersection of West Weatherford and Taylor Sts." See Schmidt to Selcer.

8. *Charter and Revised Civil and Criminal Ordinances*, FWPL.

9. For "huts," "rived boards," and "120 men," see "Report of Samuel Starr on the Condition," May 22, 1851, RG 92, NA. For "daubing and chinking," and "slab" doors, see Howard W. Peak, *A Ranger of Commerce or 52 Years on the Road* (San Antonio: Naylor Printing, 1929), p. 156.

10 See "Report of Samuel Starr on the Condition," May 22, 1851, RG 92, NA; and "Report of John Bold on the Condition," October 5, 1851, RG 92, NA. Bold also describes the rooms as being fifteen

feet square rather than the sixteen square-feet figure used by Starr.

11. "Report of John Bold on the Condition," October 5, 1851, RG 92, NA; and "Report of Samuel Starr on the Condition," May 22, 1851, RG 92, NA.

12 See Carl C. Rister, "Fort Griffin," *WTHAYB*, Vol. 1, June, 1925, p. 18.

13. Sam H. Starr to Mrs. Starr, January 6, 1850, Starr Papers, CAH, UT, Austin.

14. For measurements, see "Samuel Starr Report on the Condition," May 22, 1851, RG 92, NA. Lt. Bold gives the measurements as eleven-by-thirty feet. "Dilapidation" is also from "Report of John Bold on the Condition," October 5, 1851, RG 92, NA.

15. "Report of Whiting's Reconnaissance," Senate Executive Document No. 64, p. 241.

16. 32nd Congress, 1st Session, House Executive Document No. 2, Pt. 1, p. 270.

17. Report of Lt. Starr, 32nd Congress, 1st Session, House Executive Document No. 2, Pt. 1, p. 270.

18. All descriptions of commissary and quartermaster storehouses, adjutant's office, guard house, and workshops are from reports by Lt. Starr and Lt. Bold.

19. Lt. Bold describes the dimensions of this building in his report as being two rooms, each ten feet square, and a ten-foot-wide passageway. "Report of John Bold on the Condition," October 5, 1851, RG 92, NA.

20. *Ibid.*

21. The only first-person testimony that Fort Worth's window coverings were shutters and not glass panes comes from Howard W. Peak, *A Ranger of Commerce*, p. 156. For Fort Richardson, see J.U. Salvant and Robert M. Utley, *If These Walls Could Speak: Historic Forts of Texas* (Austin: University of Texas Press, 1985), p. 36.

22. Salvant and Utley, *If These Walls Could Speak,* p. 36.

23. Freeman, "Report of Inspection," October 1, 1853, RG 94, NA.

24. See report of Bvt. Maj. H.W. Merrill, Commanding and Acting Assistant Quartermaster, Fort Worth, to Maj. Gen. Thomas Jesup, Quartermaster General, Washington, D.C., August 20, 1853, in RG 92, Office of the Quartermaster General, Consolidated Correspondence File, 1794-1915, Box 1262, Entry 225, RG 92, NA.

25. For "limited capacity," see H.W. Merrill to Maj. Gen. Thomas S. Jesup, Quartermaster General, Washington, D.C., August 20, 1853, typescript copy in "Fort Worth," vertical files, TCHC. Other quotations from "Report of John Bold on the Condition," October 5, 1851, RG 92, NA.

26. Salvant and Utley, *If These Walls Could Speak*, p 36.

27. For 1853 dimensions of stable, see Freeman "Report of Inspection," p. 96 (legend to diagram), RG 94, NA.

28. For Fort Concho hospital quarters, see Salvant and Utley, *If These Walls Could Speak*, p. 51.

29. Sam H. Starr to Mrs. Starr, January 6, 1850, Starr Papers, CAH, UT, Austin.

30. "Report of John Bold on the Condition," October 5, 1851, RG 92, NA. Dimensions given here are from Starr and Freeman. Bold gives the dimensions of the hospital as thirty-five-by-seventeen feet and of the dispensary as ten-by-ten feet.

31. Post Returns, Fort Worth, October, 1852, RG 94, NA.

32. "Report of John Bold on the Condition," October 5, 1851, RG 92, NA.

33. *Ibid.*; Freeman, "Report of Inspection," RG 94, NA.

34. Freeman, "Report of Inspection," RG 94, NA.

35. *Ibid.*

36. For general information on laundresses, see Oliver Knight, *Life and Manners in the Frontier Army* (Norman: University of Oklahoma Press, 1993), pp. 6, 67, 69. For Fort Worth specifically, see Freeman "Report of Inspection," p. 96 (diagram), RG 94, NA.

37. "Report of John Bold on the Condition," October 5, 1851, RG 92, NA; and Freeman, "Report of Inspection," RG 94, NA.

38. See Swasey and Melton, "History," FWPL; "Excerpts Taken from the Scrapbook of Mrs. Augusta E. McKee," p. 3, in Tarrant County Scrapbook No. 1, CAH, UT, Austin.

39. Maj. H.W. Merrill to Thomas S. Jesup, August 20, 1853, photocopy in "Fort Worth," vertical files, TCHC.

40. "Report of John Bold on the Condition," October 5, 1851, RG 92, NA.

41. Bvt. Maj. H.W. Merrill, Commanding, Fort Worth, to Maj. Gen. Thomas S. Jesup, Quartermaster General, Washington, D.C., August 20, 1853, Office of the Quartermaster General, Consolidated Correspondence File, 1794-1915, Box 1262, Entry 225, RG 92, NA.

42. *Ibid.*

43. J. Evetts Haley, *Fort Concho and the Texas Frontier* (San Angelo: *San Angelo Standard*, 1952), p. 132.

6-OFFICERS' CALL

1. R.A. Arnold to Maj. George Deas, Assistant Adj. Gen., Eighth Department, San Antonio, July 30, 1849, in Letters Received, Adjutant General's Office, 1822-1860, M-567, RG 94, NA. Arnold's request went all the way to the War Department for an answer: Adj. Gen. Roger Jones to Paymaster General, September 10, 1849, Records of the Army Headquarters, Registers of Letters Received, 1849-1854, Vol. 66, Entry 21, RG 108, NA.

2. Sam H. Starr to Mrs. Starr, January 6, 1850, Starr Papers, CAH, UT, Austin.

3. The price of beef and hay in 1851 comes from "Report of Samuel Starr on the Condition," RG 92, NA. However, in transcribing his report into the *Congressional Record*, an error was made, listing the price of beef at 3/4 cents per pound. See 32nd Congress, 1st Session, House Executive Document No. 2, p. 270. (Also cited in *Federal Writers Project*, Vol. 5, p. 1697.) The price of beef in 1853 comes from Freeman, "Report of Inspection," p. 98, RG 94, NA. The price of corn comes from Bold to Maclay, Memorandum of Public Property Pertaining to the Quartermaster Department, Fort Worth, August 3, 1851, in Office of the Quartermaster General, Consolidated Correspondence File, 1794-1915, Box 1261, Entry 225, RG 92, NA. For a glimpse of the bidding process required in issuing an ordinary hay contract, see correspondence in *ibid.*, June-July, 1851.

4. For Starr's beef ration, see Starr to Maj. Gen. George Gibson, Commissary General of Subsistence, U.S. Army, Washington, D.C., April 22, 1851, in "Office of Quartermaster General, Consolidated Correspondence File, 1794-1915," Box 1261, Entry 225, RG 92, NA. For reduced beef ration, see Freeman, "Report of Inspection," p. 98, RG 94, NA.

5. For quantities of supplies, see "memorandum" from Lt. John Bold, Eighth Infantry, Acting Assistant Commissary Supply, to Captain R.P. Maclay, Commanding Post, July 31, 1851, in Office of the Quartermaster General, Consolidated Correspondence File, RG 92, NA. "Log buildings" from Freeman, "Report of Inspection," p. 98, RG 94, NA.

6. Leonard's Mill was burned to the ground at the beginning of the Civil War, rebuilt after the war, and in its second incarnation became known as "Randol Mill." See "Archibald Franklin and Mary A. Leonard, Tarrant County Pioneers," in Tarrant County Scrapbook, File 3L405, CAH, UT, Austin. For salt and cow peas, see Starr to Gibson, April 22, 1851, Office of Quartermaster General, Consolidated Correspondence File, RG 92, NA.

7. Howard W. Peak, *A Ranger of Commerce or 52 Years on the Road* (San Antonio: Naylor Printing, 1929), p. 159.

8. General Orders No. 1, issued January 8, 1851, received at Fort

Worth, March 5. See Post Returns, Fort Worth, March, 1851, RG 94, NA.

9. Sam H. Starr to Mrs. Elizabeth Starr, January 6, 1850, Starr Papers, CAH, UT, Austin. Curiously, the lieutenant wrote another letter on January 18 in the mistaken belief that the previous letter had gone astray, telling his wife, "The market affords milk, eggs, butter, game and vegetables all in great abundance." Either the supply of local produce had greatly increased in less than two weeks or Starr was mistaken.

10. Mae Biddison Benson, "Tales of Early Days Here Are Recalled by Women Pioneers," interview with Mrs. Clara Peak Walden, undated and unidentified newspaper clipping in "Fort Worth," vertical files, TCHC.

11. For Fort Worth, see Freeman, "Report of the Inspection," p. 97, RG 94, NA. For Fort McKavett, see J.U. Salvant and Robert M. Utley, *If These Walls Could Speak: Historic Forts of Texas* (Austin: University of Texas Press, 1985), p. 27. For Fort Griffin, see Carl C. Rister, "Fort Griffin," *WTHAYB,* Vol. 1, June, 1925, pp. 22-23.

12. Starr to Gibson, April 22, 1851, RG 92, NA.

13. *Texas State Gazette* (Austin), May 18, 1851, p. 1.

14. Leonora Barrett, "Transportation, Supplies, and Quarters for the West Texas Frontier Under the Federal Military System 1848-1861," *WTHAYB,* Vol. 5, June, 1929, p. 91.

15. Information on routes and charges from, 32nd Congress, 1st Session, House Executive Document No. 2, Pt. 1, Quartermaster Report of Lt. Samuel Starr, pp. 270-271.

16. Barrett, "Transportation, Supplies, and Quarters for the West Texas Frontier Under the Federal Military System, 1848-1861," *WTHAYB,* p. 91.

17. "Report of Whiting's Reconnaissance," Senate Executive Document No.64.

18. *Ibid.,* p. 241. Compare the report of the Quartermaster General of the Army in 1851 that "there was not then in all of Texas . . . a steamboat line, or a railroad, or even a turnpike road," in R.C. Crane, "Some Aspects of the History of West and Northwest Texas Since 1845," *SWHQ,* Vol. 26, July, 1922, p. 33.

19. "Report of Samuel Starr on the Condition," May, 1851, RG 92, NA.

20. Report of Secretary of War, 1851, 32nd Congress, 1st Session, Senate Executive Document 1-C, p. 271.

21. It is unclear from the historical records whether the man known as "Press" Farmer to his contemporaries was John Press Farmer, Presley Farmer, or George Preston Farmer. See 1850 Census; Schmidt to Selcer; *Texas Writers' Project,* Vol. 2, p. 617; Vol. 3, p. 870; Vol. 5, p. 1706; Vol. 48, p. 19,181.

22. For White, see Mae Biddison Benson, "Tales of Early Days Here Are Recalled by Women Pioneers," interview with Mrs. Clara Peak Walden, undated and unidentified newspaper clipping in "Fort Worth," vertical files, TCHC. For Walsh, see "Excerpts Taken from the Scrapbook of Mrs. Augusta E. McKee," p. 2, both in Tarrant County Scrapbook No. 1, Archives and Manuscripts, CAH, UT, Austin.

23. Freeman, "Report of Inspection," p. 98, RG 94, NA.

24. Fort Worth was designed for just one company, according to the "Report of Whiting's Reconnaissance," Senate Executive Document No. 64, p. 241. For company numbers, see Robert M. Utley, *Frontiersmen in Blue: The United States and the Indian, 1848-1865* (Lincoln: University of Nebraska Press, 1981), pp. 22-23.

25. Post Returns, Fort Worth, June-September, 1849, RG 94, NA.

26. Arnold to Maj. Gen. Roger Jones, Adjutant General U.S. Army, Washington, D.C., from Fort Worth, June 15, 1849. Copy in "Fort Worth," vertical files, TCHC. This company roll provides the only list of names of the soldiers who first came to the banks of the Trinity to build Fort Worth.

27. Arnold to Maj. Gen. Roger Jones, Adj. Gen., U.S. Army, September 1, 1849, Letters Received, Adjutant General's Office, M-567, RG 94, NA.

28. *Ibid.*

29. Francis B. Heitman, *Historical Register and Dictionary of the United States Army* (Washington, D.C.: Government Printing Office, 1903), Vol. 1, p. 62; "Eighth Infantry Regiment Military Histories of Officers, 1838-1869," Entry 1285, RG 391, NA.

30. For Samuel Henry Starr (1810-1891), see Heitman, *Historical Register and Dictionary of the United States Army*, Vol. 1, p. 917; catalogue to Starr Papers (1848-1854, 1930), CAH, UT, Austin; Muster Rolls, Second Dragoons, Company F, Report for June 30, 1849-August 31, 1849, RG 94, NA.

31. Bvt. Maj. Gen. G.M. Brooke to War Department, November 6, 1849, Record of the Army Headquarters, Registers of Letters Received, Entry 21, RG 108, NA.

32. For "maximum," see Brooke to War Department, June 21, 1849, Record of the Army Headquarters, Registers of Letters Received, Entry 21, RG 108, NA. Other figures from Gregory J.W. Urwin, *The United States Infantry: An Illustrated History* (New York: Sterling Publishing, 1991), p. 78.

33. See Julia K. Garrett, *Fort Worth: A Frontier Triumph* (Austin: Encino Press, 1972), p. 109.

34. Bvt. Maj. H.W. Merrill, Acting Assistant Quartermaster, to Quartermaster Gen. Thomas Jesup, Washington, D.C., August 15, 1853, Office of the Quartermaster General, Consolidated Correspondence File, 1794-1915, Box 1261, Entry 225, RG 92, NA.

35. Starr to Maj. James Longstreet, Assistant Commissary of Subsistence, May 5, 1851; Captain W.B. Blair, Officer of Commissary Subsistence, to Lt. Starr, May 16, 1851; Blair to Maj. Gen. George Gibson, Commissary General, Subsistence Washington, D.C., May 16, 1851; Office of the Quartermaster General, Consolidated Correspondence File, 1794-1915, Box 1261, Entry 225, RG 92, NA.

36. Oliver Knight, *Life and Manners in the Frontier Army* (Norman: University of Oklahoma Press, 1993), pp. 124-126.

37. Robert Frazer, ed., *Mansfield on the Condition of Western Forts, 1853-1854* (Norman: University of Oklahoma Press, 1963), p. 67.

38. Samuel H. Starr to Mrs. Starr, January 6, 1850, Starr Papers CAH, UT, Austin.

39. Starr to Maj. Gen. Thomas Jesup, Quartermaster General, U.S. Army, Washington, D.C., May 26, 1851, in Office of the Quartermaster General, Consolidated Correspondence File, 1794-1915, Box 1262, Entry 225, RG 92, NA.

40. Post Returns, Fort Worth, August, 1852, RG 94, NA.

41. See Post Returns, Fort Worth, August, 1849-October, 1852, RG 94, NA.

42. Arnold to Maj. Gen. Roger Jones, Adj. Gen., U.S. Army, June 15, 1849, in Letters Received, Adjutant General's Office, 1822-1860, M-567, RG 94, NA.

43. Post Returns, Fort Worth, May, 1850, RG 94, NA.

44. Post Returns, Fort Worth, for months cited, RG 94, NA.

45. For company strengths, see Russell Weigley, *History of the United States Army*, "Wars of the United States Series," Louis Morton, ed. (New York: Macmillan, 1967), p. 169. Post Returns, Fort Worth, August, 1849-December, 1851, RG 94, NA.

46. Arnold to Maj. Gen. Roger Jones, May 2, 1852, Letters Received, Adjutant General's Office, M-567, RG 94, NA.

47. Arnold to Maj. Gen. Roger Jones, Adjutant General, U.S. Army, June 15, 1849.

48. Utley, *Frontiersmen in Blue*, p. 41.

49. Arnold to Maj. Gen. Roger Jones, January 25, 1850, Letters Received, Adjutant General's Office, 1822-1860, M-567, RG 94, NA.

50. Henry Beers, *The Western Military Frontier, 1815-1846* (Philadelphia: Porcupine Press, 1975), p. 121 (note 72).

51. Muster Rolls, Second Dragoons, Company F, RG 94, NA.

52. Freeman, "Report of Inspection," p. 69, RG 94, NA.

53. *Ibid.*, p. 97.

54. *Ibid.*

55. Carl C. Rister, "The Border Post of Phantom Hill," *WTHAYB*, Vol. 14, October, 1938, p. ii.

56. Julius Froebel, *Seven Years Travel in Central America, Northern Mexico, and the Far West of the United States* (London: n.p., 1859), p. 323.

57. Rister, "The Border Post of Phantom Hill," *WTHAYB*, pp. 7-8.

58. Post Returns, Fort Worth, August, 1850, RG 94, NA; Muster Rolls, Second Dragoons, Company F, Report of June 30-August 31, 1850, RG 94, NA.

59. All information on deserters and equipment are from Muster Rolls, Second Dragoons, Company F, December 31, 1845-December 31, 1850, RG 94, NA. See Reports of April 30-June 30, 1850 and June 30-August 31, 1850.

60. Post Returns, Fort Worth, August-December, 1850, RG 94, NA.

61. Muster Rolls, Second Dragoons, Company F, Report of April 30-June 30, 1850, RG 94, NA.

62. The bonus system changed after August, 1854, when Congress authorized the Army to pay an extra $2 per month to soldiers who signed up for a second hitch, and $1 additionally per month for every subsequent re-enlistment. See Urwin, *The United States Infantry,* p. 80.

63. Post Returns, Fort Worth, May, 1851, RG 94, NA.

64. Lt. T.G. Pitcher, Adjutant Eighth Infantry Headquarters, to Lt. W.P. Street, Eighth Infantry, Fort Worth, February 1, March 20, April 4, 1851, Eighth Infantry, Letters Sent, Adjutant General's Office, Entry 1279, RG 391, NA.

65. Muster Rolls, Company B, Second Dragoons, 1851-1855, Report of August 31-October 31, 1853, RG 94, NA.

7-GUARD MOUNTING

1. Post Returns, Fort Worth, May and June, 1851, RG 94, NA.

2. Post Returns, Fort Worth, January, 1852, *ibid.*

3. See Report of Secretary of War C.M. Conrad, December 4, 1852, 32nd Congress, 2nd Session, House Executive Document No. 1, p. 4.

4. No member of the Fort Worth garrison left a description of daily routines, but garrison life was similar all over the West. One good description of normal "daily calls" at a frontier post comes from a member of the First Dragoon Regiment in the mid-1830s. See "A Dragoon" [James Hildreth], *Dragoon Campaigns to the Rocky Mountains*, "Far Western Frontier Series," Ray A. Billington, ed. (New York: Arno Press, 1973, reprint of 1836 ed.), pp. 60-61, 96. Additional information comes from Augustus G. Robinson, a first lieutenant with the Ninth Infantry Regiment at Camp Pickett, San Juan Island, Washington Territory, just before the Civil War. See San Juan Island, Post Orders, 1861-1868, Camp Pickett, Orders No. 22, November 18, 1861, RG 393, NA. Other information in this section relating to garrison routines comes from Randy Steffen, *The Horse Soldier, 1776-1943*, Vol. 1, *The Revolution, the War of 1812, the Early Frontier, 1776-1850* (Norman: University of Oklahoma Press, 1977), Appendix 4, "Cavalry Calls," p. 187.

5. Records of the Office of the Judge Advocate General (Army), "Court Martial Case Files, 1809-1894," File HH-93, RG 153, NA; "A Dragoon," *Dragoon Campaigns*, p. 88.

6. "A Dragoon," *Dragoon Campaigns*, pp. 86-88.

7. "Report of Whiting's Reconnaissance," Senate Executive Document No. 64, p. 238.

8. Orders No. 39, September 17, 1850, and Orders No. 42, July 18, 1849, Headquarters Eighth Military Department, San Antonio, in Orders and Special Orders, Eighth Military Department, 1848-1850, Adjutant General's Office, Vol. 250, RG 94, NA.

9. Williams, "Medical Topography," Senate Executive Document No. 96, p. 374.

10. Records of the Office of the Judge Advocate General (Army), "Court Martial Case Files, 1809-1894," File HH-93, RG 153, NA.

11. Sam H. Starr to Mrs. Starr, January 25, 1850, Starr Papers, CAH, UT, Austin.

12. *Ibid.*, January 6, 17, 18, 25, April 19, July 4, 20, 1850.

13. Jerry Thompson, *Henry Hopkins Sibley: Confederate General of the West* (Natchitoches, Louisiana: Northwestern State University Press, 1987), pp. 337-338.

14. Sam H. Starr to Mrs. Starr, January 25, 1850, Starr Papers, CAH, UT, Austin.

15. Percival G. Lowe, *Five Years a Dragoon, 1849-1854, and Other Adventures on the Great Plains* (Norman: University of Oklahoma Press, 1965), p. 122.

16. Martin L. Crimmins, ed., "Col. J.K.F. Mansfield's Report on the Inspection of the Department of Texas in 1856," *SWHQ*, Vol. 42, January, 1939, p. 254.

17. Allan M. Winkler, "Drinking on the American Frontier," *Quarterly Journal of Studies on Alcohol*, Vol. 29, 1968, p. 428.

18. Petition from Citizens of Navarro, McClellan, and Ellis Counties to P.H. Bell, July, 1852, Bell Papers, Texas State Archives (cited in Thompson, *Henry Hopkins Sibley*, p. 94).

19. Crimmins, "Col. J.K.F. Mansfield's Report of the Inspection of the Department of Texas in 1856," *SWHQ*, p. 237.

20. For the case of Private John Connigland, Company F, Second Dragoons, see Records of the Office of the Judge Advocate General (Army), "Court Martial Case Files, 1809-1894," File HH-93, Orders No. 52, Headquarters Eighth Military Department, San Antonio, July-August, 1851, RG 153, NA. (The court convened at Fort Graham.)

21. Court martial record of Private Joseph Murphy, Company F, Second Dragoons, *ibid.*

22. Quoted in Carl C. Rister, "Fort Griffin," *WTHAYB*, Vol. 51, June, 1925, p. 21. See also Dabney Herndon Maury, *Recollections of a Virginian* (New York: Charles Scribners Sons, 1894), pp. 80-81. Lt. Maury, U.S. Mounted Rifles, was stationed at Fort Inge, Texas in the early 1850s.

23. Freeman, "Report of the Inspection," p. 97, RG 94, NA. The American Society for the Promotion of Temperance was founded in 1826 and its influence spread rapidly in the 1830s. See Winkler, "Drinking on the American Frontier," *Quarterly Journal of Studies on Alcohol*, pp. 417, 438-439.

24. J. Evetts Haley, *Fort Concho and the Texas Frontier* (San Angelo: *San Angelo Standard*, 1952), pp. 301-305.

25. The one-mile radius around the fort kept out not just liquor sales but all "merchandising" in competition with the post sutler according to early pioneer John Peter Smith. See WPA Project, "Fort Worth City Guide and History," Box 4J78, File 9, CAH, UT, Austin, p. 7.

26. William S. McFeely, *Grant: A Biography* (New York: W.W. Norton, 1981), pp. 427-429.

27. There are no official records to prove this. Sources say Farmer was simply a "wagon freighter" (see *Texas Writers Project*, Vol. 48, p. 19, 181); for "a clerk in the sutler's store," see "Excerpts Taken from the Scrapbook of Mrs. Augusta E. McKee," p. 3, in Tarrant County Scrapbook No. 1, CAH, UT, Austin. By most accounts, however, Farmer was Fort Worth's first sutler.

28. Samuel H. Starr to Mrs. Starr, January 6, 1850, Starr Papers, CAH, UT, Austin. Gouhenaught also had some practical skills as a stonemason and surveyor. He built the curious, beehive-shaped "Frenchman's Well," a few years later, named after him by the local citizens, and assembled the stone cairn over the two Arnold children who died at Fort Worth. He was eventually appointed a geological surveyor for the State. (Schmidt to Selcer.)

29. Samuel H. Starr to Mrs. Starr, July 4, 1850, Starr Papers, CAH, UT,

Austin. For pet buffalo, see J.U. Salvant and Robert M. Utley, *If These Walls Could Speak: Historic Forts of Texas* (Austin: University of Texas Press, 1985), p. 37.

30. Laundresses had been part of Army structure since Congressional authorization in 1802. Their job description, according to 1873 army Regulations, was "to do the washing for the company officers and their families" first and the enlisted men second. Oliver Knight, *Life and Manners in the Frontier Army* (Norman: University of Oklahoma Press, 1993), pp. 6, 67, 69.

31. Sam H. Starr to Mrs. Starr, January 6, 1850, Starr Papers, CAH, UT, Austin.

32. Information on living conditions at Fort Worth, including "bachelors' mess" and the hiring of personal servants, comes from Samuel H. Starr Papers, CAH, UT, Austin. See specifically, Sam H. Starr to Mrs. Starr, January 6, 1850.

33. *Ibid.*, January 25, 1850.

34. *Ibid.*, January 17, 25, July 4, 20, 1850.

35. Martin L. Crimmins, ed., "W.G. Freeman's Report on the Eighth Military Department," *SWHQ*, Vol. 53, October, 1949, pp. 206-207.

36. Steffen, *The Horse Soldier*, Vol. 1, p. 174.

37. Crimmins, "Col. J.K.F. Mansfield's Report of the Inspection of the Department of Texas in 1856," *SWHQ*, p. 376.

38. Schmidt to Selcer.

39. *Ibid.*

40. Mae Biddison Benson, "Tales of Early Days Here Are Recalled by Women Pioneers," interview with Mrs. Clara Peak Walden, undated and unidentified newspaper clipping in "Fort Worth," vertical files, TCHC.

41. Arnold to Maj. George Deas, Assistant Adjutant General, Eighth Department, San Antonio, July 30, 1849, in Letters Received, Adjutant General's Office, 1822-1860, M-567, RG 94, NA. For Arnold's servants and expenses, see Sam H. Starr to Mrs. Starr, January 6, 1850, Starr Papers, CAH, UT, Austin.

42. Sam H. Starr to Mrs. Starr, January 18, 1850, Starr Papers, CAH, UT, Austin.

43. For Special Orders No. 26, see Post Returns, Fort Graham, May, 1850, RG 94, NA. Other information on mail service from Freeman, "Report of the Inspection," p. 95, RG 94, NA.

44. Arnold to Roger Jones, January 25, 1850, in Letters Received, Adjutant General's Office, 1822-1860, M-567, RG 94, NA.

45. All military correspondence was annotated by a clerk with the date received at the War Department. There is no way, however, of telling when it was answered unless the corresponding letter can be found in Letters Sent, Adjutant General's Office (Main Series), 1800-1890 (M-565, RG 94, NA). See also Rister, "Fort Griffin," *WTHAYB*, p. 22.

46. Reported in *Texas State Gazette* (Austin), May 18, 1851; also cited in Averem B. Bender, *The March of Empire: Frontier Defense in the Southwest, 1848-1860* (Lawrence: University Press of Kansas, 1952), pp. 134-35.

47. Post Returns, Fort Worth, March, 1853, RG 94, NA.

48. Sam H. Starr to Mrs. Starr, January 18, 1850, Starr Papers, CAH, UT, Austin.

49. Muster Rolls, Second Dragoons, Company B, 1851-1855, October 31-December 31, RG 94, NA.

50. Bvt. Maj. H.W. Merrill to [Headquarters], August 8, 1853, Record of the Army Headquarters, Registers of Letters Received, Entry 21, RG 108, NA.

51. Muster Rolls, Second Dragoons, Company F, December 31, 1845-December 31, 1850, RG 94, NA.

52. Leonora Barrett, "Transportation, Supplies, and Quarters for the West Texas Frontier Under the Federal Military System 1848-1861," *WTHAYB*, Vol. 5, June, 1929, p. 96.

53. *Ibid.*

54. Maj. Johnston was appointed colonel of the Second U.S. Cavalry in March, 1855, a considerable jump in rank and prestige that

reflected his efficient and uncomplaining service in one of the Army's least glamorous jobs. See William Preston Johnston, *The Life of Albert Sidney Johnston* (New York: D. Appleton & Co., 1906), pp. 169-179, 184-185.

8-ADJUTANT'S CALL

1. James V. Reese, "The Murder of Major Ripley A. Arnold," *WTHAYB*, Vol. 41, October, 1965, pp. 144-145; Julia K. Garrett, *Fort Worth: A Frontier Triumph* (Austin: Encino Press, 1972), pp. 75-77; Tommy Thompson, "Ripley A. Arnold—Frontier Major," *The Junior Historian*, Vol. 9, May, 1949, pp. 1-2.

2. "Slayer of Fort Worth Founder . . ." *Fort Worth Star-Telegram*, October 30, 1949, p. 4; and "Excerpts from the Scrapbook of Mrs. Augusta E. McKee," in Tarrant County Scrapbook No. 1, CAH, UT, Austin.

3. Sam H. Starr to Mrs. Starr, January 6, 1850, Starr Papers, CAH, UT, Austin.

4. Memoirs of Dr. C.M. Peak, vertical files, "Fort Worth," FWPL.

5. For the case of Private Joseph Murphy, *et al*, who appeared before Maj. Arnold's court-martial in July-August, 1851, see Records of the Office of the Judge Advocate General (Army), "Court Martial Case Files, 1809-1894," August, 1851, File HH-93, Box 201, RG 153, NA. Assistant Surgeon Josephus Steiner was placed under arrest and ordered to his quarters on September 6, 1853, at Fort Graham, Texas. See James V. Reese, "The Murder of Major Ripley A. Arnold," *WTHAYB*, p. 148.

6. Records of the Office of the Judge Advocate General (Army), "Court Martial Case Files, 1809-1894," File HH-93, August, 1851, Box 201, RG 153, NA.

7. Averam B. Bender, *The March of Empire: Frontier Defense in the Southwest, 1848-1860* (Lawrence: University Press of Kansas, 1952), p. 127.

8. *Ibid*, p. 128.

9. Orders No. 59 for a General Court Martial assembled at Fort Mason, Texas, on September 15, 1853, to try 1st Lt. Samuel H. Starr. Records of the Office of Judge Advocate General (Army), "Court Martial Case Files, 1809-1894," File HH-328, Box 24, RG 153, NA.

10. For General Orders No. 3, see Post Returns, March, 1853, RG 94, NA. For Merrill's lack of discipline problems, see Freeman, "Report of Inspection," p. 97, RG 94, NA.

11. *Ibid*.

12. "Report of Whiting's Reconnaissance," Senate Executive Document No. 64, pp. 240-241.

13. Sam H. Starr to Mrs. Starr, January 6, 1850, Starr Papers, CAH, UT, Austin.

14. Joseph Schmitz, ed., "Impressions of Texas in 1860," *SWHQ*, Vol. 42, April, 1939, p. 345.

15. *History of Texas from 1685 to 1892* (St. Louis: L.E. Daniell, 1893), Vol. 2, pp. 349-350.

16. Williams, "Medical Topography," Senate Executive Document No. 96, p. 374.

17. *History of Texas from 1685 to 1892*, Vol. 2, p. 350.

18. I.C. Terry, "Reminiscences of the Fort Worth of Fifty Years Ago," p. 5, FWPL.

19. All numbers relating to the sick come from Post Returns, Fort Worth, June-December, 1849, RG 94, NA.

20. Muster Rolls, Second Dragoons, Company F, Reports of June 30-August 31, 1849, RG 94, NA.

21. "A Dragoon" [James Hildreth], *Dragoon Campaigns to the Rocky Mountains* (New York: Arno Press, 1973), pp. 113-116.

22. Lydia Spencer Lane, who spent several years in Texas before the Civil War as an officer's wife, had little respect for "contract doc-

tors," whom she characterized as being "drunk half the time and not of much service." Fortunately, she added, in peacetime most men stayed fairly healthy so there was little for the practitioners to do. Lane, *I Married a Soldier, or Old Days in the Old Army* (Albuquerque: Horn & Wallace, 1964), p. 51.

23. Pearl Foster O'Donnell, *Trek to Texas, 1770-1870* (Fort Worth: Branch-Smith, 1966), p. 156. For Standifer's job description, see Post Returns, Fort Worth, June-December, 1849, RG 94, NA. For Standifer's requisitions, see Records of the Office of the Surgeon General (Army), Central Office Correspondence, 1818-1890, Registers of Letters Received, 1822-1889, Vol. 8, RG 112, NA. For Drs. Thomas H. Williams and J.M. Steiner and for Arnold and Standifer children, see Schmidt to Selcer.

24. Records of the Office of the Surgeon General, Registers of Letters Received, 1822-1889, Vol. 8, RG 112, NA; and Orders and Special Orders, Eighth Military Department, 1848-1850, Adjutant General's Office, Vol. 250, RG 94, NA.

25. Post Returns, Fort Worth, October, 1849-September, 1853, RG 94, NA; Freeman, "Report of Inspection," p. 98, RG 94, NA.

26. Records of the Office of the Surgeon General (Army), Registers of Letters Received (1822-1889) from Drs. Thomas H. Williams and J.M. Steiner, RG 112, NA.

27. *Ibid.* (Letters received from Dr. Thomas H. Williams).

28. P.M. Ashburn, *A History of the Medical Department of the United States Army* (Boston: Houghton Mifflin Company, 1929), pp. 60-62; David A. Norris, "War's 'Wonder' Drugs," *America's Civil War*, May, 1994, p. 53.

29. Muster Rolls, Second Dragoons, Company F, Reports of December 31, 1849-February 28, 1850; April 30-June 30, 1850; and June 30-August 31, 1850, RG 94, NA.

30. Freeman, "Report of Inspection," p. 98, RG 94, NA.

31. Williams, "Medical Topography," Senate Executive Document No. 96, p. 374. Freeman says almost the same thing, which would suggest that he got his information from Dr. Williams, except that Williams had left Fort Worth taking his records with him just before Freeman arrived. Freeman, "Report of Inspection," p. 98, RG 94, NA.

32. Williams, "Medical Topography," Senate Executive Document No. 96, pp. 373-374. For "vaccine," see Thomas to Office of the Surgeon General, Fort Worth, April 28, 1850, in Records of the Office of The Surgeon General (Army), Registers of Letters Received, RG 112, NA.

33. Williams, "Medical Topography," Senate Executive Document No. 96, p. 374.

34. *Ibid.*; "Report of Whiting's Reconnaissance," Senate Executive Document No. 64, p. 241.

35. Freeman, "Report of Inspection," p. 90, RG 94, NA.

36. Report of A.W. Speight, "Resources, Soil, Climate of Texas, Tarrant County," CAH, UT, Austin.

37. From the Medical Record of Fort Griffin, 1875, Vol. 52, p. 39 (cited in Carl C Rister, "Fort Griffin," *WTHAYB*, Vol. 1, June, 1925, p. 22).

9-FORM RANKS

1. Muster Rolls, Second Dragoons, 1845-1855, Company F, Reports of April 30, June 30, and August 31, 1849, RG 94, NA. Fortunately, Ripley Arnold was more descriptive in filling out his reports than most of his fellow officers. Others tended to put "good" beside the first category on the muster roll form, and then add ditto marks for every other category that followed. By making his job more difficult, Arnold left a better picture of the troops on the Trinity between 1849 and 1853.

2. Randy Steffen, *The Horse Soldier*, Vol. 1, *The Revolution, the War of 1812, the Early Frontier, 1776-1850* (Norman: University of Oklahoma Press, 1977), pp. 90-117.

3. *Ibid.*, pp. 92-113.

4. Frederick P. Todd, *American Military Equippage, 1851-1872* (Providence, Rhode Island: The Company of Military Historians, 1977), Vol. 2, p. 362. Orders No. 76, Headquarters Eighth Military Department, San Antonio, November 24, 1849, in Records of the Adjutant General's Office, Orders and Special Orders, Eighth Military Department, 1848-1850, Vol. 250, RG 94, NA.

5. H. Charles McBarron, *Military Collector & Historian, The Journal of the Company of Military Historians*, Vol. 1, No. 1, quoted in Steffen, *The Horse Soldier*, Vol. 1, p. 96.

6. Freeman, "Report of Inspection," p. 97, RG 94, NA.

7. Randy Steffen, *The Horse Soldier, 1776-1943*, Vol. 2, *The Frontier, the Mexican War, the Civil War, the Indian Wars, 1851-1880* (Norman: University of Oklahoma Press, 1978), pp. 5-20.

8. Muster Rolls, Second Dragoons, Company B, 1851-1855, Report of August 31-October 31, 1853, RG 94, NA; see also Freeman, "Report of Inspection," p. 96, RG 94, NA.

9. Gregory J.W. Urwin, *The United States Infantry, An Illustrated History, 1775-1918* (New York: Sterling Publishing, 1991), pp. 66-67, 78-79, 82-83; Philip Katcher, *The Mexican-American War, 1846-1848*, Vol. 56, "Men-At-Arms Series," Martin Windrow, ed. (London: Osprey Publishing Ltd., 1991), pp. 8-13; Robert M. Utley, *Frontiersmen in Blue: The United States Army and the Indian, 1848-1865* (Lincoln: University of Nebraska Press, 1981), pp. 23-25.

10. Urwin, *The United States Infantry*, p. 82, quoting Sergeant Eugene Bandel of the Sixth U.S. Infantry.

11. Lt. T.G. Pitcher, Adjutant General's Office, Eighth Infantry, to Lt. W.P. Street, Commanding Eighth Infantry, Fort Worth, January 3, 1851, Letters Sent, 1848-1859, Vol. 1, Entry 1279, RG 391, NA.

12. Quoted in Urwin, *The United States Infantry*, p. 82. For general information on dragoon arms, see Steffen, *The Horse Soldier*, Vol. 1, pp. 120-126.

13. Muster Rolls, Second Dragoons, Companies F and B, RG 94, NA; Steffen, *The Horse Soldier*, Vol. 1, pp. 120-126.

14. The efficiency and firepower of this revolver made it a classic in the history of the West. For its introduction to dragoons, see Todd, *American Military Equippage, 1851-1872*, Vol. 2, p. 364

15. Post Returns, Fort Worth, May and November, 1850, Orders Received, RG 94, NA; Freeman, "Report of Inspection," p. 96, RG 94, NA. For history of the Colt revolver in U.S. cavalry service, see Steffen, *The Horse Soldier*, Vol. 1, pp. 126-130. For additional information on uniforms, arms and equipment of the troops at Fort Worth, see Philip Katcher, *The Mexican-American War, 1846-1848*, pp. 15-16, 37; and Ross M. Kimmel, "American Forces in the War with Mexico, 1846-1848," *Military Illustrated—Past & Present*, No. 44 (Great Britain), January, 1992.

16. Steffen, *The Horse Soldier*, Vol. 1, pp. 131-134.

17. Muster Rolls, Second Dragoons, Company B, RG 94, NA. For War Department circular, see Post Returns, Fort Worth, June, 1850, Orders Received, RG 94, NA. For Company B's arms in September, 1853, see Freeman, "Report of Inspection," p. 96, RG 94, NA.

18. For values of soldiers' equipment and arms, see Muster Rolls, Second Dragoons, Company F, RG 94, NA. Orders No. 52, Headquarters Eighth Military Department, San Antonio, August 10, 1849, in Records of the Adjutant General's Office, Orders and Special Orders, Eighth Military Department, 1848-1850, Vol. 250, RG 94, NA.

19. Muster Rolls, Second Dragoons, Company F, October 31 and December 31, 1849; and for all reporting periods, 1850-1852, RG 94, NA.

10-ASSEMBLY

1. Terrell's cabin was on the site of the *old* Tarrant County Criminal

Court Building. Louis J. Wortham, *A History of Texas From Wilderness to Commonwealth* (Fort Worth: Wortham-Molyneaux Company, 1924), Vol. 5, p. 235. See also C.C. Cummings, "First Days in Fort Worth," *The Bohemian*, 1904, p. 210.

2. Cummings, "First Days in Fort Worth," *The Bohemian*, 1904, p. 210.

3. "Report of Whiting's Reconnaissance," Senate Executive Document No. 64, p. 238.

4. Sam H. Starr to Mrs. Starr, January 18, 1850, Starr Papers, CAH, UT, Austin; Swasey and Melton, "History," FWPL, p. 6; Recollections of Mrs. M.A. Holloway in "Excerpts from the Scrapbook of Mrs. Grover Leigh" in Tarrant County Scrapbook No. 1, CAH, UT, Austin; U.S. Census figures cited in Julia K. Garrett, *Fort Worth: Frontier Triumph* (Austin: Encino Press, 1972), p. 109.

5. *Fort Worth Press*, July 7, 1949.

6. The farrier shod horses while the blacksmith did all sorts of skilled ironwork. The two jobs were usually combined at Army posts on the frontier. Muster Rolls, Second Dragoons, Company F, Report of June 30, 1849, RG 94, NA.

7. Post Returns, Fort Worth, August, 1851, RG 94, NA.

8. Starr to Maj. Gen. George Gibson, April 22, 1851, Entry 225, RG 92, NA.

9. Special Orders No. 42, Headquarters Eighth Military Department, San Antonio, July 9, 1849, "By order of Maj. Gen. Brooke," Orders and Special Orders, Eighth Military Department, 1848-1850, Adjutant General's Office, Vol. 250, RG 94, NA.

10. Post Returns, Fort Worth, October, 1851, RG 94, NA.

11. "Archibald Franklin and Mary A. Leonard, Tarrant County Pioneers," typescript in Tarrant County Scrapbook, File 3L405, CAH, UT, Austin.

12. Frederick Law Olmsted, *A Journey through Texas* (New York: n.p., 1859), p. 315.

13. Pearl Foster O'Donnell, *Trek to Texas, 1770-1870* (Fort Worth: Branch-Smith, Inc, 1966), p. 156. Edmund S. Terrell's name is misspelled "Terrill" in the 1850 Census and in most later accounts. Terrell's saloon may have been the same "whiskey shop" that Maj. Arnold had trouble with in 1851, although that particular establishment was described in court martial testimony as being nearly a mile from the fort. After the garrison moved out, the First and Last Chance relocated to the old post grounds, on present-day Weatherford St. one block west of the courthouse. Some accounts claim Noel Burton was the original owner and Terrill bought it from him. (Schmidt to Selcer.)

14. "Report of Samuel Starr on the Condition," May 22, 1851, RG 92, NA.

15. Report of Lt. Starr, 32nd Congress, 1st Session, House Executive Document No. 2, Pt. 1, p. 270, NA. At twenty-five cents per acre, the fertile soil and the protective presence of the army would soon bring settlers into the region.

16. Freeman, "Report of Inspection," p. 95, RG 94, NA.

17. Special Orders No. 6, received March 5, 1851. See Post Returns, Fort Worth, March, 1851, RG 94, NA.

18. Garrett, *Fort Worth*, p. 111.

19. Holloway may have been confused about the names, since Sophia Arnold died in 1850 before reaching her second birthday. Mrs. Holloway's playmates had to have been the two oldest girls, Florida, who was ten, and Katherine, who was seven in the summer of 1850. Mrs. Holloway's recollections cited in *Fort Worth Star-Telegram*, July 30, 1945. For Arnold family, see Tarrant County Census Records, 1850.

20. For Starr quote, see Sam H. Starr to Mrs. Starr, January 18, 1850, Starr Papers, CAH, UT, Austin.

21. Garrett, *Fort Worth*, p. 80; and Tommy Thompson, "Ripley A. Arnold—Frontier Major," *The Junior Historian*, Vol. 9, May, 1949, p. 3. The trip to Washington, D.C., from north Texas would have taken three weeks or more in the mid-nineteenth century.

Doubling that time for the return trip and taking into account poor seasonal traveling conditions, Mrs. Arnold would have spent as much time in transit as in the nation's capital.

22. Post Returns, Fort Worth, September, October, 1850, RG 94, NA.

23. Mrs. Webster to Mrs. Kirby Smith, August [n.d.], 1851, in Kirby Smith Papers, Southern Historical Collection, University of North Carolina, Chapel Hill. Cited in Nathaniel C. Hughes, Jr., *General William J. Hardee, Old Reliable* (Wilmington, North Carolina: Broadfoot Publishing, 1987), p. 39.

24. Interview with Howard W. Peak, son of Dr. and Mrs. Carroll M. Peak, undated clipping from *Fort Worth Record*, in vertical files, "Fort Worth," FWPL.

11-TO HORSE

1. "Allied bands" was a shortened reference often used by government officials and military officers for these agricultural tribes. See Letter of Bvt. Maj. Hamilton W. Merrill, Second Dragoons, to Maj. R. S. Neighbors, Superintendent of Indian Affairs in Texas, August 9, 1853 (in Crimmins, "Fort Worth Was an Early Army Post," *Frontier Times*, Vol. 16, January, 1939, p. 141).

2. Farrar to Cummings, September 23, 1893, TCHC.

3. Report of Indian Commissioners M.G. Lewis and P.M. Butler, August 8, 1846, in "Report of the Secretary of War," December, 1847, 30th Congress, 1st Session, Senate Executive Document No. 171, p. 35; Martin L. Crimmins, ed., "Col. J.F.K. Mansfield's Report of the Inspection of the Department of Texas in 1856," *SWHQ*, Vol. 42, October, 1938, pp. 126-127.

4. Crimmins, "Col. J.K.F. Mansfield's Report on the Inspection of the Department of Texas in 1856, *SWHQ*, Vol. 42, January, 1939, p. 255.

5. Howard R. Lamar, ed., *The Reader's Encyclopedia of the American West* (New York: Thomas Y. Crowell, 1977).

6. Swasey and Melton, "History," FWPL, p. 4; Crimmins, "Col. J.F.K. Mansfield's Report of the Inspection of the Department of Texas in 1856," *SWHQ*, p. 127.

7. Grant Foreman, "The Texas Comanche Treaty of 1846," *SWHQ*, Vol. 51, April, 1948, pp. 331-332.

8. George Deas, Assistant Adjutant General, Eighth Military Department, to Governor George T. Wood, July 23, 1849, in Dorman H. Winfrey and James M. Day, eds., *The Indian Papers of Texas and the Southwest, 1825-1916* (Austin: Pemberton Press, 1966), Vol. 5, pp. 40-41.

9. Maj. Ripley Arnold to Maj. Gen. George M. Brooke, commander of Eighth Military Department (cited in *Fort Worth Star-Telegram*, June 22, 1949).

10. For Brooke's "Requisition," see Asst. Adj. Gen. L. Thomas to Bvt. Maj. Gen. G.M. Brooke, September 1, 1849, Record of the Army Headquarters, Registers of Letters Received, Entry 21, RG 108, NA. For warnings, see Post Returns, Fort Graham, June, 1850, RG 94, NA, citing a dispatch from Headquarters Eighth Military Department, furnishing "information to Commanding officers of Posts of murders committed by the Indians in Texas."

11. R.C. Crane, "Some Aspects of the History of the West and Northwest Texas Since 1845," *SWHQ*, Vol. 26, July, 1922, p. 35.

12. Notation amended to Post Returns, Fort Worth, May 1, 1850, RG 94, NA.

13. Post Returns, Fort Worth, June, 1850, *ibid*.

14. Post Returns, Fort Graham, June, 1850, *ibid*.

15. Headquarters circular received, October 21, 1850, in Post Returns, Fort Worth, October, 1850, *ibid*.

16. Orders No. 69, received at Fort Worth January 6, 1851, in Post Returns, Fort Worth, January, 1851, *ibid*.

17. "Report of Whiting's Reconnaissance," Senate Executive Document No. 64, p. 242.

18. Williams, "Medical Topography," Senate Executive Document No. 96, p. 374.

19. Nathaniel C. Hughes, *General William J. Hardee, Old Reliable* (Wilmington, North Carolina: Broadfoot Publishing, 1987), p. 39.

20. Post Returns, Fort Worth, May, 1851, RG 94, NA.

21. The Smith quotation comes from an interview in the *Fort Worth Advance*, 1893 (exact date unknown), typescript in the "John Peter Smith," p. 3, vertical files, FWPL. The Harris story comes from George L. Harris, "Remarks on Early History of Fort Worth," typescript affidavit, pp. 6-7, vertical files, FWPL.

22. John James Woody, "Early Merchandising Days in Fort Worth," interview for Civil Works Administration project, 1934, Tarrant County Scrapbook No. 1, CAH, UT, Austin, p. 1; Swasey and Melton, "History," FWPL, p. 4.

23. "Report of Whiting's Reconnaissance," Senate Executive Document No. 64, p. 243.

24. Dabney Herndon Maury, *Recollections of a Virginian* (New York: Charles Scribner's Sons, 1894), p. 76. Maury was a member of the West Point class of 1846, and like so many of the young Academy graduates of his day, after serving an apprenticeship in the Mexican War and on the frontier of Texas, he went on to greater fame as a general officer (Confederate) in the Civil War.

25. Neighbors' inflated estimate was from his own observations, as well as those of two other agents and four interpreters who were the sole representatives of the Bureau of Indian Affairs in Texas. Neighbors' Report is contained in 31st Congress, 1st Session, Senate Executive Document No. 1, p. 963. See also U.S. Census Report, 1850, p. 94; and Robert Utley, *Frontiersmen in Blue: The United States Army and the Indian, 1848-1865* (New York: Macmillan, 1967), p. 71. For Hardee's lower figures, see "Report of Lt.-Col. Hardee," August 29, 1851, in Military and Indian Affairs in Texas, 32nd Congress, 1st Session, House Executive Document No. 2, pp. 121-124; and Maj. Joseph I. Lambert, *One Hundred Years with the Second Cavalry* (Fort Riley, Kansas: The Commanding Officer, Second Cavalry, 1939), p. 49.

26. "Report of Lt.-Col. Hardee," 32nd Congress, 1st Session, House Executive Document No. 2, p. 123.

27. Merrrill to Neighbors, August 9, 1853 (Cited in Crimmins, "Fort Worth Was An Early Army Post," *Frontier Times,* p. 141).

28. "Report of Col. Cooper," June 14, 1851, in Military and Indian Affairs in Texas, 32nd Congress, 1st Session, House Executive Document No. 2, p. 121.

29. Freeman, "Report of Inspection," p. 96, RG 94, NA. For Merrill to Neighbors, August 9, 1853, see Crimmins, "Fort Worth Was An Early Army Post," *Frontier Times,* p. 141.

30. Margaret Bierschwale, "Mason County, Texas, 1845-1870," *SWHQ,* Vol. 52, April, 1949, p. 385.

31. Freeman, "Report of Inspection," pp. 95-96, RG 94, NA.

32. Post Returns, Fort Worth, May, 1853, RG 94, NA.

33. Two years earlier Lt. Col. Cooper, during his inspection tour up the Brazos, had correctly identified José María as "Chief of his own particular tribe, the Anadacos *[sic]*." See "Report of Col. Cooper," 32nd Congress, 1st Session, House Executive Document No. 2, p. 120. José María, born in Texas in 1805, received his Christian name (which he wore proudly) from the Spanish cleric who baptized him. He dealt in good faith with white Texans athough they were never so fair and honest with him. See Walter Prescott Webb, ed., *The Handbook of Texas* (Austin: Texas State Historical Association, 1952), Vol. 1, p. 929.

34. "Report of Whiting's Reconnaissance," Senate Executive Document No. 64, p. 243.

35. Like the Comanches, the Wichitas were divided into two large branches or clans, the northern Wichita, who called Oklahoma home, and the Texas Wichita who were considered part of the Caddoan family by most Texans. The northern Wichita were by far the more belligerent. Lena Clara Koch, "The Federal Indian Policy in Texas, 1845-1860," *SWHQ,* Vol. 18, January, 1925, pp. 227-228.

36. Merrill to Neighbors (Crimmins, "Fort Worth Was An Early Army Post," *Frontier Times*, p. 141).

37. Report of Jesse Stern to the Honorable L. Lea, Commissioner of Indian Affairs, Washington, D.C., 32nd Congress, 2nd Session, House Executive Document No. 1, p. 434.

38. According to family tradition, Cockerell (or Cockerel), also known as Henry Hahn (which may be an Anglicized form of Cockerell), was a ranger at Johnson's Station in 1849 and a "blood brother" to Chief Jim Ned. (Schmidt to Selcer.)

39. Howard W. Peak, *A Ranger of Commerce or 52 Years on the Road* (San Antonio: Naylor Printing, 1929), pp. 163-169.

40. According to post returns from the spring of 1850, Arnold, Maclay, and Street were never at Fort Worth at the same time. Peak also mentions the two "surgeons" by name who, he says, accompanied the soldiers: Standifer and Halliday. Dr. Standifer had not been at Fort Worth since the fall of 1849, and Halliday was a lieutenant with the dragoons, not a surgeon. Neither post returns nor regimental returns for the Second Dragoons show any casualties from Indian action during the four years of Fort Worth's existence. In 1850, no U.S. troops anywhere carried *repeating* rifles; those did not come into use until the Civil War, and then on a very limited basis. There are other, lesser points where the story fails to pass muster as genuine history.

41. The biggest Indian attack during the first half of the decade was the devastating Elm Creek Raid of 1864. One authority estimates that perhaps as many as 400 Texans, nearly all civilians, died at the hands of Indian raiders during the Civil War. David P. Smith, *Frontier Defense in the Civil War* (College Station: Texas A&M University Press, 1993). One of the Fort Worth pioneer women interviewed by newspaper columnist Edith Deen in 1932 recounted the story of a raid made in this area by Comanches in 1869, and of the killing of a family on Deer Creek that same year. The Comanches, she said, drove off some 300 settlers' horses,

leaving behind their own worn-out ponies in exchange. See *Fort Worth Star-Telegram*, March 2, 1949.

42. Merrill to Neighbors (Crimmins, "Fort Worth An Early Army Post," *Frontier Times*, p. 141).

43. Peak, *A Ranger of Commerce*, p. 164. Special Orders No. 42, issued May 4, 1851, received, Fort Worth, May 31 (Post Returns, May, 1851); and Special Orders No. 31, received, Fort Worth, August 1, 1851 (Post Returns, August, 1851), RG 94, NA.

44. Indian Agent George F. Howard, who put the operation together, claimed to have started 351 Indians on the march north. Indian trader H. Barnard at Fort Graham counted fewer than sixty when they reached the Brazos. Maj. Merrill at Fort Worth estimated the number at eighty upon their arrival there. The evidence suggests that the final numbers were closer to sixty than to 351. See Rupert N. Richardson, "Removal of Indians from Texas in 1853: A Fiasco," *WTHAYB*, Vol. 20, October, 1944, p. 89.

45. H.P.N. Gammel, *The Laws of Texas, 1822-1897* (Austin: Gammel Book Co., 1898), Vol. 3, p. 812.

46. Richardson, "Removal of Indians from Texas," *WTHAYB*, p. 90.

47. "Report of the Secretary of War," December 4, 1854, 33rd Congress, 2nd Session, House Executive Document No. 1, p. 371.

48. The Terry quote is from *Fort Worth Star-Telegram*, October 30, 1942. The staff writer incorrectly attributes the quote to Mrs. Terry's daughter, Elizabeth Terry Chapman.

49. According to authority W. Eugene Hollon, Marcy "drafted the first reasonably accurate maps of the Southwest and his advice led to the establishment of a chain of 'Cross Timbers' forts from eastern Oklahoma to western Texas." See Lamar, ed., *The Reader's Encyclopedia of the American West*, p. 705.

50. In 1870, Marcy wrote in his Journal while traveling between Phantom Hill and Jacksboro, "This rich and beautiful section does not contain today so many white people as it did when I visited it eighteen years ago." Quoted in Carl C. Rister, "The

Border Post of Phantom Hill," *WTHAYB*, Vol. 14, October, 1938, p. 5.

51. *Fort Worth Daily Gazette*, September 5, 1889, p. 8.

12-TATTOO

1. Orders No. 50, Headquarters Eighth Military Department, August 20, 1853, signed by Bvt. Maj. Gen. Persifor Smith, "Fort Worth," vertical files, TCHC. Compare Post Returns for August, 1853, Orders No. 12, issued August 20, 1853, from Headquarters Eighth Military Department, received at Fort Worth on August 30, as the official communique that announced the end of Fort Worth. As both the copy of Orders No. 50 and the Post Returns are primary documents, there is no accounting for this discrepancy.

2. Quoted in *Niles' Weekly Register*, Vol. 73, January 22, 1848, p. 334.

3. Freeman, "Report of the Inspection," p. 96, RG 94, NA; also, Schmidt to Selcer.

4. See Joseph I. Lambert, *One Hundred Years with the Second Cavalry* (Fort Riley, Kansas: The Commanding Officer, Second Cavalry, l939), p. 57. Compare Wolf W. Schmoekel, *The Dragoon's Story* (Washington, D.C.: Randall Printing, 1958), p. 37, which says that Company F was sent from Fort Worth to Fort Belknap as soon as the former was abandoned. This is incorrect; they went to Forts McKavett and Chadbourne first.

5. Orders No. 50, Headquarters Eighth Military Department, August 20, 1853, Orders and Special Orders, Eighth Military Department, 1848-1850, Adjutant General's Office, Vol. 250, RG 94, NA. Ray Miller, *Ray Miller's Texas Forts* (Houston: Gulf Publishing, 1985), pp. 58-62, 71-74; Lambert, *One Hundred Years with the Second Cavalry*, p. 49.

6. Muster Rolls, Company B, Second Dragoons, 1851-1855, Reports of August 31-October 31 and October 31-December 31, 1853, RG 94, NA.

7. The rocker exists today in possession of the Dallas County Historical Society. (Schmidt to Selcer.)

8. Maj. H.W. Merrill to Maj. Gen. Thomas S. Jesup, Quartermaster General, August 15, 1853, in "Office of the Quartermaster General, Consolidated Corresopndence File, 1794-1915," Box 1261, Entry 225, RG 92, NA.

9. Maj. Gen. Thomas S. Jesup, Quartermaster General, to Maj. H.W. Merrill, Fort Worth, Texas, September 21, 1853, and January 23, 1854, in Letters Sent by the Office of the Quartermaster General, Main Series, 1818-1870, M-745, RG 92, NA.

10. For the number and names of families in 1849, see recollections of Mrs. A.S. Dingee in Mae Biddison Benson, "Tales of Early Days Here Are Recalled by Women Pioneers," undated and unidentified newspaper clipping in "Fort Worth," vertical files, TCHC. For number of citizens in 1853 and later see *Charter and Revised Civil and Criminal Ordinances*, p. v, FWPL. According to Dingee, in 1849 there were, in addition to those living around the fort, at least three more families living northwest of town in the White Settlement area: the Connelleys, the Ventulas, and the Whites.

11. *Charter and Revised Civil and Criminal Ordinances*, p. v, FWPL.

12. Howard Peak, "Recollections of Fort Worth," *Fort Worth Star-Telegram*, June 11, 1922. Both Julia K. Garrett and Oliver Knight say Daggett's stables-cum-hotel was the same place that became Lawrence Steele's hotel and, after that, Andrews *[sic]* Tavern. Evidence from deed records suggests, however, that Steele's two-story, four-room hostelry on the bluff was a later addition to the little community separate from Daggett's original hotel. See Julia K. Garrett, *Fort Worth: A Frontier Triumph* (Austin: Encino Press, 1972), p. 128; Oliver Knight, *Fort Worth: Outpost on the Trinity* (Norman: University of Oklahoma Press, 1953), p. 27; see Allen to Schmidt, TCHC.

13. For Smith, see Allen to Schmidt, TCHC. For Feild, see *Texas*

Writers Project, Vol. 3, p. 876, FWPL. Information on the others comes from Schmidt to Selcer. Compare Knight, *Fort Worth*, p. 27. Dr. Carroll M. Peak was the father of Howard W. Peak, who later claimed the distinction of being the first white male child born in Fort Worth.

14. *Fort Worth Star-Telegram,* March 11, 1925.

15. Report of Secretary of War, December 1, 1855, 34th Congress, 1st Session, Senate Executive Document No. 1, Pt. 2, pp. 8, 22-23. Cited in Leonora Barrett, "Transportation, Supplies, and Quarters," *WTHAYB*, Vol. 5, June, 1929, p. 97.

16. C.C. Cummings, "First Days in Fort Worth," *The Bohemian*, 1904, p. 210; and Farrar to Cummings, September 23, 1893, TCHC.

17. Harris always claimed to be a member of the original party of dragoons who came up from Fort Graham with Arnold, and most citizens accepted this claim as genuine. However, his name is not listed on the first roster the major sent to headquarters from the Trinity. The first replacements at Fort Worth did not arrive until October, and those were eleven infantrymen of the Eighth under Captain R.P. Maclay. The first dragoon replacements did not arrive until December with Lt. Samuel Starr. Harris' claim is therefore suspect, although he could rightly claim to be among the *early* soldiers at Fort Worth without being one of the first. For Abe Harris' longevity and place in the city's history, see B.B. Paddock, *Early Days in Fort Worth, Much of Which I Saw and Part of Which I Was* (Fort Worth: Texas Printing Company, n.d.), p. 2.

18. Swasey and Melton, "History," FWPL, p. 5.

19. George L. Harris, "Remarks on Early History of Fort Worth," typescript affidavit, p. 2, vertical files, FWPL.

20. Farrar to Cummings, September 23, 1893, TCHC.

21. *Ibid.*

22. "Premises" quote from *Charter and Revised Civil and Criminal Ordinances*, p. vi, FWPL. According to one local researcher in recent times, a deed record from June, 1855, exists showing some land sold by Johnson to E.M. Daggett on the site of the abandoned fort. This writer has not seen that deed, but, assuming it exists, the legality of the transaction or Johnson's right to sell the land is still questionable. Cited in Allen to Schmidt, TCHC.

23. Swasey and Melton, "History," FWPL, p. 5.

24. In 1841, W.S. Peters "and associates" of Kentucky secured a land grant from the Republic of Texas to bring immigrants into north central Texas. By 1848 the struggling Peters Colony encompassed nearly two million acres, including all of Tarrant County. Eventually, more than 150 settlers were issued land certificates under the grant. Speculation in those certificates was "rampant." Dee Barker, "The Peters Colony in Tarrant County," manuscript prepared for Texas Historical Marker application, in vertical files, TCHC.

25. Barker, "The Peters Colony," *ibid.*; and George L. Harris, "Remarks on Early History of Fort Worth," typescript affidavit, p. 2, vertical files, FWPL.

26. See Survey Map of Tarrant County, issued by General Land Office, Austin, Texas, September 2, 1942, vertical files, TCHC; *Abstract of All Original Texas Land Titles Comprising Grants and Locations to August 31, 1941* (Austin: General Land Office, 1942), pp. 779, 788; *Abstract of Land Titles, Tarrant County, Texas* (Fort Worth: Genealogical Society, n. d.) pp. 46, 77; and Abstract No. 124, "The State of Texas to Middleton T. Johnson, Assignee of Mitchell Baugh" (Fort Worth: Elliott & Waldron Abstract Companies, n.d.), TCHC.

27. Swasey and Melton, "History," FWPL. See also "Some Interesting Facts About the City and Its Past History," *Fort Worth Daily Gazette*, September 5, 1889, p. 8; Mae Biddison Benson, "Tales of Early Days Here Are Recalled by Women Pioneers," undated and unidentified newspaper clipping in "Fort Worth," vertical files, TCHC; and Peak, "The Story of Old Fort Worth," p. 3, FWPL.

28. B.B. Paddock, *History of Texas: Fort Worth and the Texas Northwest Edition* (New York: Lewis Publishing Company, 1922), Vol. 2, p. 600.

13-TAPS

1. Local lore says the post closed in September, 1853. This is incorrect, however, according to both Post and Regimental Returns. The official demise of Fort Worth occurred in August.

2. Census records for 1850 show Ripley and Kate Arnold with three children, Florida, age ten, Katharan [sic], age seven, and Sophia, age one year. Local tradition says they also had a son, Willis, who died at Fort Worth, date unknown. According to the recollections of Mrs. M.A. Holloway, who came to Fort Worth with her parents in December, 1849, "Maj. Arnold's little boy died while they were here and he was the first white person buried in what is now known as Pioneers Rest." (From Holloway, "Fort Worth as Seen in 1853," in Tarrant County Scrapbook No. 1, CAH, UT, Austin.) Sophia and Willis are buried just a few feet from their father in Pioneers Rest Cemetery.

3. *Fort Worth Press*, June 6, 1947, citing the recollections of Mrs. W.H. Thompson, Maj. Arnold's granddaughter. Credibility of this story requires acceptance of the proposition that the citizens of early Fort Worth were tolerant enough to bury a black man in an otherwise all-white cemetery. Return of Arnold's body to Fort Worth from *Texas State Gazette* (Austin), June 30, 1855; and Schmidt to Selcer.

4. *New York Times*, August 21, 1859, from "unknown correspondent." Cited in Edwin Thompson, "San Juan Island National Historical Park, Historic Resource Study," Pt. 1, "A Social and Political Outline," p. 89, San Juan Island National Historic Park, Washington.

5. L.U. Reavis, *The Life and Military Services of General William Selby Harney* (St. Louis: Bryan, Brand & Co., 1878). His obituary appeared locally in *Dallas Morning News*, May 10, 1889, p. 2.

6. M.L. Crimmins, "Major Hamilton Wilcox Merrill in Texas," *WTHAYB*, Vol. 13, October, 1937, pp. 96-97. See also "Fort Merrill" entry in Ray Miller, *Ray Miller's Texas Forts* (Houston: Gulf Publishing, 1985), p. 49.

7. Stewart Sifakis, *Who Was Who in the Civil War* (New York: Facts on File Publications, 1988), p. 420; and Richard N. Current, ed., *Encyclopedia of the Confederacy* (New York: Simon & Schuster, 1993), Vol. 3, pp. 974-975.

8. Jon L. Wakelyn, *Biographical Dictionary of the Confederacy* (Westport, Connecticut: Greenwood Press, 1977), pp. 441-442; Philip Ketcher, *The Army of Robert E. Lee* (London: Arms and Armour Press, 1994), p. 161; Register of Military Service of Medical Officers, 1849-1853, Vol. 2, pp. 375-376, Entry 86, RG 112, NA.

9. Francis B. Heitman, *Historical Register and Dictionary of the United States Army* (Washington, D.C.: Government Printing Office, 1903), Vol. 1, p. 917. For details of Starr's run-in with the Army at Fort Mason, see Margaret Bierschwale, "Mason County, Texas, 1845-1870," *SWHQ*, Vol. 52, April, 1949, p. 384; and Records of the Office of Judge Advocate General (Army), "Court Martial Case Files, 1809-1894," Box 214, File HH-328, RG 153, NA. For Civil War career, see Paul M. Shevchuk, "Cut to Pieces: The Cavalry Fight at Fairfield, Pennsylvania, July 3rd, 1863," *Gettysburg Magazine*, July, 1989, pp. 105-117; William B. Skelton, *An American Profession of Arms: The Army Officer Corps, 1784-1861* (Lawrence: University Press of Kansas, 1992).

10. Heitman, *Historical Register*, Vol. 1, p. 436.

11. Teresa Griffin Viele, *Following the Drum: A Glimpse of Frontier Life* (Lincoln: University of Nebraska Press, 1984, reprint of 1858 edition), p. 174.

12. Quotation attributed to Virginian John S. Wise, in Alfred Roman,

Military Operations of General Beauregard (New York: Harper & Brothers, 1884), Vol. 2, p. 209.

13. For biographical information on Whiting, see Lawrence L. Hewitt, "William Henry Chase Whiting," *The Confederate General*, William C. Davis, ed. (Harrisburg, Pennsylvania: National Historical Society, 1991), Vol. 6, pp. 132-133. For recommendations regarding Fort Worth, see "Report of Whiting's Reconnaissance," Senate Executive Document No. 64, p. 243.

14. Secretary of War C.M. Conrad to Gen. Persifor Smith, April 30, 1851, in "Military and Indian Affairs in Texas," 32nd Congress, 1st Session, House Executive Document No. 2, p. 117.

15. W.C. Holden, "Frontier Defense, 1846-1860," *WTHAYB*, Vol. 6, 1930, pp. 49-50; Lena Clara Koch, "The Federal Indian Policy in Texas, 1845-1860," *SWHQ*, Vol. 29, July, 1925, pp. 28-29.

16. W. Eugene Hollon, *Beyond the Cross Timbers: The Travels of Randolph B. Marcy, 1812-1887* (Norman: University of Oklahoma Press, 1955), p. 170.

17. Lena Clara Koch, "The Federal Indian Policy in Texas," *SWHQ*, p. 21.

18. *Charter and Revised Civil and Criminal Ordinances*, p. v, FWPL.

19. See Swasey and Melton, "History," p. 3, FWPL.

20. See advertisement in *Texas State Gazette* (Austin), May 18, 1851, p. 8.

21. Mullin, *Stage Coach Pioneers of the Southwest* (cited in Miller, *Ray Miller's Texas Forts*, p. 52).

22. Lt. A. Croget, Acting Adjutant, Eighth Infantry, to Lt. John Bold, Commanding Fort Worth, October 17, 1850; Lt. T.G. Pitcher, Adjutant, Eighth Infantry Headquarters, to Bvt. Lt. Col. J.V. Bomford, Commanding Fort Worth, July 16, 1851, Eighth Infantry, Letters Sent, Adjutant General's Office, Entry 1279, RG 391, NA.

23. B.B. Paddock, *Early Days in Fort Worth, Much of Which I Saw and Part of Which I Was* (Fort Worth: Texas Printing Company, n.d.), p. 2.

24. Lease agreement between the Fort Worth Chamber of Commerce and the United States Army for Camp Bowie, Records of the Office of the Quartermaster General, Entry 1998, RG 92, NA.

25. Farrar to Cummings, September 23, 1893, TCHC.

BIBLIOGRAPHY

Congressional Records

House Reports, 31st Congress (1849-50), 1st Session, Report No. 280.

House Executive Documents: 32nd Congress (1851-52), 1st Session and 2nd Session.

Senate Executive Documents: 30th Congress (1847-48), 1st Session; 31st Congress (1849-50), 1st Session; 32nd Congress (1851-52), 1st Session; 34th Congress (1855-56), 3rd Session; 35th Congress (1857-58), 1st Session.

Congressional Record. Various dates

United States Government Records

Record Group 77. Records of the Office of the Chief of Engineers National Archives. Washington, D.C.

    Registers of Letters Received, Engineers Department, January 1, 1849-December 31, 1851. Entry 17.

    Letters Received, Engineers Department, January 1, 1849-December 31, 1851. Entry 17.

    Letters Received, Office of the Chief of Engineers, 1838-1866, Box No. 185, File No. 901.

    Registers of Letters Received by the Topographical Bureau of the War Department, 1824-1866. Microfilm M-505, M-506.

Record Group 92. Records of the Office of the Quartermaster General. National Archives. Washington, D.C.

    Entry 225: Consolidated Correspondence File, 1794-1915. Box 1262.

    "Report of Lt. Samuel Starr, A.A.Q.M., to Maj. Babbitt on the Condition of Facilities of the Post," May, 1851.

    "Report [by Lt. John Bold] of the Condition and of the Public Buildings at Fort Worth, Texas," October 5, 1851.

    Entry 1998: Camp Bowie, Texas.

    Letters Sent by the Office of the Quartermaster General, Main Series, 1818-1870. Microfilm M-745.

Record Group 94. Records of the Adjutant General's Office, 1780s-1917. National Archives. Washington, D.C.

    Letters Sent by the Office of the Adjutant General (Main Series), 1800-1890. Microfilm M-565.

    Letters Received by the Office of the Adjutant General (Main Series), 1822-1860. Microfilm M-567.

    Returns from U.S. Military Posts, 1800-1916. Microfilm M-617.

    Registers of Letters Received, Office of the Adjutant General, 1812-1889. Microfilm M-711.

    Entry 287: Adjutant General's Office, Miscellaneous Files,

    "Inspection Report of Col. W.G. Freeman of Eighth Military Department, Texas," File No. 282, Box 17.

Orders and Special Orders, Eighth Military Department, 1848-1850, Vol. 250.

Muster Rolls, Second Dragoons, 1845-1855.

Record Group 108. Records of Army Headquarters, Registers of Letters Received, 1849-1854. Vol. 56. National Archives. Washington, D.C.

Record Group 112. Records of the Office of the Surgeon General (Army). Registers of Letters Received, 1822-1889, Entry 10. National Archives. Washington, D.C.

Record Group 153. Records of the Office of the Judge Advocate General (Army) Court Martial Case Files, 1809-1894. National Archives. Washington, D.C.

Record Group 391. Adjutant General's Office, Letters Sent from Eighth U.S. Infantry (Regimental Letter Book). Entry 1279. National Archives. Washington, D.C.

Record Group 393. Records of the United States Army Continental Commands, 1821-1920. National Archives. Washington, D.C.

Letters Sent, Eighth Military Department, Part I, Entry 69, Vol. 46; and Entry 71, Vol. 66.

San Juan Island, Washington Territory, Post Orders, 1861-1868, Camp Pickett.

Public Records, Manuscript Collections, and Unpublished Works

Abstract of All Original Texas Land Titles Comprising Grants and Locations to August 31, 1941. Austin: General Land Office, n.d.

Abstract of Land titles, Tarrant County, Texas. Fort Worth: Fort Worth Genealogical Society, n.d.

Anonymous. "Dimensions and Location of the Military Fort, Fort Worth." Unpublished manuscript. Tarrant County Historical Commission, Fort Worth, Texas.

Anonymous. "Myth of Camp Worth in the Valley." Upublished manuscript. Tarrant County Historical Commission.

Anonymous. "The Peters Colony in Tarrant County." unpublished manuscript for Texas Historical Marker application, 1989. Tarrant County Historical Commission.

Anonymous. "The Point, Live Oak Point, Live Oak Grove, Samuels Point." Unpublished manuscript. Tarrant County Historical Commission.

Barker, Dee. "The City of Fort Worth: How It Relates to the Settlement of Tarrant County and to the Establishment of the Military Fort and Fort Worth Growth By Decades." Unpublished manuscript. Tarrant County Historical Commission.

Bold, Lt. John. "Report of Public Buildings at Fort Worth." See Record Group 92, National Archives.

Charter and Revised Civil and Criminal Ordinances of the City of Fort Worth. "By Authority." Revised and Codified by Wilson Gregg. Fort Worth: Texas Printing and Lithographing Co., 1889.

Complete Abstracts of Title to All Lands and Town Lots in Tarrant County, Texas. Fort Worth: Elliott & Waldron Abstract Companies, n.d.

Crimmins, M.L., Papers, Archives and Manuscripts. Center for American History, University of Texas, Austin.

Edmondson, Jack. "Where the West Began: The Frontier Genesis of Fort Worth, Texas." Unpublished manuscript in Richard Selcer's possession.

Fort Worth. Narrative, 1812-1939. Historical and biographical notes compiled by the Texas Writers' Project of the Work Projects Administration, Center for American History, University of Texas, Austin.

Freeman, Lt. Colonel W.G. "Report of Inspection of Eighth Military Department." See Record Group 94. National Archives.

Gammel, H.P.N. *The Laws of Texas, 1822-1897.* 10 Vols. Austin: Gammel Book Company, 1898.

Harris, George L. "Remarks on Early History of Fort Worth."

Typescript affidavit. Mary Daggett Lake Papers. 9 pp. in vertical files of Fort Worth Public Library, Central Branch, Local History and Genealogy Department.

Hawker, H.W., *et al. Soil Survey of Tarrant County, Texas*. Washington, D.C.: Government Printing Office, 1920.

Starr, Samuel H. Papers. Archives and Manuscripts. Center for American History, University of Texas, Austin.

_____. "Report on the Condition of Facilities of [Fort Worth]." See Record Group 92. National Archives.

Swasey, Charles, and W.M. Melton. "The History of the City of Fort Worth" (Introductory Essay). *Fort Worth City Directory, 1877*. Microfiche in Fort Worth Public Library, Central Branch, Genealogy and Local History Department.

Tarrant County Historical Commission. Vertical Files (various "Fort Worth"):

Allen, Frances M. to Ruby Schmidt, August 12-22, 1983.

Farrar, Simon B. to C.C. Cummings, "Palmer, Ellis County, Texas," September 23, 1893.

Tarrant County Scrapbooks. Archives and Manuscripts. Center for American History. University of Texas, Austin.

"Texas Writers' Project. Research Data: Fort Worth and Tarrant County, Texas." Seventy-seven bound typescript volmes plus eight volumes of indices. Fort Worth: Fort Worth Public Library Unit, 1941. Fort Worth Public Library, Central Branch, Local History and Genealogy Department.

Thompson, Clarence A. "Some Facts Contributing to the Growth of Fort Worth." M.A. Thesis, University of Texas, Austin, 1933.

Thompson, Edwin. "San Juan Island National Historic Park, Historic Resource Study," Pt. 1, "A Social and Political Outline." San Juan Island National Historic Park, Washington.

Uniforms of the Army of the United States, Illustrated from 1774 to 1889. Washington, D.C.: Quartermaster General (copy on file at U.S. Army Military History Institute, Carlisle, Pennsylvania).

Whiting, W.H.C. "Report of Lt. W.H.C. Whiting's Reconaissance of the Western Frontier of Texa." in Report of the Secretary of War. Senate Executive Doc. No. 64. 31st Congress. 1st Session (1850)

Woody, John James. "Early Merchandising Days in Fort Worth." Civil Works Administration Interview, 1934, 4 pp. Tarrant County Scrapbook No. 1, Center for American History, University of Texas, Austin.

Works Progress Administration. Collected Files for "Fort Worth City Guide and History." Box 4J78. Center for American History, University of Texas, Austin.

Correspondence

Ruby Schmidt, Granbury, Texas, former president of Tarrant County Historical Society to Richard Selcer, February 8, 1995.

John J. Slonaker, Chief of Historical Reference Branch, U.S. Army War College, Carlisle Barracks, Pennsylvania, to Richard Selcer, various dates, 1994-1995.

General Works

Anonymous. *History of Texas from 1685 to 1892*. 2 Vols. St. Louis: L.E. Daniell Pub., 1893 (Microfilm copy in Library of Congress).

Anonymous. *100 Year History of Fort Worth*. Pamphlet published by *Fort Worth Star-Telegram*, 1949. Files of Fort Worth Public Library, Central Branch, Genealogy and Local History Department.

Banta, William, and Caldwell, J.W., Jr. *Twenty-Seven Years on the Texas Frontier*. Rewritten and revised by L.G. Park. Council Hill, Oklahoma: Privately printed, 1933, reprint of 1893 edition.

Beers, Henry Putney. *The Western Military Frontier, 1815-1846*. Philadelphia: Porcupine Press, 1975.

Bender, Averam B. *The March of Empire: Frontier Defense in the Southwest, 1848-1860*. Lawrence: University Press of Kansas, 1952.

Brown, John. *History of Texas*. 2 Vols. St. Louis: Alebaiell Publishing Co., n.d.

Chamberlain, Samuel E. *My Confession: The Recollections of a Rogue*. Roger Butterfield, ed. Lincoln: University of Nebraska Press, 1987 (reprint).

Connor, Seymour V. *Texas: A History*. Arlington Heights, Illinois: AHM Publishing Corp., 1971.

Current, Richard N., ed. *Encyclopedia of the Confederacy*. 4 Vols. New York: Simon & Schuster, 1993.

Davis, William C., ed. *The Confederate General*. 6 Vols. Harrisburg, Pennsylvania: National Historical Society, 1991.

"Dragoon" [Hildreth, James]. *Dragoon Campaigns to the Rocky Mountains*. "Western Frontier Series," Ray A. Billington, Ed. New York: Arno Press, 1973, reprint of 1836 edition.

Elting, John R., ed. *Military Uniforms in America*. Vol. 2, *Years of Growth, 1796-1851*. San Rafael, California: Presidio Press, 1977.

Frazer, Robert W. *Forts of the West*. Norman: University of Oklahoma Press, 1972.

_____. ed. *Mansfield on the Condition of Western Forts, 1853-1854*. Norman: University of Oklahoma Press, 1963.

Froebel, Julius. *Seven Years Travel in Central America, Northern Mexico, and the Far West of the United States*. London: n.p., 1859.

Garrett, Julia Kathryn. *Fort Worth: A Frontier Triumph*. Austin: Encino Press, 1972.

Haley, J. Evetts. *Fort Concho and the Texas Frontier*. San Angelo, Texas: *San Angelo Standard*, 1952.

Handbook of Texas. Walter Prescott Webb, ed. 2 Vols. Austin: Texas State Historical Association, 1952.

Heitman, Francis B. *Historical Register and Dictionary of the United States Army*. 2 Vols. Washington, D.C.: Government Printing Office, 1903.

Hollon, W. Eugene. *Beyond the Cross Timbers: The Travels of Randolph B. Marcy, 1812-1887*. Norman: University of Oklahoma Press, 1955.

Holzman, Robert S. *Stormy Ben Butler*. New York: Macmillan, 1954.

Hughes, Natahniel C., Jr. *General Willian J. Hardee: Old Reliable*. Wilmington, N.C.: Broadfoot Publishing Company, 1987 reprint.

Irving, Washington. *A Tour on the Prairies*. John Francis McDermott, ed. Norman: University of Oklahoma Press, 1956.

Johnston, William Preston. *The Life of General Albert Sidney Johnston*. New York: D. Appleton & Company, 1906, reprint of 1878 edition.

Jones, J. William. *Life and Letters of Robert Edward Lee, Soldier and Man*. Harrisonburg, Virginia.: Sprinkle Publications, 1986, reprint of 1906 edition.

Katcher, Philip. *The Mexican-American War, 1846-1848*. "Osprey Men-At-Arms Series." Martin Windrow, Ed. London: Osprey Publishing Ltd., 1976.1

_____. *U.S. Infantry Equipments, 1775-1910*. "Osprey Men-At-Arms Series." Martin Windrow, Ed. London: Osprey Publishing Ltd., 1989.

Knight, Oliver. *Fort Worth: Outpost on the Trinity*. Norman: University of Oklahoma Press, 1953.

_____. *Life and Manners in the Frontier Army*. Norman: University of Oklahoma Press, 1993, reprint of 1978 edition.

Lamar, Howard R., ed. *The Reader's Encyclopedia of the American West*. New York: Thomas Y. Crowell Company, 1977.

Lambert, Joseph I. *One Hundred Years with the Second Cavalry*. Fort Riley, Kansas: The Commanding Officer, Second Cavalry, 1939.

Lane, Lydia Spencer. *I Married a Soldier, or Old Days in the Old Army*. Albuquerque: Horn & Wallace, 1964, reprint of 1893 edition.

Langellier, John. *U.S. Dragoons, 1833-55*. "Men-at-Arms Series," Vol. 281. Lee Johnson, ed. London: Osprey, an imprint of Reed Consumer Books, Ltd., 1995.

Longstreet, Stephen. *Indian Wars of the Great Plains*. New York: Indian Head Books, 1993, reprint of *War Cries on Horseback*, 1970.

Lowe, Percival G. *Five Years a Dragoon, '49-'54*. Kansas City, Missouri: Franklin Hudson, 1906, reprinted by University of Oklahoma Press, 1965.

Matloff, Maurice, ed. *American Military History*. "Army Historical Series." Washington, D.C.: Office of the Chief of Military History, U.S. Army, 1969.

Maury, Dabney Herndon. *Recollections of a Virginian*. New York: Charles Scribners Sons, 1894.

Miller, Ray. *Ray Miller's Texas Forts: A History and Guide*. Houston: Gulf Publishing, 1985.

Neighbours, Kenneth F. *Indian Exodus: Texas Indian Affairs, 1835-1859*. Wichita Falls, Texas: Nortex Offset Publications, 1973.

Newcomb, W.W., Jr. *The Indians of Texas: From Prehistoric to Modern Times*. Austin: University of Texas Press, 1961.

O'Donnell, Pearl Foster. *Trek to Texas, 1770-1870*. Fort Worth: Branch-Smith, Inc., 1966.

Olmsted, Frederick Law. *A Journey through Texas*. New York: n.p., 1859.

Paddock, Buckley B. *History of Texas: Fort Worth and the Texas Northwest Edition*. 4 Vols. New York: Lewis Publishing Company, 1922.

_____. *Early Days in Fort Worth, Much of Which I Saw and Part of Which I Was*. Fort Worth: Texas Printing Company, n.d. (Copy at Fort Worth Public Library, Central Branch.)

Peak, Howard W. *A Ranger of Commerce Or 52 Years on the Road*. San Antonio: Naylor Printing company, 1929.

_____. *The Story of Old Fort Worth*. Fort Worth: n.p., n.d. (In collections of Fort Worth Public Library, Central Branch)

Peterson, Charles J. *The Military Heroes of the War with Mexico With a Narrative of the War*. Philadelphia: William A. Leary, 1848.

Phares, Ross. *The Governors of Texas*. Gretna, Louisiana: Pelican Publishing Co., 1976.

Pirtle, Caleb, and Michael F. Cusack. *The Lonely Sentinel, Fort Clark: On Texas's Western Frontier*. Austin: Eakin Press, 1985.

Roberts, Robert B. *Encyclopedia of Historic Forts*. New York: Macmillan Publishing Company, 1988.

Rodenbough, T.F. *From Everglade to Ca·on with the Second Dragoons*. New York: D. Van Nostrand, 1875.

Roman, Alfred. *Military Operations of General Beauregard*. 2 Vols. New York: Harper & Brothers, 1884.

Salvant, J.U. and Utley, Robert M. *If These Walls Could Speak: Historic Forts of Texas*. Austin: University of Texas Press, 1985.

Schmoekel, Wolf W. *The Dragoons' Story: A History of the 2nd Armored Cavalry Regiment*. Washington, D.C.: Randall Printing Co., 1958.

Sifakis, Stewart. *Who Was Who in the Civil War*. New York: Facts on File Publications, 1988.

Simpson, Harold B. *Cry Comanche: The 2nd U.S. Cavalry in Texas, 1855-1861*. Hillsboro, Texas: Hill Junior College Press, 1979.

Skelton, William B. *An American Profession of Arms: The Army Officer Corps, 1784-1861*. Lawrence: University Press of Kansas, 1992.

Smith, David P. *Frontier Defense in the Civil War*. College Station: Texas A&M University Press, 1993.

Smith, Edward J. *The Capitalist; Or The City of Fort Worth, A Parody of "The Mikado."* Fort Worth: n.p., 1888. Yale University, Bienecke Rare Book and Manuscript Library, New Haven, Coonecticut.

Smith, Thomas Tyree. *Fort Inge: Sharps, Spurs, and Sabers on the Texas Frontier, 1849-1869*. Austin: Eakin Press, 1993.

Sowell, A.J. *Rangers and Pioneers of Texas*. Austin: State House Press, 1991, reprint of 1884 edition.

Steffen, Randy. *The Horse Soldier, 1776-1943*. 4 Vols. Norman: University of Oklahoma Press, 1977-79. See Vol. 1, *The Revolution, the War of 1812, the Early Frontier, 1776-1850* (1977); Vol. 2, *The Frontier, the Mexican War, the Civil War, the Indian Wars, 1851-1880* (1978).

Stubbs, Mary Lee, and Connor, Stanley Russell. *Armor-Cavalry. Part 1: Regular Army and Army Reserve. 2nd Armored Cavalry (Second*

Dragoons). "Army Lineage Series." Washington, D.C.: Office of the Chief of Military History, U.S. Army, 1969.

Thian, Raphael P., comp. *Notes Illustrating the Military Geography of the United States, 1813-1880.* Washington, D.C.: Government Printing Office, 1881, reprinted by University of Texas Press, 1979.

Todd, Frederick P. *American Military Equippage, 1851-1872.* 3 Vols. Providence, Rhode Island: The Company of Military Historians, 1977.

Urwin, Gregory J.W. *The United States Infantry: An Illustrated History, 1775-1918.* New York: Sterling Publishing Co., Inc., 1988.

Utley, Robert M. *Frontiersmen in Blue: The United States Army and the Indian, 1848-1865.* Lincoln: University of Nebraska Press, 1981. Reprint of 1967 edition.

_____. *The Indian Frontier of the American West, 1846-1890.* Albuquerque: University of New Mexico Press, 1984.

Viele, Teresa Griffin. *Following the Drum, A Glimpse of Frontier Life.* Lincoln: University of Nebraska Press, 1984, reprint of 1858 edition.

Wallace, Edward S. *General William Jenkins Worth: Monterey's Forgotten Hero.* Dallas: Southern Methodist University Press, 1953.

Weigley, Russell F. *History of the United States Army.* "Wars of the United States Series," Louis Morton, Ed. New York: Macmillan, 1967.

Werlich, Robert. *"Beast" Butler: The Incredible Career of Major General Benjamin Franklin Butler.* Washington, D.C.: Quaker Press, 1962.

Wilhelm, Thomas. *Synopsis of the History of the Eighth U.S. Infantry.* New York: n.p., 1871.

Winfrey, Dorman H. and James M. Day, eds. *The Indian Papers of Texas and the Southwest, 1825-1916.* 5 Vols. Austin: Pembertons Press, 1966

Wooten, Dudley Goodall, ed. *A Comprehensive History of Texas.* 2 Vols. Dallas: G. Scarf, 1898.

Wortham, Louis J. *A History of Texas: From Wilderness to Commonwealth.* 5 Vols. Fort Worth: Wortham-Molyneaux Co., 1924.

Newspapers and Periodicals

Barrett, Arrie. "Western Frontier Forts of Texas." *West Texas Historical Association Year Book*. Vol. 7, 1939. pp. 115-139.

Barrett, Leonora. "Transportation, Supplies, and Quarters for the West Texas Frontier Under the Federal Military System, 1848-1861." *West Texas Historical Association Year Book*. Vol. 5, June, 1929, pp. 87-99.

Bender, Averam B. "Opening Routes Across West Texas, 1848-1850." *Southwestern Historical Quarterly*. Vol. 37. October, 1933, pp. 116-135.

Benson, Mae Biddison. "Tales of Early Days Here Are Recalled by Women Pioneers." Interview with Mrs. Clara Peak Walden. Undated and unidentified newspaper clipping in vertical files of Tarrant County Historical Commission.

Bierschwale, Margaret. "Mason Country, Texas, 1845-1870." *Southwestern Historical Quarterly*. Vol. 52, No. 4. April, 1949, pp. 379-397.

Braley, Earl Burk. "Fort Belknap of the Texas Frontier." *West Texas Historical Association Year Book*. Vol. 30, 1954, pp. 83-114.

Brockway, Michael D. "Fort Martin Scott . . . Last Civilized Outpost on the Old El Paso Road." *Wild West Magazine*. June, 1993, pp. 66-70.

Crane, R.C. "Some Aspects of the History of the West and Northwest Texas Since 1845." *Southwestern Historical Quaterly*. Vol. 26. July, 1922, pp. 30-43.

Crimmins, M.L., ed. "Colonel J.K.F. Mansfield's Report of the Inspection of the Department of Texas in 1856." *Southwestern Historical Quarterly*. In 3 Parts: Vol. 42, No. 2, July 1938, pp. 122-148; No. 3, January, 1939, pp. 215-257; No. 4, April, 1939, pp. 351-387.

_____. "The First Line of Army Posts Established in West Texas in 1849." *West Texas Historical Association Year Book*. Vol. 19, October, 1943, pp. 121-127.

_____. "Fort Worth Was an Early Army Post." *Frontier Times*. Vol. 16, No. 4. January, 1939, pp. 139-141.

_____. "The Second Dragoon Indian Campaign in Texas." *West Texas Historical Association Year Book*. Vol. 21, October, 1945, pp. 50-56.

Cummings, C.C. "First Days in Fort Worth." *The Bohemian*. Souvenir Edition, 1904, p. 210.

Foreman, Grant. "The Texas Comanche Treaty of 1846." *Southwestern Historical Quarterly*. Vol. 51, No. 4. April, 1948, pp. 313-332.

Fort Worth Daily Gazette. September 5, 1889, p. 8, col. 2.

Fort Worth Press. Various dates.

Fort Worth Record. February 18, 1917.

Fort Worth Star-Telegram. Various dates.

Freeman, W.G. "W.G. Freeman's Report on the Eighth Military Department." ed. by M.L. Crimmins. *Southwestern Historical Quarterly*. Vol. 51, Nos. 1, July, 1947, pp. 54-58; and 4, April, 1948, pp. 350-357; Vol. 52, Nos. 4, April, 1949, pp. 444-447; and 5, January, 1949, pp. 349-353; Vol. 53, Nos. 1, July, 1949, pp. 71-77; 2, October, 1949, pp. 202-208; 3, January, 1950, pp. 308-319; and 4, April, 1950, pp. 443-473; and Vol. 54, No. 2, October, 1950, pp. 204-218.

Holden, William C. "Frontier Defense, 1846-1860." *West Texas Historical Association Year Book*. Vol. 6, 1930, pp.35-64.

Kimmel, Ross M. "American Forces in the War with Mexico, 1846-48." *Military Illustrated—Past & Present*. No. 44, January, 1992, pp. 9-14.

Kliger, Paul I. "The Confederate Invasion of New Mexico." *Blue & Gray Magazine*. Vol. 11, No. 5, June, 1994, pp. 8-20, ff.

Koch, Lena Clara. "The Federal Indian Policy in Texas, 1845-1860." *Southwestern Historical Quarterly*. Pt. 1: Vol. 28, No. 3, January, 1925; Pt. 2: Vol. 28, No. 4, April, 1925; Part 3, Vol. 29, No. 1, July, 1925, pp. 19-35.

Kutchinski, Marjorie. "Petticoats at Frontier Posts," *Wild West Magazine*, December, 1993, pp. 58-64.

Niles' Weekly Register (Baltimore).

Norris, David A. "War's 'Wonder' Drugs." *America's Civil War*. May, 1994, pp. 51-57.

Peak, Howard W. "History and Progress at Fort Worth." *Epic Century Magazine*. Vol. 3, No. 1, April, 1936, pp. 48-62.

Reese, James V. "The Murder of Major Ripley A. Arnold." *West Texas Historical Association Year Book*. Vol. 41, October, 1965, pp. 144-155.

Richardson, Rupert N. "Removal of Indians from Texas in 1853: A Fiasco." *West Texas Historical Association Year Book*. Vol. 20, October, 1944, pp. 86-91.

Rister, Carl C. "Fort Griffin." *West Texas Historical Association Year Book*. Vol. 1, June, 1925, pp. 15-24.

_____. "The Border Post of Phantom Hill." *West Texas Historical Association Year Book*. Vol. 14, October, 1938, pp. 3-13.

Ritchie, E.B., ed. "Copy of Report of Colonel Samuel Cooper, Assistant Adjutant General of the United States, of Inspection Trip from Fort Graham to the Indian Villages on the Upper Brazos Made in June, 1851." *Southwestern Historical Quarterly*. Vol. 42, No. 4, April, 1939, pp. 327-333.

Schmitz, Joseph, ed. "Impressions of Texas in 1860" [anonoymous journal dated fall 1859 through May 1860]. *Southwestern Historical Quarterly*. Vol. 42, April, 1939, pp. 334-350.

Seginski, Tincia. "Anadarko Chief Jose Maria . . . at Peace with Indians and Whites Alike." *Wild West Magazine*. April, 1994, pp. 26-29, ff.

Sibley, Henry Hopkins. "Recollections of Cadet Life Forty Years Ago," *Popular Monthly*. June 17, 1881, pp. 12-16.

Tate, Michael L. "Frontier Defense on the Comanche Ranges of Northwest Texas, 1846-1860." *Great Plains Journal*. Vol. 2, No. 1, Fall, 1971, pp. 41-56.

Texas State Gazette (Austin). Various dates.

Thompson, Tommy. "Ripley A. Arnold—Frontier Major." *The Junior Historian*. Vol. 9, No. 6, May, 1949, pp. 1-4.

Winkler, Allan M. "Drinking on the American Frontier." *Quarterly Journal of Studies on Alcohol*. Vol. 29, 1968, pp. 413-445.

INDEX

William B. Potter, a native of Fort Worth, provided the inspiration for this volume. He holds the Bachelor of Fine Arts degree from Texas Christian University. Potter's intricate recreations of the post were originally intended as blueprints for a life-size replica of the post—an undertaking yet to be realized. Mr. Potter has made a career in architectural delineation, industrial design, and heraldic art. In addition to his historical interests, Potter is an avid bird watcher.

Historian Richard Selcer holds the Ph.D. from Texas Christian University and currently teaches at Northlake College, Dallas, Texas, and at International Christian University in Vienna, Austria, and Kiev, Ukraine. Selcer is the author of *Hell's Half Acre: The Life and Legend of a Red-Light District* (TCU Press, 1991) and the biography, *"Faithfully Yours"—General George E. Pickett, C.S.A.* (Gettysburg: Farnsworth House, 1995), as well as numerous articles about the American Civil War.